D1479222

PRESUMED GUILTY

PRESUMED GUILTY

Lee Harvey Oswald
in the
Assassination of President Kennedy

Howard Roffman

Rutherford • Madison • Teaneck
Fairleigh Dickinson University Press

London: Associated University Presses

Associated University Presses, Inc.
Cranbury, New Jersey 08512

Associated University Presses
108 New Bond Street
London W1Y OQX, England

Library of Congress Cataloging in Publication Data

Roffman, Howard, 1953-
    Presumed guilty: Lee Harvey Oswald in the assassination of President Kennedy.

    Bibliography: p.
    1. Kennedy, John Fitzgerald, Pres. U. S., 1917-1963—Assassination. 2. Oswald, Lee Harvey. I. Title.
E842.9.R5B   973.'922'092'4   74-1119
ISBN 0-8386-1526-0

To my parents, Anita and Daniel

PRINTED IN THE UNITED STATES OF AMERICA

Contents

14877

Preface

Whoever killed President John F. Kennedy got away with it because the Warren Commission, the executive commission responsible for investigating the murder, engaged in a cover-up of the truth and issued a report that misrepresented or distorted almost every relevant fact about the crime. The Warren Commission, in turn, got away with disseminating falsehood and covering up because virtually every institution in our society that is supposed to make sure that the government works properly and honestly failed to function in the face of a profound challenge; the Congress, the law, and the press all failed to do a single meaningful thing to correct the massive abuse committed by the Warren Commission. To anyone who understood these basic facts, and there were few who did, the frightening abuses of the Nixon Administration that have come to be known as "Watergate" were not unexpected and were surprising only in their nature and degree.

This is not a presumptuous statement. I do not mean to imply that anyone who knew what the Warren Commission did could predict the events that have taken place in the last few years. My point is that the reaction to the Warren Report, if properly understood, demonstrated that our society had *nothing* that could be depended upon to protect it from the abuses of

power that have long been inherent in the Presidency.
The dynamics of our system of government are such
that every check on the abuse of power is vital; if the
executive branch were to be trusted as the sole guard-
ian of the best interests of the people, we would not
have a constitution that divides power among three
branches of government to act as checks on each other,
and we would need no Bill of Rights. Power invites
abuses and excesses, and at least since the presidency
of Franklin Roosevelt, an enormous amount of power
has been assumed and acquired by the president.

Political deception is an abuse that democracy invites; in a system where the leaders are ultimately ac-
countable to the people, where their political future is
decided by the people, there is inevitably the tempta-
tion to deceive, to speak with the primary interest of
pleasing the people and preserving political power.
There probably has not been a president who has not
lied for political reasons. I need only cite some more recent examples:

Franklin Roosevelt assured the parents of America
in October 1940 that "your boys are not going to be
sent into foreign wars"; at the time he knew that
American involvement in World War II was inevitable,
even imminent, but he chose not to be frank with the
people for fear of losing the 1940 election.

Dwight Eisenhower in 1960 denied that the American aircraft shot down by the Russians over their ter-
ritory was a spy-plane, when he *and* the Russians
knew very well that the plane, a U-2, had been on a
CIA reconnaissance flight;

John F. Kennedy had the American ambassador at
the United Nations deny that the unsuccessful invasion
of Cuba at the Bay of Pigs was an American responsibility when exactly the opposite was true.

So, deception and cover-up per se did not originate

with the Warren Commission in 1964 or the Nixon
administration in 1972. They had always been an unfortunate part of our political system. With the Warren
Commission they entered a new and more dangerous
phase. Never before, to my knowledge, had there been
such a systematic plan for a cover-up, or had such an
extensive and pervasive amount of deception been attempted. And certainly never before had our government collaborated to deny the public the true story of
how its leader was assassinated.

In the face of this new and monumental abuse of authority by the executive, all the institutions that are
supposed to protect society from such abuses failed and,
in effect, helped perpetrate the abuse itself. As with
Watergate, numerous lawyers were involved with the
Warren Commission; in neither case did these lawyers
act as lawyers. Rather, they participated in a cover-up
and acted as accessories in serious crimes. The Congress accepted the Warren Report as the final solution
to the assassination and thus acquiesced in the cover-
up of a President's murder. And, perhaps most funda-
mentally, the press failed in its responsibility to the
people and became, in effect, an unofficial mouthpiece
of the government. For a short time the press publi-
cized some of the inconsistencies between the Warren
Report's conclusions and the evidence; yet never did
the press seriously question the legitimacy of the official findings on the assassination or attempt to ascertain why the Johnson administration lied about the
murder that brought it into power and what was hidden by those lies.

It was only a small body of powerless and unheralded
citizens who undertook to critically examine the official
investigation of President Kennedy's murder, and
among them it was still fewer who clearly understood
the ominous meaning of a whitewashed inquiry that

was accepted virtually without question. It was only these few who asked what would happen to our country if an executive disposed to abuse its authority could do so with impunity.

It was in 1966, long before the press and the public saw through the thicket of deception with which we had been led into a war in Vietnam, long before this country was to suffer the horrors of Watergate, that a leading assassination researcher, Harold Weisberg, wrote and published the following words:

> If the government can manufacture, suppress and lie when a President is cut down—and get away with it —what cannot follow? Of what is it not capable, regardless of motive. . .?
> This government *did* manufacture, suppress and lie when it pretended to investigate the assassination of John F. Kennedy.
> If it can do that, it can do anything.
> And will, if we let it.

Weisberg, in effect, warned that the executive would inevitably commit wrongdoing beyond imagination so long as there was no institution of government or society that was willing to stop it. That one man of modest means could make this simple deduction in 1966 is less a credit to him than it is an indictment of a whole system of institutions that failed in their fundamental responsibility to society.

My political maturity began to develop only in the past few years; all of my research on the assassination was conducted while I was a teenager. Yet the basic knowledge that my government could get away with what it did at the murder of a president made me fearful of the future. On October 10, 1971, when I was eighteen years old, I wrote what I hoped would be the last letter in a long and fruitless correspondence with a

lawyer who had participated in the official cover-up as
an investigator for the Warren Commission. I concluded that letter with these words:

> I ask myself if this country can survive when men like
> you, who are supposed to represent law and justice, are
> the foremost merchants of official falsification, deceit, and
> criminality.

It was to take three years and the worst political
crisis in our history for the press and the public to even
begin to awaken to the great dangers a democracy
faces when lawyers are criminals.

It is with pain and not pride that I look back and see
that so few were able to understand what the Warren
Commission and the acceptance of its fraudulent Report meant for this country. This was not omniscience,
but simple deduction from basic facts. I cannot escape
the conviction that had the Congress, or the lawyers, or
especially the press seriously endeavored to establish
the basic facts and then considered the implications of
these facts, we all might have been spared the frightening and threatening abuses of Watergate. If the institutions designed to protect society from such excesses of power had functioned in 1964, it is possible that
they would not have had to mobilize so incompletely
and almost ineffectively in 1972 and 1973.

Watergate has brought us into a new era, hopefully
one in which all institutions will work diligently to see
that our government functions properly and honestly.
As of now, the reasons for optimism are still limited. It
was not the press as an institution that probed beneath
the official lies about Watergate and demanded answers; essentially, it was *one* newspaper, the
Washington Post, that, true to its obligations, bulldog-
ged the story that most of the nation's press buried

until it became a national scandal. It was not the law
as an institution that insisted on the truth; it was one
judge, John Sirica, who best served the law by settling
for no less than the whole truth, and he was and continues to be deceived and lied to by those whose responsibility it is to uphold and defend the law.
Whether Congress will adequately respond to the
crimes and abuses of the Nixon administration remains
to be seen.

Our very system of government and law faces its
most profound challenge today. A nation that did not
learn from the Warren Commission has survived to re-
live a far worse version of that past in Watergate. It
would do well to live by the wisdom of Santayana, for
it is doubtful that American democracy could survive
another Watergate.

Howard Roffman

Acknowledgments

I wish to thank the following publishers for having given me permission to quote from published works:

The Bobbs-Merrill Company, Inc., for permission to quote from *Accessories After the Fact,* copyright © 1967 by Sylvia Meagher, reprinted by permission of the publisher, The Bobbs-Merrill Company, Inc.

CBS News, for permission to quote from *CBS News Extra: "November 22 and the Warren Report",* 1964, and *CBS News Inquiry: "The Warren Report",* 1967.

Harold Weisberg, for permission to quote from his books *Whitewash,* 1965, *Whitewash II,* 1966, *Photographic Whitewash,* 1967, and *Oswald in New Orleans,* 1967.

I would also like to express my deepest gratitude to Dick Bernabei and Harold Weisberg, who gave so unselfishly of themselves to help further my research and my personal development. Special thanks go to Sylvia Meagher for her encouragement and assistance with my manuscript, and to Halpert Fillinger for his time and invaluable advice concerning the medical/ballistics aspects of this study. To those too numerous to name who helped in so many ways, I offer my thanks and appreciation.

Introduction

Alabama Governor George Wallace, E. C. Dothard, Nicholas Zarvos, and Dora Thompson were not the only victims of Arthur Bremer's bullets on May 15, 1972. As has been the case in virtually all instances of political violence in the past eleven years, especially assassination, truth was the first casualty. When George Wallace was gunned•down, the media and the "experts" immediately groped for answers. But, beyond the obvious fact that Bremer was the man who pulled the trigger, nothing was really answered, and, instead, history was falsely revised.

Immediately, parallels were sought between Bremer, a "loner" and a "nut," and other political assassins in recent American history.[1] For the sake of convenience, if nothing worse, facts were abandoned and a massive rewriting of history took place. To the media it was a "fact" that Lee Harvey Oswald was the sole assassin of President Kennedy. No one mentioned that Oswald had never been declared legally guilty, or that the report of a "fact-finding" presidential commission that named Oswald as the assassin was deemed inadmissible as evidence in court.[2] Rarely was it mentioned that any controversy had surrounded the John Kennedy assassination, even though a bitter one raged over a period of years and was never resolved. Suddenly, too, James Earl Ray became the lone assassin of Martin Luther King; again, conspiracy was discounted. No one pointed

out that Ray, while pleading guilty to the legal charge
of murder, never admitted that he fired the bullet that
killed King and, in fact, stated in court that he did not
agree with officials who asserted that King was not killed by a conspiracy.[3] Ray's "minitrial," which was de-
nounced by the press as a mockery of justice,[4] was suddenly approved, and all the loose ends and inconsistencies in the King murder were swept under the rug and
forgotten.[5] Also, suddenly, there was no doubt that
Sirhan Sirhan was without aid or influence of any sort
when he murdered Robert Kennedy. Although Sirhan
has been found guilty of the murder, no court has ruled
that he was not part of a conspiracy or that he was not
influenced by others. Again, anyone who read the
newspapers or watched television after Wallace was
shot was led to believe that no elements of doubt surrounded Robert Kennedy's murder;[6] whatever con-
flicted with the notion that Sirhan was a lone
lunatic—for example, a grand jury investigation into
charges of evidence-tampering in the case,[7]—was simply ignored. Thus, with unresolved controversies, unin-
vestigated leads, and conflicting information neatly
tucked away, Americans were assured that they were
still a sane and decent people and that only the loners
and the madmen among them commit the heinous
crime of political assassination. Indeed, within two
hours of the Wallace shooting, before it was known
who had fired the bullets, a commentator for a major
radio news network announced *his* conclusion that
there was no political motive in the crime because
those who kill political figures are demented ego-
maniacs who cannot understand politics.[8]

The falsehoods and misrepresentations disseminated
by the government and the media concerning political
assassinations over the past eleven years are, in my

opinion, almost as odious in our society as the assassinations themselves. It is beyond the capability of the
average citizen to discover the truth about the murders
that threaten the nation's political stability, largely because the government has operated in a cloud of secrecy repugnant to the ideal of an open society. Yet the
freedoms guaranteed under the law are without meaning unless the people are honestly and competently informed.

In this book I present evidence that disproves the
central myth about the assassination of President
Kennedy, namely, that Lee Harvey Oswald was the assassin. The truth about John Kennedy's murder remains untold and doubtless unknown, thanks to an extensive and dishonest effort by the government to
frame Oswald as the lone assassin. As I here document,
the local and federal authorities who investigated the
Kennedy assassination assumed from the very beginning that Oswald was guilty, without regard to, and in
contradiction of, the evidence.

It has been many years since the assassination of
President Kennedy was the focus of great public attention. A brief historical review will refresh the memory.

President Kennedy was shot to death at 12:30 P.M.,
c.s.t., on November 22, 1963, as he rode through the
streets of Dallas, Texas, in a motorcade. Texas Governor John Connally, seated in the President's open
limousine, received serious bullet wounds in the shooting. Immediately, the motorcade sped to nearby Parkland Hospital, where a team of doctors tried in vain to
save the President's life. The President's death was announced, and, over the objections of the local authorities, who then had exclusive jurisdiction in the
crime, the body was forcefully removed from the hospital and flown back to Washington. Before the plane

bearing the President's body took off, Vice-President Lyndon Johnson, who had ridden in the motorcade, took the oath of office and assumed the duties of President. Within forty-five minutes of the assassination, a Dallas Police officer, J. D. Tippit, was shot to death in a Dallas suburb. A half-hour later, Lee Harvey Oswald was arrested in a movie theater near the site of the Tippit murder. He was first suspected of killing only Tippit, but by that evening he became the prime suspect in the murder of the President as well. Throughout that hectic weekend, the Dallas police made repeated public accusations of Oswald's guilt. Oswald steadfastly maintained that he was innocent and said he would prove it when he was brought to trial.

The trial never came, however. On November 24, Oswald, still in police custody, was shot to death by Jack Ruby.

Elimination of the only suspect in the assassination precluded a trial that might have turned up facts about the President's murder through the adversary system of justice. In its stead, President Johnson on November 29 appointed a commission to "evaluate and report upon the facts relating to the assassination. . .and the subsequent violent death of the man charged with the assassination" (R471). Earl Warren, then Chief Justice of the Supreme Court, presided over this commission, whose members included Senators Richard Russell and John Sherman Cooper, Representative Hale Boggs and Gerald Ford, Allen Dulles (former head of the CIA), and John J. McCloy. This panel, which became known as the Warren Commission, appointed a General Counsel, J. Lee Rankin, who headed a group of fourteen Assistant Counsels and twelve staff members. Throughout the Warren Commission's ten-month investigation, it was this staff of lawyers under Rankin who took virtually all the testimony and composed the final report.

The Commission's task was not executed by its prestigious but preoccupied members. In the words of the Warren Report, it was the staff that "undertook the work of the Commission with a wealth of legal and investigative experience." "Highly qualified personnel from several Federal agencies, assigned to the Commission at its request" also assisted in the investigation (Rxi). Members of the legal staff, divided by subject into teams, were responsible for analyzing and summarizing much of the information originally received from the various agencies, and for "determin[ing] the issues, sort[ing] out the unresolved problems, and recommend[ing] additional investigation to the Commission" (Rxii). "Because of the diligence, cooperation, and facilities of Federal investigative agencies," says the Report, "it was unnecessary for the Commission to employ investigators other than the members of the Commission's legal staff" (Rxiii). Thus, the validity of the Report rests largely on the integrity of the staff. While the distinguished members of the Commission may be held responsible for the actions of those working under them, the actual blame for an invalid or unsatisfactory investigation may be laid on the staff, just as any praise for exceptional work would properly be theirs.

On September 24, 1964, the Warren Commission submitted an 888-page report to the President. (This report was later to become known as the Warren Report.) The Commission concluded that Lee Harvey Oswald alone had assassinated President Kennedy, and maintained that it had seen no evidence indicating that Oswald and Jack Ruby, together or alone, had been part of a conspiracy to murder the President. Two months after the issuance of its Report, the Commission published as a massive appendix the evidence upon which the report was allegedly based, including transcripts of witness testimony, evidential exhibits, and thousands of documents. This evidence is contained in twenty-six large volumes.

Immediately upon its release, the Warren Report was met by an overwhelmingly favorable response from the nation's "establishment" press.[9] This response, analyzed objectively, was in fact a blatant instance of irresponsible journalism, for newsmen lavished praise on the Report before they could have read and analyzed it—*two months* before the evidence upon which it rested was released to the public.

Nevertheless, the Warren Report, which was introduced to the public as the definitive and final word on the assassination, was soon to be seriously questioned; a national controversy would erupt in which the Warren Commission, its Report, its evidence, and its workings would be challenged by a broad range of critics.

Criticism of the Commission and doubts about the assassination existed prior to the issuance of the Report, although the origins were primarily foreign and of the political left. Thomas Buchanan questioned Oswald's lone guilt and put forth a conspiracy theory in *Who Killed Kennedy?*, first published in London in May 1964. Joachim Joesten posed the question in the title of his book, *Oswald: Assassin or Fall Guy?* A French reporter, Nerin Gun, wrote a right-wing interpretation of a conspiracy to murder the President in *The Red Roses of Dallas*.

The January and March 1965 editions of *Liberation* magazine, a small left-of-center American publication, featured lengthy articles by Vincent Salandria questioning the medical/ballistics evidence in the assassination. At the same time, *The Oswald Affair* by Leo Sauvage was published in France; Sauvage attempted to prove Oswald's innocence. In August 1965, Harold

Weisberg copyrighted *Whitewash,* the first full-length book to examine in detail the Commission's investigation. *The Unanswered Questions About President Kennedy's Assassination,* a hasty critical analysis by Sylvan Fox, appeared in October 1965. It was *Whitewash* that bore the unenviable task of "breaking" the subject of Warren Report criticism in the United States. From March 1965 through April 1966, Weisberg futilely sought a publisher; many praised his book as a major work of great significance, but none would handle it. Finally, in April 1966, Weisberg published his book in a private printing at his own expense. Shortly after *Whitewash* appeared as an "underground" book, several other works critical of the official version of the assassination were published: *Inquest,* by Edward Jay Epstein (June 1966); *Rush to Judgement,* by Mark Lane (August 1966; Lane had been among the first to defend the dead Oswald, and, at his own urging, gave testimony before the Warren Commission); *The Second Oswald,* by Richard Popkin (September 1966); *Whitewash II* (December 1966) and *Photographic Whitewash* (May 1967), both private printings by Weisberg (Dell printed *Whitewash I* and *Whitewash II* in paperback in December 1966 and May 1967 respectively); *Accessories After the Fact* by Sylvia Meagher (September 1967); and *Oswald in New Orleans* by Weisberg (November 1967). Late in 1967, *Six Seconds In Dallas* by Josiah Thompson was published; Thompson maintained that his book presented a "radically different" approach in critical assassination literature.[10]

These books were widely reviewed and often appeared on best-seller lists. They were responsible for generating a considerable national controversy over the findings of the Warren Commission, in which several responsible periodicals called for a new investigation[11] and about two-thirds of the public rejected the allegation of Oswald's lone guilt.[12]

The controversy also produced numerous defenses of the Warren Commission and its Report, although these seldom addressed the evidence and were usually based upon platitudes about the "integrity" of the Commission and the questionable behavior of some of the critics. In 1967, two books appeared defending the official version: *The Truth About the Assassination,* by Charles Roberts, a short, hastily prepared work that attempted to bolster the Warren Report by citing errors in the works of Lane and Epstein, and *The Scavangers and Critics of the Warren Report,* by Richard Lewis and Lawrence Schiller, which inpugned the integrity of the critics. In June 1967 CBS News presented a four-part series, which amounted to little more than a televised version of the Warren Report and addressed itself to only a small fraction of the many serious criticisms leveled against the Report.[13] Governor Connally declared, based on his recollection of the event, that the Commission was wrong in its reconstruction of the shots; at the same time he expressed his confidence that the Report was correct—although he admitted he never read it.[14] In a similar vein, one of the Kennedy autopsy surgeons attempted to defend the official conclusions by "admitting" (three years too late) that his original autopsy notes were in error.[15]

Early in 1967, New Orleans District Attorney Jim Garrison made the dubitable announcement that his office, after conducting an extensive investigation, had "solved" the assassination.[16] One figure in the plot alleged by Garrison died immediately before he was to be arrested.[17] Soon after, a New Orleans businessman, Clay Shaw, was arrested and charged with conspiring to murder President Kennedy.[18] Finally the assassina-

tion was to get its day in court. But Shaw did not come
to trial until January 1969, and he was easily acquit-
ted after a two-month proceeding in which all the
shocking evidence against him promised by Garrison
failed to materialize.[19] Garrison was in consequence
widely condemned by the media, and the New Orleans
fiasco caused the virtual destruction of whatever foundation for credibility had previously been established
by the critics of the Warren Report. Garrison did not
refute, nor in any tangible way diminish the legitimacy
of several responsible and documented criticisms of the
official version of the assassination. But his unethical
behavior and the mockery of justice (involving only
Shaw) perpetrated under him was "bad press"; it left
the public and the media highly suspicious of Warren
Report criticism.

Although there is a general lack of interest in and,
in some quarters, overt distaste for discussion of President Kennedy's assassination, the need for honest discussion is as great today as it has been since the time
of the murder. The crime remains unsolved, and as I
illustrate here, the federal government played a direct
and deliberate role in assuring that it would remain
unsolved. Surely this is intolerable. One of the few remedies available to the average citizen is to set the record straight, however and wherever it can be done.

To set the record straight is the purpose of this book,
which draws together many facets of works published
long ago by other critics in addition to presenting my
own research and analysis. Here I present documented
proof of two points essential to any understanding of
the assassination and its official "investigation":

1. Lee Harvey Oswald did not fire any shots in the assassination:

2. The Warren Commission considered no possibility

other than that Oswald was the lone assassin, and consciously endeavored to fabricate a case against Oswald. These are serious charges. The implications of these charges are equally serious, for they place in jeopardy the integrity of our government.

A Word about Context

The focus of this study is admittedly narrow, limited to factual matters demanding nothing less than impartiality and objectivity. However, I think it is important that the reader, before he is presented with the facts, be prepared to understand the evidence and the conclusions it dictates in the proper context. The assassination did not take place in a vacuum, nor was it investigated in a vacuum. When a president of the United States is murdered, the implications and repercussions are inevitably far-reaching, regardless of the motive behind the murder. When an executive commission is authorized to come up with the definitive answer to every question about a president's murder and, instead, it is seen to have framed an innocent man, tacitly allowing presidential assassins to run free, that too has countless implications. Should any study avoid consideration of these implications, it would deny the great significance of the assassination and its official investigation.

The most obvious and the most important context is political. The assassination of President Kennedy was a political crime, whether or not it was so intended. The murder of an American president brings into question the legitimacy of the administration coming into power as a result of the crime. If that administration was in any way involved in the crime that made its accession

possible, then it cannot be legitimate. Thus, in our society, when the government investigates the murder of
a President, it investigates its own legitimacy. When
the Warren Commission investigated the Kennedy assassination, it sought, in effect, the credentials for
Lyndon Johnson.

But the Commission never produced those credentials; it never gave the stamp of legitimacy to the
Johnson administration because it never conducted an
honest, unprejudiced search for the truth. As this book
documents, the Commission named the wrong man as
the assassin of President Kennedy. Although I do not
allege that the Commission or its staff knew that Lee
Harvey Oswald was not the assassin, the documents
presented here reveal that no possibility other than
Oswald as the assassin was ever considered in the investigation. What this means, regardless of motives
(about which I am not competent to speculate), is that
the Commission left President Kennedy's murder unsolved, tacitly allowed the real assassins to go free, and
failed to absolve the Johnson administration of any
possible involvement in the assassination. I do not wish
to imply that any high government official, especially
anyone on a policy level, had a hand in the planning or
execution of the assassination. My point is that the
Warren Commission, because it failed to solve the
crime, has left a historical record that does not permit
the hoped-for conclusion that no one within the government was in any way responsible for the murder of
John Kennedy.

In a way, the Commission put itself into a political
trap that virtually insured that its investigation would
fail to establish the truth. The people who did the least
of the Commission's work were the Commission members themselves, all but one of whom were men whose

public and private responsibilities left them little or no
time to devote to the enormous task of investigating
the assassination. As I mentioned in the preface above,
and as the Commission admitted in its report, a staff of
lawyers headed by a general counsel "undertook the
work of the Commission" (Rxi). Virtually everything
that reached the Commission members had already
been selected, digested, and analyzed by the staff; in
this way the Commission members were really at the
mercy of the staff.

However, the staff, in turn, put itself at the mercy of
those agencies within the executive branch of the federal government which had an unmistakable political
interest to protect. Virtually all the information available to the staff came from the FBI, the Secret Service,
and, to a lesser degree, other executive agencies, including the CIA. It was these agencies to which the
staff usually turned when it desired additional investigation. Yet the FBI, the Secret Service, and the CIA
were left holding the bag when President Kennedy was
killed, and it would not be unreasonable to expect each
agency to protect itself, whether or not it was involved
in the murder. The President was killed in Dallas; that
city's police were partly responsible for assuring his
safety; they failed. The Secret Service had the direct
responsibility of protecting the President wherever he
went; they too failed. Both the FBI and the Secret Service knew of Oswald and of what they alleged to be his
"pro-Communist" and other "subversive" characteristics; neither agency made the slightest attempt to protect Kennedy from Oswald. Immediately, it was ru-
mored that Oswald had served as a government agent,
which meant that the alleged assassin may have been
on the payroll of the FBI, the CIA, or possibly other
agencies.

Thus, the material that came to the investigating staff risked being tainted by self-justification on the part of people intent on proving themselves not responsible for the tragedy and by self-interest on the part of agencies seeking to maintain or to regain good reputations. As Harold Weisberg succinctly puts it, all of these agencies "had one objective, to take the heat off themselves."[20] Through the staff, the Commission, and the Report, they succeeded. "But," Weisberg adds, "they left an unsolved crime, the most important that can be committed in this country."[21]

Each of the major critical works has formulated its own context in which it attempts to study the assassination and the Commission's investigation. As I see it, two basic approaches have been made with respect to the question of context. On the one hand, Mark Lane, Edward J. Epstein, and Richard Popkin sought to treat the assassination as if it had virtually no implications for society or government. To my way of thinking, they are at least guilty of naiveté in believing that the assassination and its official investigation could be divorced from a political context. Although Epstein, and Popkin after him, postulate that the Commission was concerned with "political truth," they carry this thesis no further and ignore the implications of this "political truth," which is their euphemism for untruth. On the other hand, Harold Weisberg and Sylvia Meagher have, in somewhat different ways, realistically dealt with the societal and political implications of the assassination and its prejudiced, if not fraudulent, investigation.

So that the reader can better appreciate what I consider the proper as well as the improper context, I will elaborate.

The basic context or focus of Mrs. Meagher's book is

set forth in its very appropriate title, *Accessories After
the Fact: The Warren Commission, The Authorities and
The Report.* Mrs. Meagher scrupulously contrasts the
statements contained in the Warren Report with the
Commission's published Hearings and Exhibits. She
finds that:

> The first pronounces Oswald guilty; the second, instead of
> corroborating the verdict reached by the Warren Commis-
> sion, creates a reasonable doubt of Oswald's guilt and
> even a powerful presumption of his complete innocence of
> all the crimes of which he was accused.[22]

As stated by Mrs. Meagher, the corollary to this finding is as follows:

> Because of the nature of the investigation, it is probable
> that the assassins who shot down President John F. Ken-
> nedy have gone free, undetected. The Warren Report has
> served merely to delay their identification and the process
> of justice.[23]

This is to say that the Warren Commission and the
federal authorities, regardless of their motives or con-
scious intent, made themselves accessories after the
fact in the President's murder by constructing a false
solution that allowed the real criminals to go free. Mrs.
Meagher does not go to great lengths to develop this
context, for her book is undeviatingly documentary and
a firm, irrefutable historical record that attests to the
lack of correlation between the assertions of the Warren Report and the Commission's evidence. However, it
is important that her work was framed in a context
that does not deny the implications of the Commission's failure to establish the truth, and that
does not offer apologies for the Commission based on

nothing more than an unwillingness to consider government officials capable of malfeasance or political evil. There is, however, nothing in Mrs. Meagher's or my own conception of the proper context that was not first conceived and published by Harold Weisberg. Weisberg has written, with passion, seven books about the Warren Commission's investigation.[24] The style of his writing, although objectionable to some, does not undermine the validity of the facts he presents or of his analyses thereof. He has consistently placed his work within a context that emphasizes the significant implications of the assassination and its fraudulent investigation as they relate to the integrity of our society and of our government. Indeed, the first sentence of his first book, written in 1965, reads: "Assassination is a political crime."[25] Because there is almost nothing I would add to Weisberg's formulation of context, I present verbatim quotations from three of his published works. I believe that his words, stating obvious yet often overlooked truths, will help the reader to appreciate the seriousness and significance of this subject.

In its approach, operations and Report, the Commission considered one possibility alone—that Lee Harvey Oswald, without assistance, assassinated the President and killed Officer Tippit. Never has such a tremendous array of power been turned against a single man, and he was dead. Yet even without opposition the Commission failed. . . .

A crime such as the assassination of the President of the United States cannot be left as the Report. . . has left it, without even the probability of a solution, with assassins and murderers free, and free to repeat their crimes and enjoy what benefits they may have expected to enjoy therefrom. [This was written before such crimes were repeated.] No President is ever safe if Presidential assas-

sins are exculpated. Yet that is what the Commission has
done. In finding Oswald "guilty," it has found those who
assassinated him "innocent." If the President is not safe,
then neither is the country.[26]

Nothing can happen to [the President] or the institution of the Presidency that does not in some degree affect
everyone in the entire world.

Much more does it relate to each individual American,
to the integrity of the institutions of our society, when
anything happens to any president—especially when he is
assassinated.

The consignment of President John F. Kennedy to history with the dubious epitaph of the whitewashed investigation is a grievous event.[27]

Above all, the Report leaves in jeopardy the rights of all
Americans and the honor of the nation. When what happened to Oswald once he was in the hands of the public
authority can occur in this country with neither re-
primand nor question, no one is safe. When the Federal
government puts its stamp of approval on such unabashed
and open denial of the most basic legal rights of any
American, no matter how insignificant he may be, then no
American can depend on having these rights, no matter
what his power or connections. The rights of all Americans, as the Commission's chairman said when wearing
his Chief Justice's hat, depend upon each American's en-
joyment of these same rights.[28]

Can these things [the improprieties in the official
investigation] happen in a democratic society? They did.

They happened not in the pro-forma police investigation
of the violent end of an unknown, a man without friends
or influence, although it would not be tolerable in a democratic society if he had been an unwanted bum.

These things happened when a man over whom millions
wept the bitterest tears was murdered. They happened
when a President was assassinated. . . .

If the government can manufacture, suppress and lie

when a President is cut down—and get away with it-
—what cannot follow? Of what is it not capable, regardless of motive. . .?

This government *did* manufacture, suppress and lie
when it pretended to investigate the assassination of John
F. Kennedy.

If it can do that, it can do anything.

And will, if we let it.[29]

The context enunciated by Harold Weisberg and Sylvia Meagher was constantly avoided and ignored during those few years in which the news media presented
the assassination controversy to the American public.
Instead, the media embraced those critics whose works
denied the basic truths, lacked the essential context,
and contrived dishonest and immature excuses for the
failure of the Warren Commission.

For Mark Lane, in his "No. 1 Bestseller" *Rush to
Judgement,* there was no Commission staff. Throughout his book they are hidden and thus protected. Where
their questioning of particular witnesses is quoted,
their names are replaced by an anonymous "Q." His
book mentions only two minor staff lawyers by name,
and is totally silent about those lawyers who did most
of the work, such as Joseph Ball, David Belin, Wesley
Liebeler, Norman Redlich, and Arlen Specter. The in-
troduction to *Rush to Judgement* by Professor Hugh
Trevor-Roper states: "It is clear that the bulk of the
work fell upon the Chairman and upon the assistant
counsel and staff [who, for Lane's readers, are
nameless]."[30] This assertion unjustly singles out Earl
Warren for blame, although he never came close to
doing "the bulk of the work."

Lane allowed his book to be introduced in a way that
would make it appear that the failure of the entire
government was a regrettable, inadvertent mistake.

"The crux of the matter," says Trevor-Roper, "is a question of confidence. We have to admit that we lack confidence in the evidence submitted to the Commission and the Commission's handling of it."[31] This lack of confidence is the crux of nothing. We are immediately assured that "moderate, rational men will naturally and...rightly" reject the idea that the Commission and the "existing agencies" "sought to reach a certain conclusion at the expense of the facts...that they... were   dishonest... [that   the]   Commission...engaged in a conspiracy to cover up a crime...."[32]

Like the Commission, Lane and Trevor-Roper have rushed to their own judgment without regard for the facts. It is nice to know that both impute no dishonesty or prefabrication to the Commission, but it is disturbing that the evidence they present *proves* both. "I do not suppose that the Commission itself was consciously working towards a preconceived answer. I assume that all its members were conscientiously looking for the truth," says Trevor-Roper.[33] The lines that follow this supposition also disprove it: "I believe with Mr. Lane that their examination was defective and their argument unsound: defective because they overlooked inconvenient evidence [if nothing was "preconceived" and "truth" was sought, there could have been no "inconvenient" evidence]; unsound because they applied different standards to the evidence which they accepted [does this not imply a "preconceived" conclusion?]"[34]

Edward J. Epstein rode high on his critique of the inner workings of the Commission, entitled *Inquest,* while in reality he was defending the official investigation and assuming the virtue of the investigators. His book "attempts to answer the question: How did the Commission go about searching for...the truth?"[35] This assumes what is not true: that the Commission at any time searched for the truth. It never did, nor could it have, since truth does not emerge from an "investigation" predisposed toward a set conclusion. Epstein's defense is that the Warren Commission was involved in a situation that might have excused lying in the "national interest." He rightly asserts that "the nation's faith in its own institutions was held to be at stake."[36] But, at the conclusion of the book, he says that "in establishing its version of the truth, the Warren Commission acted to reassure the nation and protect the national interest."[37] This, he thinks, justified the failure to make "it clear that very substantial evidence indicated the presence of a second assassin."[38] Although I deplore it, I will not bicker with Epstein's notion of what "national security" entails and what the government can do it protect it. But it seems nonsensical to assert that the Commission could reassure a nation whose faith in its institutions was "at stake" by causing those very institutions to fail.

The Second Oswald, by Richard Popkin, never achieved the notoriety of the first books by Weisberg, Epstein, and Lane, but has been considered one of the basic books attacking the Commission's findings.[39] As a historical record it reflects, in general, Epstein's thesis, for it attempts to whitewash the Commission's investigation just as the Commission whitewashed the assassination. Indeed, Epstein is quite openly identified as the hero of Popkin's book.[40] The nonhero of the book, according to my impression, is Harold Weisberg, who is very infrequently mentioned in the text. Anyone familiar with the critical assassination literature would certainly be aghast at the unscholarly claim by Popkin that his book "provides the one element that has been missing in all criticism of the Warren Commission thus

far: the first systematic theory suggesting how Oswald
may have conspired with others to assassinate President Kennedy."[41] The "systematic theory" is that
someone, resembling and posing as Oswald, planted incriminating circumstantial evidence during the two
months before the assassination. However, the theory
is not Popkin's. It was conceived and copyrighted by
Weisberg over a year before Popkin published his book;
chapter 11 of *Whitewash* is entitled "The False Oswald." But Weisberg is unacknowledged by Popkin,
who wrongly claims singular and original credit.[42]

It is not surprising, considering his unscholarly approach, his apparent contempt for Weisberg, and his
respect for Epstein, that Popkin closes his book as follows:

> the Commission did a poor job. . .But Weisberg's constant
> charge that the Commission was malevolent is, I believe,
> quite unfounded. Until Epstein came along, one searched
> for some possible explanation for the deficiencies of the
> Dallas Police, the FBI, and the Commission. Epstein has
> at least explained the failings of the last group. They did
> a rush job, a slapdash one, defending a politically accepta-
> ble explanation.[43]

Popkin thus presents himself as a "reasonable" critic
by distorting the issues and ignoring the facts. Weisberg, to my knowledge after reading his every published word on the assassination and working closely
with him over the past three years, has never charged
the Commission with "malevolence." He has trans-
cended both the fictions of Lane and Trevor-Roper that
the Commission had no preconceived conclusions and
honestly sought the truth, and the unsupported
apologies of Epstein and Popkin that the Commission
sought nothing worse that to reassure the American

people by disseminating a very palatable, if inadvertently false, version of "political truth." Rather, what Weisberg has specifically said (and as the documents discovered by him and presented in this book prove) is that the Commission consciously pursued a conclusion already formulated by the Dallas Police and the FBI in advance of any investigation. Weisberg has never stated that the Commission members, as distinguished from the staff, ever felt that what they were doing was "bad" or not in the best interests of the country. But the record is incontrovertible that the truth was not sought, that Oswald was consciously and deliberately presumed guilty by the Commission. The motives of the Commissioners, whether "political" or "malevolent" or anything else, are actually irrelevant in terms of what *was* done and the implications of what was done. Lane, Epstein, and Popkin are guilty, in the very least, of putting the cart before the horse and formulating a context that *begins* with the presumption that the Commission operated with good intentions.

So that my purpose here is not misunderstood, let me emphasize that I do not wish to make personal attacks on individual critics of the Warren Report, nor do I wish to endorse or condemn, as a whole, any book. I am now dealing solely with the question of context and doctrine. In this respect, I must condemn the books by Lane, Epstein, and Popkin as having been set in a context that is factually wrong, politically deceiving, and wholly unscholarly.

It is not the critic's responsibility to explain the motives of the Commission members or their staff. The only responsibility of the critic is to deal with the facts and never to avoid or attempt to modify, without factual basis, the implications of the evidence. So, when the Commissioners decided in advance that the wrong man was the lone assassin, whatever their intentions, they protected the real assassins. Through their staff, they misinformed the American public and falsified history. Regardless of whether their false solution to the crime was a "politically acceptable explanation," they did nothing to rectify the politically "unacceptable" solution. When a government can get away with what ours did on the death of its president, then the presidency is betrayed; it is subject to whim and illegality, and is reduced to a position of no real security or stability.

The actions of the Commission betrayed the institution of the Presidency no more than they betrayed the rights of every American. No one's rights can be safe when an executive commission, including the Chief Justice of the Supreme Court, Congressmen, and a score of respected lawyers, operates on a presumption of guilt and conducts an investigation that, in plain language, frames an innocent man who was dead and could not defend himself.

And what will be said of our country by those future historians, not so concerned with defending anyone's presumed "good motives," when they study the records of Lyndon Johnson's accession to the Presidency and find that the Commission, which failed to identify those responsible for John Kennedy's murder, also failed to eliminate the possibility that Johnson or anyone in his administration was involved?

And, besides the implications for our history, how do the actions of the Commission and its staff speak for the integrity of our society and of our government? With the Warren Report, the government sacrificed its credibility, and undermined any legitimate basis the people might have had for confidence in it. Very simply, a government that disseminates blatant falsehoods

about the murder of its chief executive and frames an
innocent man whether he be dead or alive, rich or poor,
does not deserve the confidence of the people.

This is a disquieting reality, but it is a reality that
must be faced if integrity is to be restored to our government and its institutions. The government must
function properly, with decency, honesty, and respect
for the law. In framing Oswald and exculpating Presidential assassins, the Commission mocked the law and
every principle of justice. In the words of a decision by
a U.S. Court of Appeals judge, "In a government of
laws, the very existence of the government will be im-
periled if it fails to observe the law scrupulously."[44]

If those citizens who have a legitimate concern that
the institutions of our government are not working
properly be condemned as unreasonable or unpatriotic,
then I fear that it cannot be honestly said that we in-
habit "the land of the free and the home of the brave."
Men cannot be free when they allow the freedom of
others to be usurped by sheer power; they cannot be
brave when they assume a posture of cowardice or ac-
quiescence in the face of such power.

This book is not a call to the people to lose faith in
their government. It is a call to reason, so that no one
will unquestioningly accept governmental assurances
without first checking the facts. In the end, we must
face reality; we must reckon with truth no matter
where it is found.

A Note on Citations

References to the 26-volume *Hearings Before the President's Commission on the Assassination of President Kennedy* follow this form: volume number, H, page number; thus, for example, 4H165 refers to volume 4, page 165. Exhibits introduced in evidence before the Commission are designated CE and a number; CE399, for example, refers to the Commission's 399th exhibit. References to the *Report of the President's Commission on the Assassination of President Kennedy* (Washington, D.C.: Government Printing Office, 1964) follow this form: R, page number; R150, for example, indicates page 150 of the Report. Most references to the Commission's unpublished files deposited in the National Archives follow this form: CD, number: page number; CD5:260, for example, indicates page 260 of Commission Document 5.

PRESUMED GUILTY

PART I:

THE PRESUMPTION OF GUILT

1

Assassination: The Official Case

As stated in its Report, one of the Warren
Commission's main objectives was "to identify the person or persons responsible for both the assassination of
President Kennedy and the killing of Oswald through
an examination of the evidence" (Rxiv). Accordingly,
the Commission produced one person whom it claimed
to be solely responsible for the assassination: Lee Harvey Oswald (R18-23). Because the scope of the present
study is limited to Oswald's role in the shooting, it is
vital that we first understand the foundations for the
Commission's conclusion that Oswald was guilty.

In this chapter I will deal solely with the evidence
that is alleged to prove Oswald's guilt, as presented in
the Report. I will make no attempt to criticize the
selection of evidence, but rather will take the final report at face value, probing its logic and structure so
that it can be judged whether the determination of
Oswald's guilt is warranted by the "facts" set forth.

The first and most vital step in determining who
shot at the President involved ascertaining the
location(s) and weapon(s) from which the shots came.
In a chapter entitled "The Shots From the Texas School
Book Depository," the Commission "analyzes the evidence and sets forth its conclusions concerning the
45

source, effect, number and timing of the shots that killed President Kennedy and wounded Governor Connally" (R61).

The Scene

   The scene of the assassination was Dealey Plaza, the
so-called heart of Dallas, made up of three streets that
converge at a railroad overpass. At the opposite side of
the plaza are several buildings, many city owned.
Along each side leading to the underpass are grassy
banks adorned with shrubbery and masonry structures.
Two grassy plots separate the three streets—Elm,
Main, and Commerce—all of which intersect with
Houston at the head of the plaza. The shooting occurred as the Presidential limousine cruised down
Elm Street toward the underpass.

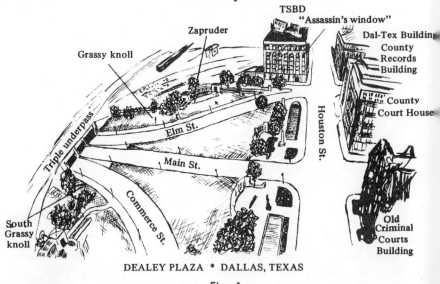

DEALEY PLAZA * DALLAS, TEXAS

Fig. 1

   One of the major conclusions of the Commission is
that the shots "were fired from the sixth floor window

at the southeast corner of the Texas School Book Depository" (R18), a book warehouse located on the northwest corner of Elm and Houston. (Oswald was employed in this building.) Several factors influenced this conclusion.

The Report first calls upon the witnesses who indicated in some way that the shots originated from this source. It refers to two spectators who claimed to see "a rifle being fired" from the Depository window, two others who "saw a rifle in this window immediately after the assassination," and "three employees of the Depository, observing the parade from the fifth floor," who "heard the shots fired from the floor immediately above them" (R61).

The Limousine

Discussed next is the presidential automobile (R76-77). On the night of the assassination, Secret Service agents found two relatively large bullet fragments in the front seat of the car—one consisting of the nose portion of a bullet, the other a section of the base portion. An examination of the limousine on November 23 by FBI agents disclosed three very small lead particles on the rug beneath the left jump seat, which had been occupied by Mrs. Connally, and a small lead residue on the inside surface of the windshield, with a corresponding series of cracks on the outer surface. All of the metallic pieces were compared by spectrographic analysis by the FBI and "found to be similar in metallic composition, but it was not possible to determine whether two or more of the fragments came from the same bullet." The physical characteristics of the windshield damage indicated that it was struck on the inside surface from behind, by a bullet fragment traveling at "fairly high velocity."

THE PRESIDENTIAL LIMOUSINE:
November 22, 1963

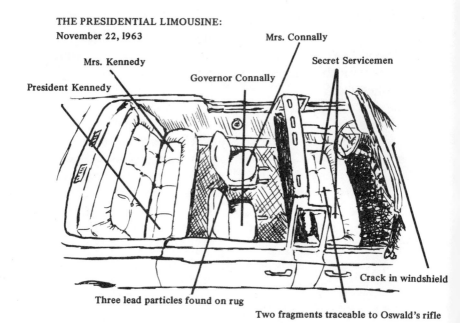

Fig. 2

Ballistics

In a crime involving firearms, the ballistics evidence is always of vital importance. This was especially true of the ballistics evidence adduced by the Commission relating to the President's murder. As used in the Report, this evidence seems to have a clarifying effect, bringing together loose ends and creating a circumstantial but superficially persuasive case. The relevant discussion is summarized in the Report as follows, based on unanimous expert testimony:

> The nearly whole bullet found on Governor Connally's stretcher at Parkland Memorial Hospital [the President and the Governor were rushed to this hospital after the shooting] and the two bullet fragments found on the

front seat of the Presidential limousine were fired from the 6.5-millimeter Mannlicher-Carcano rifle found on the sixth floor of the Depository Building to the exclusion of all other weapons.

The three used cartridge cases found near the window on the sixth floor at the southeast corner of the building were fired from the same rifle which fired the above-described bullet and fragments, to the exclusion of all other weapons. (R18)

Here the Commission has related a rifle and three spent cartridge cases found at the scene of the crime to a bullet found in a location presumably occupied by Governor Connally as well as to fragments found in the car in which both victims rode. The circumstantial aspect of the ballistics evidence presented by the Commission is this: it does not directly relate the weapon to a specific shooter nor the bullet specimens to a specific victim's body.

Autopsy

An autopsy is a central piece of evidence in violent or unnatural death. In the case of death by gunshot wounds, an autopsy can reveal a wealth of information, indicating the type(s) of ammunition used by the assailant(s), as well as the general relationship of the gun to the victim's body. Bullets or fragments found in the body can sometimes conclusively establish the specific weapon used in the crime. The medical evidence used by the Commission emanated from (a) the doctors who observed the President's and the Governor's wounds at Parkland Hospital, (b) the autopsy on the President performed at the Bethesda Naval Hospital, Maryland, on the night of the assassination, (c) the clothing worn by the two victims, and (d) ballistics tests conducted with the Carcano found in the Depository and ammunition of the same type as

that found in the hospital and the car. From this information the Commission drew the following conclusions:

> The nature of the bullet wounds suffered by President
> Kennedy and Governor Connally and the location of the
> car at the time of the shots establish that the bullets were
> fired from above and behind the Presidential limousine,
> striking the President and the Governor as follows:
> (1) President Kennedy was first struck by a bullet
> which entered at the back of his neck and exited through
> the lower front portion of his neck, causing a wound
> which would not necessarily have been lethal. The Presi-
> dent was struck a second time by a bullet which entered
> the right-rear portion of his head, causing a massive and
> fatal wound.
> (2) Governor Connally was struck by a bullet which en-
> tered on the right side of his back and travelled downward
> through the right side of his chest, exiting below his right
> nipple. This bullet then passed through his right wrist
> and entered his left thigh where it caused a superficial
> wound. (R18-19)

For each set of wounds, the Report cites ballistics tests
in support of the notion that the injuries observed were
consistent with bullets fired from the Carcano (R87, 91,
94-95). In two instances it is asserted that the tests
further indicated that the wounds could have been produced by the bullet specimens traceable to the *specific*
Carcano found in the Depository, as opposed to merely
being consistent with a *similar* rifle firing similar ammunition (R87, 95).

The Trajectory
   "The trajectory" is the next topic of discussion in the
Report, which says: "...to insure that all data were
consistent with the shots having been fired from the
sixth floor window, the Commission requested addi-

tional investigation, including analysis of motion picture films of the assassination and on-site tests" (R96). The films referred to by the Commission were those taken of the assassination by spectators Abraham Zapruder, Orville Nix, and Mary Muchmore. Only Zapruder's film, taken from the President's side of the street, provided a photographic record of the entire shooting. (Zapruder's position is shown in the sketch of Dealey Plaza.)

Motion picture footage is composed of a series of still pictures called "frames" taken in extremely rapid succession which, when projected at approximately the same speed of exposure, create the illusion of motion. The frames of the Zapruder film were numbered by the FBI for convenient reference, and it is not until frame 130 that the President's car appears in the film. From that point on, this is basically what we see in terms of frames: The car continues down Elm for a brief period, gradually approaching a road sign that loomed in Zapruder's view. At frame 210, President Kennedy goes out of view behind this sign. Governor Connally, also temporarily blocked from Zapruder's sight, first reappears in frame 222. At 225 the President comes into view again, and he has obviously been wounded, for his face has a grimace and his hands are rising toward his chin. Within about ten frames, the Governor is struck; he manifests a violent reaction. In the succeeding frames we see Mrs. Kennedy reach over to help her husband, her attention temporarily diverted by Connally, who is screaming. Finally, at frame 313, the President is struck in the head, as can be clearly seen by the great rupturing of skull and brain tissues. Mrs. Kennedy scrambles frantically onto the trunk of the limousine and is forced back into her seat by a Secret Service agent who had run to the car from the follow-up vehicle. Subsequent to the head shot, the limousine accelerated in its approach toward the underpass. Once the car is out of view, the film stops. The Nix and Muchmore films depict sequences immediately before, during, and after the head shot.

Examination of Zapruder's camera by the FBI established that an average of 18.3 film frames was exposed during each second of operation; thus the timing of certain events could be calculated by allowing 1/18.3 seconds for the action depicted from one frame to the next. Tests of the "assassin's" rifle disclosed that at least 2.3 seconds (or 41-42 film frames) were required between shots (R97).

The on-site tests were conducted by the FBI and Secret Service in Dealey Plaza on May 24, 1964. A car simulating the Presidential limousine was driven down Elm Street, as depicted in the various assassination films, with stand-ins occupying the general positions of the President and the Governor. An agent situated in the sixth-floor window tracked the car through the telescopic sight on the Carcano as the assassin allegedly did on November 22. Films depicting the "assassin's view" were made through the rifle scope (R97). During these tests it was ascertained that the foliage of a live oak tree would have blocked a sixth-floor view of the President during his span of travel corresponding to frames 166 through 210. An opening among the leaves permitted viewing the President's back at frame 186, for a duration of about 1/18 second (R98).

The Commission concluded that the first shot to wound the President in the neck occurred between frames 210 to 225, largely because (a) a sixth-floor gunman could not have shot at the President for a substantial time prior to 210 because of the tree, and (b) the President seems to show an obvious reaction to his neck wounds at 225. Exact determination of the time of impact was prevented because Mr. Kennedy was blocked from Zapruder's view by a road sign from 210 to 224 (R98, 105).

The Report next argues that the trajectory from the sixth-floor window strongly indicated that a bullet exiting from the President's throat and traveling at a substantial velocity would not have missed both the car and its occupants. No damage to the limousine was found consistent with the impact of such a missile. "Since [the bullet] did not hit the automobile, [FBI expert] Frazier testified that it probably struck Governor Connally," says the Report, adding, "The relative positions of President Kennedy and Governor Connally at the time when the President was struck in the neck confirm that the same bullet probably passed through both men" (R105). The evidence allegedly supporting this double-hit theory is then discussed, and the Commission concludes that one bullet probably was responsible for all the nonfatal wounds to the two victims (R19).

Number of Shots

"The weight of the evidence indicates that there were three shots fired," declares the Report (R19). This conclusion is based not so much on witness recollections as on the physical evidence at the scene—namely, the presence of three cartridge cases (R110-11). The Commission reasons that, because (a) one shot passed through the President's neck and probably went on to wound the Governor, (b) a subsequent shot penetrated the President's head, (c) no other shot struck the car, and (d) three shots were fired, "it follows that one shot probably missed the car and its occupants. The evidence is inconclusive as to whether it was the first, second, or third shot which missed" (R111).

Time Span

Determination of the time span of the shots, according to the Commission's theory, is dependent on which of the three shots missed. As calculated by use of the Zapruder film, the time span from the first shot to wound the President to the one that killed him was 4.8 to 5.6 seconds. Had the missed shot occurred between these two, says the Report, all the shots could still have been fired from the Carcano, which required at least 2.3 seconds (or 42 frames) between successive shots. If the first or third shots missed, the time span grows to at least 7.1 to 7.9 seconds for the three shots.

Thus, the Commission concluded

> that the shots which killed President Kennedy and wounded Governor Connally were fired from the sixth-floor window at the southeast corner of the Texas School Book Depository Building. Two bullets probably caused all the wounds suffered by President Kennedy and Governor Connally. Since the preponderance of the evidence indicated that three shots were fired, the Commission concluded that one shot probably missed the Presidential limousine and its occupants, and that the three shots were fired in a time period ranging from approximately 4.8 to in excess of 7 seconds. (R117)

The Assassin

In a preface to its discussion of the evidence relevant to the identity of President Kennedy's assassin, the Report adds a new conclusion to those of its preceding chapter. Here it asserts not only that it has established the source of the shots as the specific Depository window, but also "that the weapon which fired [the] bullets was a Mannlicher-Carcano 6.5-millimeter Italian rifle bearing the serial number C2766" (R118). Although it had previously traced the found bullet specimens to this rifle discovered in the Depository, the Report never specifically concluded that these bullets were responsible for the wounds. Making such an assertion at this point provided the premise for associating the owner of that rifle with the murder.

Who owned the rifle? The Report announces:

> Having reviewed the evidence that (1) Lee Harvey Oswald purchased the rifle used in the assassination [although the name under which the rifle was ordered was "A. Hidell," the order forms were in Oswald's handwriting (R118-119)], (2) Oswald's palmprint was on the rifle in a position which shows that he had handled it while it was disassembled, (3) fibers found on the rifle most probably came from the shirt Oswald was wearing on the day of the assassination [although the Commission's expert felt that these fibers had been picked up "in the recent past," he could not say definitely how long they had adhered to the rifle (R125)]. The Commission never considered the possibility that they were deposited on the rifle subsequent to Oswald's arrest.], (4) a photograph taken in the yard of Oswald's apartment shows him holding this rifle [the photographic expert could render no opinion as to whether the rifle shown in these pictures was the C2766 and not another rifle of the same configuration (R127)], and (5) the rifle was kept among Oswald's possessions from the time of its purchase until the day of the assassination [The Commission cites no evidence that the specific C2766 rifle was in Oswald's possession.], the Commission concluded that the rifle used to assassinate President Kennedy and wound Governor Connally was owned and possessed by Lee Harvey Oswald. (R129)

At this point the Commission has related Oswald to the President's murder in two ways. It has posited the source of the shots at a location accessible to Oswald, and has named as the assassination weapon a rifle purchased and possibly possessed by Oswald. This, although circumstantial, obviously laid the foundation for the ultimate conclusion that Oswald was the assassin. Now his activities on the day of the shooting had to be considered in light of this charge.

In a section headed "The Rifle in the Building," the
Report takes up the problem of how the C2766 rifle
was brought into the Depository. The search for an
answer was not difficult for the Commission. Between
Thursday night, November 21, and Friday morning,
Oswald had engaged in what could have been con-
strued as incriminating behavior. As the Report ex-
plains,

> During October and November of 1963, Lee Harvey Os-
> wald lived in a roominghouse in Dallas while his wife and
> children lived in Irving, at the home of Ruth Paine, ap-
> proximately 15 miles from Oswald's place of work at the
> ... Depository. Oswald travelled between Dallas and Irv-
> ing on weekends in a car driven by a neighbor of the
> Paine's, Buell Wesley Frazier, who also worked at the De-
> pository. Oswald generally would go to Irving on Friday
> afternoon and return to Dallas Monday morning. (R129)

On Thursday, November 21, Oswald asked Frazier
whether he could ride home with him to Irving that
afternoon, saying that he had to pick up some curtain
rods for his apartment. The Report would lead us to believe that Oswald's Irving visit on the day prior to the
assassination was a departure from his normal
schedule. Adding further suspicion to this visit, the
Report asserts "It would appear, however, that obtaining curtain rods was not the purpose of Oswald's trip to
Irving on November 21," noting that Oswald's apartment, according to his landlady, did not need curtains
or rods, and no curtain rods were discovered in the Depository after the assassination (R130).

By seeming to disprove Oswald's excuse for the
weekday trip to Irving, the Report establishes a basis
for more sinister explanations; they hinge on the assumption that the rifle was stored in the Paine garage.
Asserting that Oswald had the opportunity to enter the

garage Thursday night without being detected, the Report emphasizes that, by the afternoon of November 22 the rifle was missing from "its accustomed place." The implication is that Oswald removed it (R130-31).

To top off this progression of hypotheses is the fact that Oswald carried a "long and bulky package" to work on the morning of the assassination. As he walked to Frazier's house for a ride to the Depository, Frazier's sister, Linnie May Randle, saw him carrying a package that she estimated to be about 28 inches long and 8 inches wide. Frazier was the next to see the brown paper container, as he got into the car and again as he and Oswald walked toward the Depository after parking in a nearby lot. He thought the package was around 2 feet long and 5 or 6 inches wide, recalling that Oswald held it cupped in his right hand with the upper end wedged in his right armpit. The Report expresses its apparent exasperation that both Frazier's and Mrs. Randle's estimates and descriptions were of a package shorter than the longest component of the Carcano which, when disassembled, is 34.8 inches in length. It asserts that "Mrs. Randle saw the bag fleetingly" and quotes Frazier as saying that he paid it little attention, and concludes that the two "are mistaken as to the length of the bag" (R131-34). Had they not been "mistaken" in their recollections, Oswald's package could not have contained the rifle.

"A handmade bag of wrapping paper and tape was found in the southeast corner of the sixth floor alongside the window from which the shots were fired (R134)," says the Report, citing scientific evidence that this bag was (a) made from materials obtained in the Depository's shipping room, and (b) handled by Oswald so that he left a palmprint and fingerprint on it. After connecting this sack with the "assassin's" window and

Oswald, the Report attempts a further connection with
the rifle by asserting that some fibers found inside the
bag matched some of those which composed the blanket
in which the rifle was allegedly stored, suggesting that
perhaps the rifle "picked up the fibers from the blanket
and transferred them to the paper bag." This feeble
evidence is all the Commission could produce to suggest a connection between the rifle and the bag. A
Commission staff lawyer, Wesley Liebeler, called it
"very thin."[1] Likewise, the Commission asserts that
Oswald *constructed* this bag, while it presents evidence
only that he *handled* it (R134-37).

One may indeed express concern that, on the basis of
the above-cited evidence, the Commission asserts, "The
preponderance of the evidence supports the conclusions
that" Oswald: "(1) told the curtain rod story to Frazier
to explain both the return to Irving on a Thursday and
the obvious bulk of the package he intended to bring to
work the next day," even thought no explanation other
than the transporting of the rifle was considered by the
Commission (*e.g.,* that perhaps Oswald told the "curtain rod story" to Frazier to cover a personal reason
such as making up with his wife, with whom he had
quarreled earlier that week, bringing a large package
the following morning to substantiate the false excuse);
"(2) took paper and tape from the wrapping bench of
the Depository and fashioned a bag large enough to
carry the disassembled rifle," although no evidence is
offered that Oswald ever constructed the bag, "(3) removed the rifle from the Paine's garage on Thursday
evening," citing no evidence that it might not have
been someone other than Oswald who removed the
rifle, if it was ever there at all, "(4) carried the rifle
into the Depository Building, concealed in the bag,"
even though, to make this assertion, it had to reject the

stories of the only witnesses who saw the package, and could produce no direct evidence that the rifle had been in the bag; and "(5) left the bag alongside the window from which the shots were fired," offering no substantiation that it was Oswald who left the bag in this position (R137). The Commission's conclusion from this evidence is that "Oswald carried [his] rifle into the Depository building on the morning of November 22, 1963" (R19), although the prefabrication of the bag demands premeditation of the murder, and the presence of the bag by the "assassin's" window implies, according to the Report, that Oswald brought the rifle to this window.

Because its logic was faulty, the Commission's interpretation of "the preponderance of the evidence" loses substantial foundation. Not one of the five above-quoted subconclusions relating to the rifle in the building is confirmed by evidence; a conclusive determination is precluded by insufficient evidence. The most the Commission could fairly have asserted from the facts presented is that, although there was no conclusive evidence that Oswald brought his rifle to the Depository, there was likewise no conclusive disproof, that is, the state of the evidence could not dictate a reliable conclusion.

As the Commission edged toward its ultimate conclusion that Oswald was the lone assassin, it reached a comfortable position in having concluded that Oswald brought his rifle to the Depositiory. It next had to consider the question of Oswald's presence at the right window at the right time. Assured that Oswald "worked principally on the first and sixth floors of the building," we learn that "the Commission evaluated the physical evidence found near the window after the assassination and the testimony of eyewitnesses in deciding whether Lee Harvey Oswald was present at this window at the time of the assassination" (R137).

The Report presents only one form of "physical evidence"—fingerprints—asserting that a total of four of Oswald's prints were left on two boxes near the window and on the paper sack found in that area. In evaluating the significance of this evidence,

> the Commission considered the possibility that Oswald handled these cartons as part of his normal duties . . . .Although a person could handle a carton and not leave identifiable prints, none of these employees [who might have handled the cartons] except Oswald left identifiable prints on the cartons. This finding, in addition to the freshness of one of the prints. . .led the Commission to attach some probative value to the fingerprint and palmprint identifications in reaching the conclusion that Oswald was present at the window from which the shots were fired, although the prints do not establish the exact time he was there. (R141)

The Report's reasoning is that the presence of Oswald's prints on objects present at the sixth-floor window is probative evidence of his presence at this window at some time. Liebeler felt that this evidence "seems to have very little significance indeed," and pointed out that the absence of other employees' fingerprints "does not help to convince me that [Oswald] moved [the boxes] in connection with the assassination. It shows the opposite just as well."[2] Both Liebeler and the Report avoid the logical, and the only precise, meaning of these fingerprint data: the presence of Oswald's prints on the cartons and the bag means *only* that he handled them; it does not disclose *when* or *where*. Oswald *could* have touched these objects on the first floor of the Depository prior to the time when they were moved to their location by the "assassin's" window, perhaps by another person. Thus, this evidence does not connect Oswald with the source of the shots and is meaningless, because Oswald normally handled such cartons in the building as part of his work.

"Additional testimony linking Oswald with the point from which the shots were fired was provided by the testimony of Charles Givens," the Report continues, "who was the last known employee to see Oswald inside the building prior to the assassination." According to the Report, Givens saw Oswald walking *away* from the southeast corner of the sixth floor at 11:55, 35 minutes before the shooting (R143). That Oswald was seen where he normally worked such a substantial amount of the time prior to the shots connects him with nothing except his expected routine. That "none of the Depository employees is known to have seen Oswald again until after the shooting," if true, is likewise of little significance, especially since most of the employees had left the building to view the motorcade.

In its next section relevant to the discussion of "Oswald at Window," the Report—best expressed in colloquial terms—"pulls a fast one." This section is entitled "Eyewitness Identification of Assassin," but contains *no* identification accepted by the Commission (R143-49). The first eyewitness mentioned is Howard Brennan who, 120 feet from the window, said he saw a man fire at the President. "During the evening of November 22, Brennan identified Oswald as the person in the [police] lineup who bore the closest resemblance to the man in the window but said he was unable to make a positive identification." Prior to this lineup, Brennan had seen Oswald's picture on television. In the months before his Warren Commission testimony, Brennan underwent some serious changes of heart. A month after the assassination he was suddenly positive that the man he saw was Oswald. Three weeks later, he was again unable to make a positive identification. In two months, when he appeared before the Commission, he was again ready to swear that the man was Oswald, claiming to have been capable of such an identification all along. Brennan's vacillation on the crucial matter of identifying Oswald renders all of his varying statements unworthy of credence. The Report recognized the worthlessness of Brennan's after-the-fact identification, although it managed to use his testimony for the most it could yield:

> `Although the record indicates that Brennan was an accurate observer, he declined to make a positive identification of Oswald when he first saw him in the police lineup. *The Commission therefore, does not base its conclusion concerning the identity of the assassin on Brennan's subsequent certain identification of Lee Harvey Oswald as the man he saw fire the rifle.* . . .The Commission is satisfied that. . .Brennan saw a man in the window who closely resembled. . .Oswald. (R145-46; emphasis added)

If the Commission did not base its conclusion as to Oswald's presence at the window on Brennan's identification, upon whose "eyewitness identification of assassin" did it rely? Under this section it presents three additional witnesses who saw a man in the window, all of whom gave sketchy descriptions, and *none* of whom were able to identify the man. Thus, the Report, having rejected Brennan's story, could offer *no* eyewitness capable of identifying the assassin.

In pulling its "fast one," the Commission sticks to its justified rejection of Brennan's identification for only 11 pages for, when the conclusion to the "Oswald at Window" section is drawn, his incredible identification is suddenly accepted. Here the Commission concludes "that Oswald, at the time of the assassination, was present at the window from which the shots were fired" on the basis of findings stipulated above. One of these "findings" involves "an eyewitness to the shooting" who "identified Oswald in a lineup as the man most nearly resembling the man he saw and later identified Oswald as the man he observed" (R156). Through this double standard the Report manifests itself to be no more credible than Brennan.

"In considering whether Oswald was at the southeast corner window at the time the shots were fired, the Commission. . .reviewed the testimony of witnesses who saw Oswald in the building within minutes after the assassination" (R149). Immediately after the shots, Patrolman M. L. Baker, riding a motorcycle in the procession, drove to a point near the front entrance of the Depository, entered the building, and sought assistance in reaching the roof, for he "had it in mind that the shots came from the top of this building." He met manager Roy Truly, and the two ran up the steps toward the roof. Baker stopped on the second floor and saw Oswald entering the lunchroom there. This encounter in the lunchroom presented a problem to the Commission:

> In an effort to determine whether Oswald could have descended to the lunchroom from the sixth floor by the time Baker and Truly arrived, Commission counsel asked Baker and Truly to repeat their movements from the time of the shot until Baker came upon Oswald in the lunchroom. . . .On the first test, the elapsed time between the simulated first shot and Baker's arrival on the second-floor stair landing was one minute and 30 seconds. The second test run required one minute and 15 seconds.
>
> A test was also conducted to determine the time required to walk from the southeast corner of the sixth floor to the second-floor lunchroom by stairway [Oswald could not have used the elevator.]. . . .The first test, run at normal walking pace, required one minute, 18 seconds; the second test, at a "fast walk" took one minute, 14 seconds. (R152)

Thus, as presented in the Report, these tests could prove that Oswald was *not* at the sixth-floor window, for had his time of descent been one minute, 18 seconds and Baker's time of ascent been one minute, *14* seconds, Oswald would have arrived at the lunchroom *after* Baker, which was not the case on November 22. Recognizing this, the Report assures us that the reconstruction of Baker's movements was invalid in that it failed to simulate actions that would have lengthened Baker's time. Thus, it is able to conclude "that Oswald could have fired the shots and still have been present in the second floor lunchroom when seen by Baker and Truly" (R152-53).

Here the Commission is playing games. It tells us that its reconstructions could support or destroy the assumption of Oswald's presence at the window. This point is crucial in determining the identity of the assassin, for it could potentially have provided Oswald with an alibi. Instead of conducting the tests properly, the Commission tells us that it neglected to simulate some of Baker's actions, and on the premise that its test was invalid, draws a conclusion incriminating Oswald. One of the factors mentioned by the Report as influencing the conclusion that Oswald was at the window is that his actions after the assassination "are consistent with" his having been there. Because the premise of an invalid reconstruction makes debatable any inferences drawn from it, and because Oswald's actions after the shooting were consistent with his having been almost *anywhere* in the building, this aspect of the Report's conclusion is a *non sequitur*.

The Report ultimately attempts to combine its four logically deficient arguments in support of the conclusion that Oswald was present during the assassination at the window from which the shots were fired. The facts presented are not sufficient to support such a conclusion. The fingerprint evidence does not place Oswald at that window, for the objects on which he left prints were mobile and therefore may have been in a location other than the window when he handled them. That someone saw Oswald near this area 35 minutes before the shots does not mean he was there during the shots, nor does the alleged fact that no one else saw Oswald eliminate the possibility of his having been elsewhere. The one witness who claimed to have seen Oswald in the window could do so only at intervals, rendering his story incredible. Oswald's actions after the assassination do not place him at any specific location during the shots and might even preclude his having been at the window.

The only fair conclusion from the facts presented is that there is no evidence that Oswald was at the window at the time of the assassination.

At this point in the development of the Commission's case, Oswald "officially" possessed the murder weapon, brought it to the Depository on the day of the assassination, and was present at the "assassin's" window during the shots. There would seem to be only one additional consideration relevant to the proof of his guilt: his capability with a rifle. This issue is addressed only after several unrelated matters are considered.

The Commission's conclusion that Oswald was the assassin is not based on a constant set of considerations. The chapter "The Assassin" draws its conclusion from eight factors (R195). The chapter "Summary and Conclusions" omits two of these factors and adds another. The eight-part conclusion states that:

On the basis of the evidence reviewed in this chapter, the Commission has found that Lee Harvey Oswald (1) owned and possessed the rifle used to kill President Kennedy and wound Governor Connally, (2) brought this rifle

to the Depository Building on the morning of the assassination, (3) was present, at the time of the assassination,
at the window from which the shots were fired, (4) killed
Dallas Police Officer J. D. Tippit in an apparent attempt
to escape, (5) resisted arrest by drawing a fully loaded pistol and attempting to shoot another police officer, (6) lied
to the police after his arrest concerning important sub-
stantive matters, (7) attempted, in April 1963, to kill
Major General Edwin A. Walker, and (8) possessed the
capability with a rifle which would have enabled him to
commit the assassination. On the basis of these findings
the Commission has concluded that Lee Harvey Oswald
was the assassin of President Kennedy. (R195)

Obviously, considerations 4, 5, 6, and 7 do not relate to
the question of whether Oswald did or did not pull the
trigger of the gun that killed the President and
wounded the Governor. In the alternate version of the
Commission's conclusions, 4 and 5 are omitted from the
factors upon which the guilty "verdict" is based. Added
in this section is the consideration that the
Mannlicher-Carcano and the paper sack were found on
the sixth floor subsequent to the shooting (R19-20).

"In deciding whether Lee Harvey Oswald fired the
shots. . .," says the Report, "the Commission considered
whether Oswald, using his own rifle, possessed the
capability to hit his target with two out of three shots
under the conditions described in Chapter III
[concerning the source of the shots]" (R189). The
Commission's previous conclusions leave little room for
an assertion other than one indicating that Oswald had
the capability to fire the assassination shots. If he
could not have done this from lack of sufficient skill,
the other factors seeming to relate him to the assassination will have to be accounted for by some other explanation.

First considered under this section is the nature of
the shots (R189-91). Several experts are quoted as say-

ing that the shots, fired at ranges of 177 to 266 feet and employing a four-power scope, were "not...particularly difficult" and "very easy." However, in no case did the experts take into account the time element involved in the assassination shots. Without this consideration, Wesley Liebeler could not understand the basis for any conclusion on the nature of the shots. He wrote:

> The section on the nature of the shots deals basically with the range and the effect of a telescopic sight. Several experts conclude that the shots were easy. There is, however, no consideration given here to the time allowed for the shots. I do not see how someone can conclude that a shot is easy or hard unless he knows something about how long the firer has to shoot, i.e., how much time is allotted for the shots.[3]

Liebeler's criticism had no effect on the final report, which ignores the time question in evaluating the nature of the shots. The evaluation of the shots as "easy" should therefore be considered void and all inferences based on it at best questionable.

In considering "Oswald's Marine Training," the Report deceives its readers by use of common and frequent *non sequiturs*. First it includes, as relevant to Oswald's *rifle* capability, his training in the use of weapons other than rifles, such as pistols and shotguns. Of this Liebeler said bluntly, "That is completely irrevelant to the question of his ability to fire a rifle....It is, furthermore, prejudicial to some extent."[4] The Report then reveals with total dispassion Oswald's official Marine Corps evaluation based on firing tests: when first tested in the Marines, Oswald was "a fairly good shot"; on the basis of his last recorded test he was a *"rather poor shot."* A Marine marksmanship expert

who had absolutely no association with Oswald is next
quoted as offering various excuses for the "poor shot"
rating, including bad weather and lack of motivation.
No substantiation in any form is put forth to buttress
these "excuses." As the record presented in the Report
stands, Oswald left the Marines a "fairly poor shot."
However, the unqualified use of the expert's unsubstantiated hypothesizing gives the impression that Oswald was not such a "poor shot." On the basis of this
questionable premise, the Report quotes more experts
who, in meaningless comparisons, contradicted the official evaluation of Oswald's performance with a rifle
and called him "a good to excellent shot" (R191-92).
One may indeed question the state of our national "defense" when "rather poor shots" from the Marines are
considered "excellent" marksmen.

In discussing "Oswald's Rifle Practice Outside the
Marines" (R192-93), the Report cites a total of 11 instances in which Oswald could be physically associated
with a firearm. Most of these instances involved hunting trips, six of which took place in the Soviet Union.
However, as Liebeler pointed out in his critical
memorandum, Oswald used a shotgun when hunting in
Russia. Liebeler's concern can be sensed in his question
"Under what theory do we include activities concerning
a *shotgun* under a heading relating to *rifle* practice,
and then presume not to advise the reader of that?"[5]
The latest time the Report places a weapon in Oswald's
hands is May 1963, when his wife, Marina, said he
practiced operating the bolt and looking through the
scope *on a screened porch at night*. Liebeler thought
"the support for that proposition is thin indeed," adding
that "Marina Oswald first testified that she did not
know what he was doing out there and then she was
clearly led into the only answer that gives any support

to this proposition."[6] The Report evoked its own support, noting that the cartridge cases found in the Depository "had been previously loaded and ejected from the assassination rifle, which would indicate that Oswald practiced opening the bolt." Marks on these cases could not show that *Oswald,* to the exclusion of all other people, loaded and ejected the cases.

In the end, the Commission was able to cite only two instances in which Oswald handled the Carcano, both based on Marina's tenuous assertions. It produced *no* evidence that Oswald ever fired his rifle. Despite this and the other major gaps in its arguments, the Report concludes that "Oswald's Marine training in marksmanship, his other rifle experience and his established familiarity with this particular weapon show that he possessed ample capability to commit the assassination" (R195). Because the Report offers no evidence to support it, this conclusion is necessarily dishonest. Liebeler cautioned the Commission on this point but was apparently ignored. He wrote:

> The statements concerning Oswald's practice with the assassination weapon are misleading. They tend to give the impression that he did more practicing than the record suggests he did. My recollection is that there is only one specific time when he might have practiced. We should be more precise in this area, because the Commission is going to have its work in this area examined very closely.[7]

That a shooter can be only as good as the weapon he fires is a much-repeated expression. In fact, the proficiency of the shooter and the quality of his shooting apparatus combine to affect the outcome of the shot. To test the accuracy of the assassination rifle, the Commission did not put the weapon in the hands of one whose marksmanship was as "poor" as Oswald's and whose known practice prior to firing was virtually nil. Its test firers were all experts—men whose daily routines involved working with and shooting firearms. Liebeler, as a member of the Commission's investigatory staff, was one of the severest critics of the rifle tests. The following paragraphs, again from Liebeler's memorandum, provide a good analysis of those tests as represented in the Report:

As I read through the section on rifle capability it appears that 15 different sets of three shots were fired by supposedly expert riflemen of the FBI and other places. According to my calculations those 15 sets of shots took a total of 93.8 seconds to be fired. The average of all 15 is a little over 6.2 seconds. Assuming that time calculated is commencing with the firing of the first shot, that means the average time it took to fire two remaining shots was about 6.2 seconds. That comes to about 3.1 seconds for each shot, not counting the time consumed by the actual firing, which would not be very much. I recall that Chapter Three said that the minimum time that had to elapse between shots was 2.25 seconds, which is pretty close to the one set of fast shots fired by Frazier of the FBI.

The conclusion indicates that Oswald had the capability to fire 3 shots with two hits in from 4.8 to 5.6 seconds. Of the fifteen sets of three shots described above, only *three* were fired within 4.8 seconds. A total of five sets, including the three just mentioned, were fired within a total of 5.6 seconds. The conclusion at its most extreme states Oswald could fire faster than the Commission experts fired in 12 of their 15 tries and that in any event he could fire faster than the experts did in 10 out of their 15 tries. . . .

The problems raised by the above analysis should be met at some point in the text of the Report. The figure of 2.25 as a minimum firing time for each shot is used throughout Chapter 3. The present discussion of rifle capability shows that expert riflemen could not fire the assassination weapon that fast. Only one of the experts managed to do so, and his shots, like those of the other

FBI experts, were high and to the right of the target. The fact is that most of the experts were much more proficient with a rifle than Oswald could ever be expected to be, and the record indicates that fact.[8]

Despite the obvious meaning of Liebeler's analysis, the rifle tests are used in the Report to buttress the notion that it was within Oswald's capability to fire the assassination shots (R195). The kindest thing that can be said of this one-sided presentation of the evidence was written by Liebeler himself: "To put it bluntly, that sort of selection from the record could seriously affect the integrity and credibility of the entire Report . . . .These conclusions will never be accepted by critical persons anyway."[9]

The only possible conclusion warranted by the evidence set forth in the Report is that Oswald left the Marines a "rather poor shot" and, unless a major aspect of his life within a few months prior to the assassination has been so well concealed as not to emerge through the efforts of several investigative teams, he did not engage in any activities sufficient to improve his proficiency with his weapon to the extent of enabling him to murder the President and wound the Governor unaided.

This is the official case, the development of the "proof" that Oswald, alone and unaided, committed the assassination. To avoid the detailed discussion required for a rebuttal, I have assumed that the source of the shots was as the Commission postulated—the sixth-floor window of the Depository, from "Oswald's rifle."

This was as far as the Commission could go in relation to the question of Oswald's guilt. Obviously, the use of his rifle in the crime does not mean he fired it. The Commission offers, in essence, *no* evidence that Oswald brought his rifle to the Depository, *no* evidence that Oswald was present at the window during the shots, and *no* evidence that Oswald had the capability to have fired the shots. This is not to say that such evidence does not exist, but that none is presented in the Report. That, for the scope of this chapter's analysis, is significant.

The Commission's conclusion that Oswald was the assassin is invalid because it is, from beginning to end, a *non sequitur*. This analysis of the derivation of that conclusion, based solely on the evidence presented in the Report, demonstrates that evidence to be without logical relationship, used by the Commission in total disregard of logic. The Report's continued fabrication of false premises from which are drawn invalid inferences is consistent with one salient factor: that the Commission evaluated the evidence relating to the assassin's identity on the presumption that Oswald alone was guilty.

2

Presumed Guilty: The Official Disposition

The discussion in chapter 1 did not disprove the Commission's conclusion that Lee Harvey Oswald assassinated President Kennedy. It merely showed that, based on the evidence presented in the Report, Oswald's guilt was presumed, not established. The Commission argued a case that is logical only on the premise that Oswald alone was guilty.

The official assurance is, as is to be expected, the opposite. In the Foreword to its Report, the Commission assures us that it "has functioned neither as a court presiding over an adversary proceeding nor as a prosecutor determined to prove a case, but as a fact finding agency committed to the ascertainment of the truth" (Rxiv). This is to say that neither innocence nor guilt was presumed from the outset of the inquiry, in effect stating that the Commission conducted a "chips-fall-where-they-may" investigation.

At no time after a final bullet snuffed out the life of the young President did *any* agency conduct an investigation not based on the premise of Oswald's guilt. Depsite the many noble assurances of impartiality, the fact remains that from the time when he was in police custody, Oswald was officially thought to be Kennedy's sole assassin. In violation of his every right and as a

73

guarantee that virtually no citizen would think otherwise, the official belief of Oswald's guilt was shame-
fully offered to a public grieved by the violent death of
its leader, and anxious to find and prosecute the per-
petrator of the crime.

The Police Presumption

Two days after the assassination, the *New York
Times* ran a banner headline that read, in part, "Police
Say Prisoner is the Assassin," with a smaller—but
likewise front-page—heading, "Evidence Against Oswald Described as Conclusive." The article quoted Captain Will Fritz of the Dallas Police Homicide Bureau as
having said, "We're convinced beyond any doubt that
he killed the President. . . .I think the case is cinched."[1]

Other newspapers echoed the *Times* that day. The
Philadelphia Inquirer reported: "Police on Saturday
said they have an airtight case against pro-Castro
Marxist Lee Harvey Oswald as the assassin of Presi-
dent Kennedy."[2] On the front page of the *St. Louis
Post-Dispatch* was the headline "Dallas Police Insist
Evidence Proves Oswald Killed Kennedy."

> Dallas police said today that Lee Harvey Oswald
> . . .assassinated President John F. Kennedy and
> they have the evidence to prove it. . . ."The man killed
> President Kennedy. We are convinced without any doubt
> that he did the killing. There were no accomplices,"
> [Captain] Fritz asserted.
>   Police Chief Jesse E. Curry outlined this web of evi-
> dence that, he said, showed Oswald was the sniper.[3]

The following day, November 25, was the occasion
for yet another banner headline in the *Times*. In one
fell swoop, there was no longer any doubt; it was no
longer just the Dallas police who were prematurely
convinced of Oswald's guilt. "President's Assassin Shot

to Death in Jail Corridor by a Dallas Citizen," the headline proclaimed. There was no room for such qualifiers as "alleged" or "accused." Yet, in this very issue, the *Times* included a strong editorial that criticized the police pronouncement of guilt:

> The Dallas authorities, abetted and encouraged by the newspaper, TV and radio press, trampled on every principle of justice in their handling of Lee Harvey Oswald. . . .The heinousness of the crime Oswald was alleged to have committed made it doubly important that there be no cloud over the establishment of his guilt.
> Yet—before any indictment had been returned or any evidence presented and in the face of continued denials by the prisoner—the chief of police and the district attorney pronounced Oswald guilty.[4]

It is unfortunate that this proper condemnation applies equally to the source that issued it.

Transcripts of various police interviews and press conferences over the weekend of the assassination (which confirm the above newspaper accounts) demonstrate that, in addition to forming a bias against Oswald through the press, the police made extensive use of the electronic media to spread their improper and premature conclusion.

On Friday night, November 22, NBC-TV broadcast a press interview with District Attorney Henry Wade, whose comments included these: "I figure we have sufficient evidence to convict him [Oswald] . . . there's no one else but him" (24H751). The next day, Chief Curry, though he cautioned that the evidence was not yet "positive," said that he was convinced. In an interview carried by NBC, Curry asserted, "Personally, I think we have the right man" (24H754). In another interview broadcast by local station WFAA-TV, Curry was asked, "Is there any doubt in your mind, Chief, that Oswald is the man who killed the President?" His response was: "I think this is the man who killed the President" (24H764). In another interview that Saturday, Captain Fritz made the absolute statement:

> There is only one thing that I can tell you without going into the evidence before first talking to the District Attorney. I can tell you that this case is cinched—that this man killed the President. There's no question in my mind about it. . . ." I don't want to get into the evidence. I just want to tell you that we are convinced beyond any doubt that he did the killing. (24H787)

By November 24, Curry's remarks became much stronger. Local station KRLD-TV aired this remark: "This is the man, we are sure, that murdered the patrolman and murdered—assassinated the President" (24H772). Fritz stuck to his earlier conviction that Oswald was the assassin (24H788). Now D.A. Henry Wade joined in pronouncing the verdict before trial or indictment:

> WADE: I would say that without any doubt he's the killer—the law says beyond a reasonable doubt and to a moral certainty which I—there's no question that he was the killer of President Kennedy.
> Q. That case is closed in your mind?
> WADE: As far as Oswald is concerned, yes. (24H823)

The FBI Presumption

That same day the FBI announced, contrary to the police assertion, that the case was still open and that its investigation, begun the day of the shooting, would continue.[5] This continued investigation climaxed after a duration just short of three weeks. In a series of contrived news "leaks," the Bureau added to the propaganda campaign started by the Dallas Police.

The decision of the FBI and the Commission was to

keep the first FBI Summary Report on the assassination secret.[6] However, even prior to the completion of this report, the newspapers carried frequent "leaked" stories telling in advance what the report would contain. The Commission met in executive session on December 5, 1963, and questioned Deputy Attorney General Nicholas Katzenbach about these leaks. Katzenbach spoke bluntly. FBI Director Hoover, he related, denied that the leaks originated within the FBI, but "I say with candor to this committee, I can't think of anybody else it could have come from, because I don't know of anybody else that knew that information."[7]

On December 9, Katzenbach transmitted the completed FBI Report to the Commission. In his covering letter of that date, he again expressed the Justice Department's desire to keep the Report secret, although he felt that "the Commission should consider releasing—or allowing the Department of Justice to release—a short press statement which would briefly make the following points." Katzenbach wanted the Commission to assure the public that the FBI had turned up no evidence of conspiracy and that "the FBI report through scientific examination of evidence, testimony and intensive investigation, establishes beyond a reasonable doubt that Lee Harvey Oswald shot President Kennedy."[8]

Although the Commission released no such statement, the conclusions of which the Justice Department felt the public should be informed were widely disseminated by the press, through leaks which, according to Katzenbach, must have originated with the FBI. On December 1, the *Washington Post* in a major article told its readers that "all the police agencies with a hand in the investigation. . .insist that [the case against Oswald] is an unshakable one."[9] *Time* magazine, in the week before the FBI report was forwarded to the Commission, said of the report, "it will indicate that Oswald, acting in his own lunatic loneliness, was indeed the President's assassin."[10] *Newsweek* reported that "the report holds to the central conclusion that Federal and local probers had long since reached: that Oswald was the assassin."[11] The *New York Times* was privy to the most specific leak concerning the FBI report. On December 10 it ran a front-page story headed "Oswald Assassin Beyond a Doubt, FBI Concludes." This article, by Joseph Loftus, began as follows:

> A Federal Bureau of Investigation report went to a special Presidential commission today and named Lee H. Oswald as the assassin of President Kennedy.
> The Report is known to emphasize that Oswald was beyond doubt the assassin and that he acted alone. . . .
> The Department of Justice, declining all comment on the content of the report, announced only that on instruction of President Johnson the report was sent directly to the special Commission.[12]

All of these news stories, especially that which appeared in the *Times,* accurately reflect those findings of the FBI report which Katzenbach felt should be made public. The FBI has long claimed that it does not draw conclusions in its reports. The FBI report on the assassination disproves this one of many FBI myths. This report *does* draw conclusions, as the press reported. In the preface to this once-secret report (released in 1965), the FBI stated:

> Part I briefly relates the assassination of the President and the identification of Oswald as his slayer.
> Part II sets forth the evidence conclusively showing that Oswald did assassinate the President. (CD 1)

The Commission, in secret executive sessions, expressed its exasperation at the leak of the FBI report. On December 16, Chairman Warren stated:

> CHAIRMAN: Well, gentlemen, to be very frank about it, I have read that report two or three times and I have not seen anything in there yet that has not been in the press.
>
> SEN. RUSSELL: I couldn't agree with that more. I have read it through once very carefully, and I went through it again at places I had marked, and practically everything in there has come out in the press at one time or another, a bit here and a bit there.[13]

It should be noted here that even a casual reading of this FBI report and its sequel, the "Supplemental Report" dated January 13, 1964, discloses that neither establishes Oswald's guilt, nor even adequately accounts for all the known facts of the assassination. In neither report is there mention of or accounting for the President's anterior neck wound which, by the night of November 22, was public knowledge around the world. The Supplemental Report, in attempting to associate Oswald with the crime, asserts that a full-jacketed bullet traveling at approximately 2,000 feet per second stopped short after penetrating "less than a finger length" of the President's back. One need not be an expert to discern that this is an impossible event, and indeed later tests confirmed that seventy-two inches of flesh were insufficient to stop such a bullet (5H78). The Commission members themselves, in private, grumbled about the unsatisfactory nature of the FBI report, as the following passage from the December 16 Executive Session reveals:

> MR. MC CLOY: ...The grammar is bad and you can see

they did not polish it all up. It does leave you some
loopholes in this thing but I think you have to realize
they put this thing together very fast.

REP. BOGGS: There's nothing in there about Governor
Connally.

CHAIRMAN: No.

SEN. COOPER: And whether or not they found any bullets
in him.

MR. MC CLOY: This bullet business leaves me confused.

CHAIRMAN: It's totally inconclusive.[14]

Thus, by January 1964, the American public had
been assured by both the Dallas Police and the FBI
that Oswald was the assassin beyond all doubt. For
those who had not taken the time to probe the evidence, who were not aware of its inadequacies and
limitations, such a conclusion was easy to accept.

The Commission Presumption

Today there can be no doubt that, despite their assurances of impartiality, the Commission and its staff
consciously planned and executed their work under the
presumption that Oswald was guilty. The once-secret
working papers of the Commission explicitly reveal the
prejudice of the entire investigation.

General Counsel Rankin did not organize a staff of
lawyers under him until early in January 1964. Until
that time, the Commission had done essentially no
work, and had merely received investigative reports
from other agencies. Now, Rankin and Warren drew up
the plans for the organization of the work that the staff
was to undertake for the Commission. In a "Progress
Report" dated January 11, from the Chairman to the
other members, Warren referred to a "tentative outline
prepared by Mr. Rankin which I think will assist in
organizing the evaluation of the investigative materials received by the Commission."[15] Two subject head-

ings in this outline are of concern here: "(2) Lee Harvey Oswald as the Assassin of President Kennedy; (3) Lee Harvey Oswald: Background and Possible Motives."[16] Thus, it is painfully apparent that the Commission did, from the very beginning, plan its work with a distinct bias. It would evaluate the evidence from the perspective of "Oswald as the assassin," and it would search for his "possible motives."

Attached to Warren's "Progress Report" was a copy of the "Tentative Outline of the Work of the President's Commission." This outline reveals in detail the extent to which the conclusion of Oswald's guilt was predetermined. Section II, "Lee Harvey Oswald as the Assassin of President Kennedy," begins by outlining Oswald's movements on the day of the assassination. Under the heading "Murder of Tippit," there is the subheading "Evidence demonstrating Oswald's guilt."[17] Even the FBI had refrained from drawing a conclusion as to whether or not Oswald had murdered Officer Tippit. Yet, at this very early point in its investigation, the Commission was convinced it could muster "evidence demonstrating Oswald's guilt."

Another heading under Section II of the outline is "Evidence Identifying Oswald as the Assassin of President Kennedy," again a presumptive designation made by a commission that had not yet analyzed a single bit ot evidence. The listings of evidence under this heading are sketchy and hardly conclusive, and further reveal the biases of the Commission. Some of the evidence that was to "identify Oswald as the assassin" was "prior similar acts: a) General Walker attack, b) General Eisenhower threat."[18] Thus we learn that Oswald was also presumed guilty in the attempted shooting of the right-wing General Walker in April 1963.

Under the additional heading "Evidence Implicating

Others in Assassination or Suggesting Accomplices,"
the Commission was to consider only the possibility
that others worked with *Oswald* in planning or execut-
ing the assassination. The outline further reveals that
it had been concluded in advance that Oswald had no
accomplices, for the last category under this heading
suggests that the evidence be evaluated for the "refutation of allegations."[19]

The Commission was preoccupied with the question
of motive. According to the initial outline of its work, it
had decided to investigate Oswald's motives for killing
the President *before* it determined whether Oswald had
in fact been involved in the assassination *in any capacity*. At the executive session of January 21, 1964, an illuminating discussion took place between Chairman
Warren, General Counsel Rankin, and member Dulles.
Dulles wanted to be sure that every possible action was
taken to determine Oswald's motive:

> Mr. Dulles: I suggested to Mr. Rankin, Mr. Chairman,
> that I thought it would be very useful for us, if the rest of
> you agree, that as items come in that deal with motive,
> and I have seen, I suppose, 20 or 30 of them already in
> these various reports, those be pulled together by one of
> these men, maybe Mr. Rankin himself so that we could
> see that which would be so important to us.
> Chairman Warren: In other words, to see what we are
> running down on the question of motive.
> Mr. Dulles: Just on the question of motive I found a
> dozen or more statements of the various people as to why
> they thought he [Oswald] did it.
> Warren: Yes.
> Mr. Dulles: Or what his character was, what his aim,
> and so forth that go into motive and I think it would be
> very useful to pull that together, under one of these head-
> ings, not under a separate heading necessarily.
> Warren: Well, I think that that would probably come
> under Mr. [Albert] Jenner, wouldn't that, Lee [Rankin],

isn't he the one who is bringing together all the facts concerning the life of Oswald?

Mr. Rankin: Yes, yes. We can get that done. We will see that that is taken care of.

Warren: Yes.[20]

The staff, working under the direction of Rankin, was likewise predisposed to the conclusion that Oswald was guilty. Staff lawyer W. David Slawson wrote a memorandum dated January 27 concerning the "timing of rifle shots." He suggested that:

> In figuring the timing of the rifle shots, we should take into account the distance travelled by the Presidential car between the first and third shots. This tends to shorten the time slightly during which *Oswald* would have had to pull the trigger three times on his rifle.[21] (emphasis added)

At this early point in the investigation, long before any of the relevant testimony had been adduced, Slawson was positive that Oswald "pulled the trigger three times on his rifle."

Another staff lawyer, Arlen Specter, expressed the bias of the investigation in a memorandum, dated January 30, in which he offered suggestions for the questioning of Oswald's widow, Marina. Specter felt that certain questions "might provide some insight on whether Oswald learned of the motorcade route from newspapers." He added that "perhaps [Oswald] was inspired, in part by President Kennedy's anti-Castro speech which was reported on November 19 on the front page of the Dallas Times Herald."[22] The implication here is obvious that the President's speech "inspired" Oswald to commit the assassination. Again, it must be emphasized that until Oswald's guilt was a proven fact, which it was *not* at the time these memoranda were composed, it was mere folly to investigate the factors that supposedly "inspired" Oswald. Such fraudulent investigative efforts demonstrate that Oswald's guilt was taken for granted.

Rankin had assigned teams of two staff lawyers each to evaluate the evidence according to the five divisions of his "Tentative Outline." Working in Area II, "Lee Harvey Oswald as the Assassin of President Kennedy," were Joseph Ball as the senior lawyer and David Belin as the junior.[23] On January 30, Belin wrote a very revealing memorandum to Rankin, concerning "Oswald's knowledge that Connally would be in the Presidential car and his intended target."[24] This memorandum leaves no doubt that Belin was quite sure of Oswald's guilt *before* he began his assigned investigation. He was concerned that Oswald might not have known that Governor Connally was to ride in the presidential limousine because this "bears on the motive of the assassination and also on the degree of marksmanship required, which in turn affects the determination that Oswald was the assassin and that it was not too difficult to hit the intended target two out of three times in this particular situation." The alternatives, as stated by Belin, were as follows:

> In determining the accuracy of Oswald, we have three major possibilities: Oswald was shooting at Connally and missed two of the three shots, two misses striking Kennedy; Oswald was shooting at both Kennedy and Connally and all three shots struck their intended targets; Oswald was shooting only at Kennedy and the second bullet missed its intended target and hit Connally instead.[25]

Belin could not have been more explicit: Three shots were fired and Oswald, whatever his motive, fired them all. Of course, at that point Belin could not possibly have *proved* that Oswald was the assassin. He merely presumed it and worked on that basis.

It is important to keep this January 30 Belin memorandum in mind when we consider the 233-page "BALL - BELIN REPORT #1" dated February 25, 1964, and submitted by the authors as a summation of all the evidence they had evaluated up to that point. The "tentative" conclusion reached in this report is that "Lee Harvey Oswald is the assassin of President John F. Kennedy."[26] However, Ball and Belin were careful to include here a new interpretation of their assigned area of work. They wrote:

> We should also point out that the tentative memorandum of January 23 substantially differs from the original outline of our work in this area which had as its subject, "Lee Harvey Oswald as the Assassin of President Kennedy," and which examined the evidence from that standpoint. At no time have we assumed that Lee Harvey Oswald was the assassin of President Kennedy. Rather, our entire study has been based on an independent examination of all the evidence in an effort to determine who was the assassin of President Kennedy.[27]

Although this new formulation was no doubt the proper one, the Warren Report makes it abundantly clear that Ball and Belin failed to follow the course outlined in their "Report #1." As we have seen, the only context in which the evidence is presented in the Report is "Lee Harvey Oswald as the Assassin of President Kennedy," even though that blatant description is not used (as it was in the secret working papers). Furthermore, that Belin a month before could write so confidently that Oswald was the assassin completely refutes this belatedly professed intention to examine the evidence without preconceptions. It would appear that in including this passage in "Report #1," Ball and

Belin were more interested in leaving a record that
they could later cite in their own defense than in conducting an honest, unbiased investigation. Indeed,
Belin has quoted this passage publicly to illustrate the
impartiality of his work, while neglecting to mention
his memorandum of January 30.[28]

The Warren Report was not completed until late in
September 1964, with hearings and investigations extending into the period during which the Report was
set in type. Yet outlines for the final Report were
drawn up as early as mid-*March*. These outlines demonstrate that Oswald's guilt was a definite conclusion
at the time that sworn testimony was first being taken
by the Commission. The first outline was submitted to
Rankin at his request by staff lawyer Alfred Goldberg
on approximately March 14, according to notations on
the outline.[29] Under Goldberg's plan, Chapter Four of
the Commission's report would be entitled "Lee Harvey
Oswald as the Assassin." Goldberg elaborated:

> This section should state the facts which lead to the
> conclusion that Oswald pulled the trigger and should indi-
> cate the elements in the case which have either not been
> proven or are based on doubtful testimony. Each of the
> facts listed below should be reviewed in that light.[30]

The "facts" enumerated by Goldberg are precarious.
Indeed, as of March 14, 1964, no testimony had been
adduced on almost all of the "facts" that Goldberg outlined as contributing to the "conclusion that Oswald
pulled the trigger." Goldberg felt that this chapter of
the Report should identify Oswald's rifle "as the murder weapon." Under this category he listed "Ballistics"
and "Capability of Rifle." Yet the first ballistics testimony was not heard by the Commission until March
31 (3H390ff.). Another of Goldberg's categories is "Evi-

dence of Oswald Carrying Weapon to Texas School Book Depository." Here he does not specify which evidence he had in mind. However, the expert testimony that *might* have supported the thesis that Oswald carried his rifle to work on the morning of the assassination was not adduced until April 2 and 3 (4H1ff.). This pattern runs through several other factors that Goldberg felt established Oswald's guilt *before* they were scrutinized by the Commission or the staff. To illustrate: "Testimony of eyewitnesses and employees on fifth floor"—this testimony was not taken until March 24, at which time the witnesses contradicted several of their previous statements to the federal authorities (3H161ff.); "Medical testimony"—the autopsy surgeons testified on March 16 (2H347ff.), and medical/ballistics testimony concerning tests with Oswald's rifle was not taken until mid-May (5H74ff.); "Eyewitness Identification of Oswald Shooting Rifle"—only one witness claimed to make such an identification, and he gave testimony on March 24 (3H140ff.) that was subsequently rejected by the Commission (R145-46).

On March 26, staff lawyer Norman Redlich submitted another outline of the final Report to Rankin; in almost all respects, Redlich's outline is identical with Goldberg's. Chapter Four is entitled "Lee H. Oswald as the Assassin," with the notation that "this section should state the facts which lead to the conclusion that Oswald pulled the trigger. . . ."[31] In general, Redlich is vaguer than Goldberg in his listing of those "facts" which should be presented to support the conclusion of Oswald's guilt. However, he does specify what he considers to be "evidence of Oswald carrying weapon to building." One factor, he wrote, is the "fake curtain rod story." Yet, when Redlich submitted this outline, no investigation had been conducted into the veracity of the "curtain rod story." The first information relevant to this is contained in an FBI report dated March 28 (24H460-61), and it was not until the last day in *August* that further inquiry was made (CE2640).

The pattern is consistent. The Commission outlined its work and concluded that Oswald was guilty before it did any investigation or took any testimony. The Report was outlined, including a chapter concluding that Oswald was guilty, before the bulk of the Commission's work was completed. Most notably, these conclusions were drafted *before* the staff arranged a series of tests that were to demonstrate whether the official theories about how the shooting occurred were physically possible. A series of ballistics tests using Oswald's rifle, and an on-site reconstruction of the crime in Dealey Plaza were conducted in May; the Report was outlined in March. On April 27, Redlich wrote Rankin a memorandum "to explain the reasons why certain members of the staff feel that it is important" to reconstruct the events in Dealey Plaza as depicted in motion pictures of the assassination. Redlich stated that the Report would "presumably" set forth a version of the assassination shots concluding "that the bullets were fired by one person located in the sixth floor southeast corner window of the TSBD building." He then pointed out:

> As our investigation now stands, however, we have not shown that these events could possibly have occurred in the manner suggested above. All we have is a reasonable hypothesis which appears to be supported by the medical testimony but which has not been checked out against the physical facts at the scene of the assassination.[32]

Thus, Redlich admitted that the Commission did not know if the conclusions already outlined were even physically possible. But his suggestion of on-site tests should not be taken to indicate his desire to establish the untainted truth, for he explicitly denied such a purpose in his memorandum. Instead, he wrote:

> Our intention is not to establish the point with complete accuracy, but merely to substantiate the hypothesis which underlies the conclusions that Oswald was the sole assassin.[33]

This is as unambiguous a statement as can be imagined. The reconstruction was not to determine whether it was physically possible for Oswald to have committed the murder as described by the Commission; it was "merely to substantitate" the preconceived conclusion "that Oswald was the sole assassin."

On April 30, three days after Redlich composed the above-quoted memorandum, the Commission met in another secret executive session. Here Rankin added to the abundant proof that the Commission had already concluded that Oswald was guilty. The following exchange was provoked when Dulles expressed his well-voiced preoccupation with biographical data relating to Oswald:

> Mr. Dulles: Detailed biography of Lee Harvey Oswald—I think that ought to be somewhere.
> Mr. Rankin: We thought it would be too voluminous to be in the body of the report. We thought it would be helpful as supplementary material at the end.
> Mr. Dulles: Well, I don't feel too strongly about where it should be. This would be—I think some of the biography of Lee Harvey Oswald, though, ought to be in the main report.
> Mr. Rankin: *Some of it will be necessary to tell the story and to show why it is reasonable to assume that he did what the Commission concludes that he did do.*[34] (emphasis added)

As late as the middle of May, long after the Commission and the staff had decided, in advance of analyzing the evidence, that Oswald was guilty, Commission member McCloy expressed his feeling that the conclusion as to Oswald's guilt was not being pursued with enough vigor by the staff. McCloy was not interested in a fair and objective report. This story was related by David Belin in his memorandum of May 15, which described his trip to Dallas with certain Commission members, McCloy included. One night in Dallas, Belin persuaded McCloy to read "Ball-Belin Report #1," which by then was almost three months old. Belin recounts McCloy's reactions:

> He seemed to misunderstand the basic purpose of the report, for he suggested that we did not point up enough arguments to show why Oswald was the assassin ....Commissioner McCloy did state that in the final report he thought that we should be rather complete in developing reasons and affirmative statements why Oswald was the assassin—he did not believe that it should just merely be a factual restatement of what we had found.[35]

As quoted at the opening of this chapter, the Warren Report asserted that the Commission functioned not "as a prosecutor determined to prove a case, but as a fact finding agency committed to the ascertainment of the truth." This statement is clearly a misrepresentation of the Commission's real position, as expressed in private by McCloy when he told Belin that he wanted a report that argued a prosecution case, and not simply "a factual restatement."

The Dallas Police and the FBI both announced their "conclusion" before it could have been adequately substantiated by facts and, in so doing, almost irrevocably prejudiced the American public against Oswald and thwarted an honest and unbiased investigation. The Commission operated under a facade of impartiality. Yet it examined the evidence—and subsequently presented it—on the premise that Oswald was guilty, a premise openly stated in secret staff memoranda and reinforced when the members met in secret sessions. Now, as the curtain of secrecy that once sheltered the working papers of the investigation is lifted, the ugly and improper presumption of guilt becomes obvious. Wesley Liebeler expressed the prejudice of the entire "investigation" when he argued to Rankin in a once-secret memorandum that ". . .the best evidence that Oswald could fire as fast as he did and hit the target is the fact that he did so."[36]

PART II:

THE MEDICAL/BALLISTICS EVIDENCE

3

Suppressed Spectrography

In the final analysis, the Warren Commission had three pieces of tangible evidence that linked Lee Harvey Oswald to the assassination of President Kennedy: (1) A rifle purchased by Oswald and three empty cartridge cases fired in that rifle were discovered on the sixth floor of the Texas School Book Depository, (2) a nearly whole bullet that had been fired from Oswald's rifle was found on a stretcher at Parkland Hospital, and (3) two fragments of a bullet or bullets that had been fired from Oswald's rifle were found on the front seat of the presidential limousine.

Yet, there is nothing in this evidence itself to prove either that Oswald's rifle was used in the shooting or, if it was, that Oswald fired it. The whole fault in the Commission's case relating the Mannlicher-Carcano rifle to the shooting is this: bullets identifiable with that rifle were found *outside* of the victims' bodies. Pieces of metal not traceable to any rifle were found *inside* the bodies. The Report merely assumes the legitimacy of the specimens found externally and works on the assumption that these bullets and fragments had once been *inside* the bodies, and thus were involved in the shooting.

Obviously, bullets found outside the bodies are entirely circumstantial evidence, for although they may be conclusively linked with a particular weapon, their location of discovery does not link them with a particular victim. No matter how close to the victims or to the scene of the crime these bullets were found, as long as they were not *in* the actual bodies when discovered, proof is lacking that they were ever in the bodies at all. If Commission Exhibit 399, the nearly whole bullet found on a stretcher at Parkland, had been removed from Governor Connally's body, it could be asserted that it had indeed produced his wounds. Likewise, if the identifiable bullet fragments found on the front seat of the limousine had instead been located in President Kennedy's head wound, we would have the proof linking Oswald's rifle to the fatal shot.

In the case of the assassination, there was an easy and conclusive way to determine whether the bullet specimens found *outside* the bodies had ever been *inside* the victims, thus providing either the proof or the disproof of the notion that Oswald's rifle was used in the shooting. This conclusive evidence is the spectrographic comparison made between the metallic compositions of the projectiles found outside of the victims and the bits of metal removed from the wounds themselves.

Spectrography is an exact science. In spectrographic analysis, a test substance is irradiated so that all of the elements composing it emit a distinct spectrum. These spectra are recorded on film and analyzed both qualitatively (to determine exactly which elements compose the substance in question) and quantitatively (to determine the exact percentage of each element present). Through such analysis, two substances may be compared in extremely fine detail, down to the percentages of even their most minor constituents.[1]

Comparative chemical analysis such as spectrography has long been a vital tool in crime solving. The following are actual cases that illustrate the value of such comparison:

1. A deformed slug with some white metal adhering to it was found at the scene where a man had been shot, but not wounded. The white metal was first suspected to be nickel, which would have indicated a nickel-coated bullet, but was subsequently tested and found to be silver from a cigarette case that had been penetrated. The slugs in the cartridges taken from the suspect in the attack were analyzed and found to differ in composition from the projectile used in the shooting; the suspect thus escaped conviction.

2. In another case, a man escaped conviction because of dissimilarities in composition found upon comparative analysis of the bullet removed from the wounded man and bullets from cartridges seized in the suspect's house. The former contained a trace of antimony and no tin and the latter contained a comparatively large amount of tin.

3. A night watchman shot at some unidentified persons fleeing the scene of a robbery, but all escaped. Blood found at the scene the next morning indicated that one of the persons had been wounded and subsequently a man was arrested with a bullet wound in his leg for which he could provide no plausible explanation. Analysis demonstrated that lead fragments removed from the wound did not agree in composition with the slugs in the watchman's cartridges and the man was released. The impurities present in the lead were the same in each case, consisting chiefly of antimony, but the fragments from the wound contained much less antimony than the watchman's slugs.[2]

The identifiable bullets and fragments found *outside* the victims' bodies are the suspect specimens in the presidential assassination. The tiny pieces of metal found *inside* the bodies are, in effect, the control speci-

mens. All of the specimens—including those removed
from the President and the Governor—were subjected
to spectrographic analysis. The results of these
analyses hold the conclusive answer to the problem
that was the central issue in the question of Oswald's
guilt: Did the bullets from Oswald's rifle produce the
wounds of the victims?

The spectrographic analyses could solve this central
problem through minute qualitative and quantitative
comparison. If a fragment from a body was not
identical in composition with a suspect bullet, that bullet could not have entered the body and left the fragment in question. The requirements for "identical"
composition are stringent; if the exact elements are not
present in the exact percentages from one sample to
another, there is no match and the samples must have
originated from two different sources. If a fragment is
found to be identical in composition with a suspect bullet, it is possible that the bullet deposited the fragment
in the body. However, before this can be conclusively
proven, it must be demonstrated that other bullets
manufactured from the same batch of metal were not
employed in the crime.[3] Some of the major comparisons
that should have been made in the case of the
President's death are these:

1. The Commission apparently believed that the two
large bullet fragments (one containing part of a lead
core) found on the front seat of the car and traceable to
Oswald's rifle were responsible for the head wounds.
Two pieces of lead were recovered from the President's
head. The head fragments could have been compared to
the car fragment containing lead. Had the slightest difference in composition been found, the car fragments
could not have caused the head wounds.

2. The Commission believed that the two car frag-

ments were part of the same bullet. Spectrographic comparison might have determined this.

3. Copper traces were found on the bullet holes in the back of the President's coat and shirt. Since the Commission believed that bullet 399 penetrated the President's neck, the copper residues on the clothing could have been compared with the copper jacket of 399 for a conclusive answer. Any dissimilarity between the two copper samples would rule out 399.

4. The Commission believed that 399 wounded Governor Connally. Fragments of lead were removed from the Governor's wrist. These could have been compared with the lead core of 399. Again, any dissimilarity would conclusively disassociate 399 from Connally's wounds. An identical match might support the Commission's belief.

5. The lead from the Governor's wrist could have been compared with the lead from one of the identifiable car fragments to determine whether this might have caused Connally's wounds in the event that 399 did not. This could have associated "Oswald's" rifle with the wounds even if 399 had been proven "illegitimate."

6. The lead residue found on the crack in the windshield of the car could have been compared with fragments from the two bodies plus fragments from the car in an effort to determine which shot caused the windshield damage.

7. As a control, the lead and copper composition of 399 could have been compared to that of the identifiable car fragments to determine whether all were made from the same batches of metal.

The government had in its possession the conclusive proof or disproof of its theories. It is not presumptuous to assume that, had the spectrographic analyses pro-

vided the incontrovertible proof of the validity of the
Warren Report's central conclusions, they would have
been employed in the Report, eliminating virtually all
of the controversy and doubt that have raged over the
official assertions.

But the complete results of the spectrographic
analyses were never reported to the Commission; there
is no indication that the Commission ever requested or
desired them; they are not in the printed exhibits or
the Commission's unpublished files; no expert testimony relevant to them was ever adduced; and to this
day, the Department of Justice is withholding the complete results from researchers.

On November 23, 1963, FBI Director J. Edgar
Hoover sent a report to Dallas Police Chief Jesse Curry
summarizing the results of FBI laboratory examinations, including spectrographic analysis (see
24H262-64). On the matter of composition, Hoover said
only that the jackets of the found specimens were "copper alloy" and the cores and other pieces, "lead." The
element mixed with the copper to form the "alloy" is
not even mentioned. It is quite unlikely that the other
specimens were composed solely of "lead," for the lead
employed in practically all modern bullets is mixed
with small quantities of antimony, bismuth, and
arsenic.[4] The only spectrographic comparison mentioned in this report is meaningless:

> The lead metal of [exhibits] Q4 and Q5 [fragments from
> the President's head], Q9 [fragment(s) from the Governor's
> wrist], Q14 [three pieces of lead found under the left jump
> seat in the limousine] and Q15 [scraping from the
> windshield crack] is similar to the lead of the core of the
> bullet fragment, Q2 [found on the front seat of the car].

That two samples are "similar" in composition is without meaning in terms of the precise data yielded through spectrographic analysis. The crucial determination, "identical" or "not identical," is consistently avoided. Also avoided is the essential comparison between the "stretcher bullet," 399, and the metal fragments removed from the Governor's wrist.

The Commission sought virtually no testimony relevant to the spectographic analysis. When it did seek this testimony, it asked the wrong questions of the wrong people. FBI ballistics expert Robert Frazier gave testimony about these tests on May 13, 1964. At this time, he told the Commission and Arlen Specter, his interrogator, that the spectrographics examinations were performed by a spectrographer, John F. Gallager (5H67, 69). Frazier, accepted by the Commission only as a "qualified witness on firearms" (3H392), was not a spectrographic expert. His field was ballistics and firearms identification, and while he might have supplemented his findings with those from other fields, he was not qualified in spectrography, which entails expertise in physics and chemistry. Gallagher, the expert, could well be called the Commission's most-avoided witness. His testimony, the *last* taken in the entire investigation, was given in a deposition attended by a stenographer and a staff member the week before the Warren Report was submitted to President Johnson. At this time, he was not asked a single question relating to the spectrographic analyses.[5] (See 15H746ff.)

Neither Specter nor the Commission members can deny having known that Frazier was not the man qualified to testify about spectrographic analysis; Frazier stated this in his testimony:

Mr. Specter: Was it your job to analyze all of the bullets or bullet fragments which were found in the President's car?

Mr. Frazier: Yes; it was, *except for the spectrographic analysis of the composition.* (5H68; emphasis added)

Frazier added, "I don't know actually whether I am expected to give the results of (the spectrographer's) analysis or not" (5H59). If this statement fails to make it clear that Frazier was not prepared to testify about the results of the spectrographic analyses, an earlier statement by him leaves no doubt: "[The spectrographic] examination was performed by a spectrographer, John F. Gallagher, and I do not have the results of his examination here" (5H67). If Frazier did not have the actual report of the results of the tests with him when he appeared before the Commission, there was obviously no way of vouching for the accuracy of the findings to which he testified, whether he was qualified as an expert in spectrography or not. Also, Frazier's knowledge of the spectrographic analysis was merely secondhand; he was aware of the results of these tests because the spectrographer "submitted his report to me" (5H69). Thus, Frazier played no role in conducting this analysis. His only "qualification" for giving testimony about the spectrographic analyses was that he had read a report about them. Because this report is not part of the public records, we have no way of determining whether Frazier accurately related the results of the analyses, or whether the report upon which he based his testimony was competent, complete, or satisfactory. In short, we are asked to take Frazier on his word when (1) he knew of these tests only secondhand, (2) he did not have the actual results with him when he testified about them, and (3) he had no expertise in spectrography. On this basis alone, Frazier's testimony concerning the tests is not worthy of credence.

However, if we examine exactly what Frazier

specified as the results of the spectrographic analyses, it becomes apparent that his testimony, if true, is meaningless and incomplete. Frazier spoke of essentially the same comparisons that Hoover did in his letter to police chief Curry, repeating Hoover's meaningless designation that the ballistic specimens compared were "found to be similar in metallic composition" (5H67, 69, 73-74). When the *exact* composition had been determined to a minute degree and could be compared for conclusive and meaningful answers, there was no legitimate reason to accept this testimony about mere "similarities" in composition. Furthermore, Frazier offered his opinion that the spectrographic analyses were inconclusive in determining the origin of certain of the ballistics specimens (5H67, 69, 73-74). However, because Frazier was not a spectrographic expert and because the actual report of these tests is not available, his interpretation of the test results is worthless. Even at that, Frazier and his Commission interrogator, Arlen Specter, avoided mention of those comparisons affecting the legitimacy of bullet 399—namely, the copper from the President's clothing and the lead from Governor Connally's wrist as compared with the copper and lead of 399.

Frazier was cross-examined at the New Orleans conspiracy trial of Clay Shaw. Here he was pressed further on the spectrographic analysis. When asked about any "similarity" in the compositions of the various ballistic specimens he replied, "They all had the same metallic composition as far as the lead core or lead portions of these objects is concerned."[6]

This response prompts two inferences. First, Frazier specifically excluded as being the "same in metallic composition" the *copper* portions of the specimens. If this omission was necessitated by the fact that the copper of the recovered specimens did not match in composition, a significant part of the Warren Report is disproved. Second, Frazier's description of the lead as being the "same" in composition is ambiguous. Did he mean that the *elements* of the composition or the *percentages* of the elements were the "same"? In the former case, his testimony would again be meaningless, for *what* is contained in the metal is not so important as *how much* is contained. If the percentages were the same, the Report could be confirmed.

Further questioning by Attorney Oser cleared up this ambiguity.

> Mr. Oser: Am I correct in saying there is a similarity in metallic composition or they are identical?
> Mr. Frazier: It was identical as far as the metallic *elements* are concerned.[7] (emphasis added)

Here Frazier leaves no doubt that the individual *elements* in the various lead samples were identical. What he avoids saying is that the percentages of those elements were identical throughout. This is the crucial point. If anything, Frazier's specification that the *elements* were identical (when questioned about the *composition*) leads to the inference that the percentages of those elements were *not* identical, hence the recovered specimens could not be related and the Warren Report is necessarily invalid.

The Commission's failure to obtain the complete spectrographic analyses and to adduce meaningful expert testimony on them can be viewed only with suspicion. Here was the absolute proof or disproof of the official theories. If truth was the Commission's objective, there can be no explanation for the exclusion of these tests from the record. If the Commission was right in its "solution" of the assassination, for what reason could it conceivably have omitted the *proof* of its validity? One is reasonably led to believe that the spectrographic analyses proved the opposite of what the Commission asserted.

If the Commission's failure to produce the spectrographic analyses was no more than a glaring oversight, the remedy is indeed a simple one. The government need only release these tests to the public. They cannot contain the gore that makes publication of the President's autopsy pictures a matter of questionable taste. They cannot be injurious to living persons as other classified reports might be. They cannot threaten our national defense. They are merely a collection of highly scientific data that could support or destroy the entire official solution to the assassination.

The government has to this day kept them squelched.

Harold Weisberg, the first researcher to recognize the significance of the spectrographic tests and their omission from the record, has fought and continues to fight for access to the report detailing these tests. In 1967, Weisberg wrote as follows of his efforts to obtain the tests:

> On October 31, 1966, then Acting Attorney General Clark ordered that everything considered by the Commission and in the possession of the government be placed in the National Archives. I had written [J. Edgar] Hoover five months earlier, on May 23, 1966, asking for access to the spectrographic analysis of the bullet allegedly used in the assassination and the various bullet fragments, clearly the most basic evidence, but not in the printed evidence. He has not yet answered that letter. Since issuance of the Attorney General's order, I have on a number of occasions requested this evidence of the Archives. Hoover, as of March 1967, had not turned it over. Once, in my presence, one of his agents deceived the Archives by falsely reporting this analysis was in an FBI file that was accessible. Since then, silence, but no spectrographic analysis.[8]

Weisberg's efforts have continued. In 1970, he made

available to me all of his government correspondence. I saw, over the signatures of then Attorney General John Mitchell and Deputy Attorney General Richard Kleindienst, the government's constant refusal to release the spectrographic analyses.[9] Having exhausted his administrative remedies, Weisberg took the Justice Department to court, suing for release under provisions of the "Freedom of Information" law. The U.S. District Court for the District of Columbia ruled against Weisberg in this case, Civil Action No. 712-70. Weisberg and his attorney appealed this decision, and the appeal, brief No. 71-1026, is currently before the U.S. Court of Appeats for the District of Columbia Circuit.

Without the spectrographic analyses, there is *no* evidence to associate Oswald's rifle with the wounds suffered by President Kennedy and Governor Connally. Nothing was found in the body of either victim that would suggest a connection between that specific Mannlicher-Carcano and the wounds. The spectrographic tests might establish such a connection; they might also conclusively *dissociate* that rifle from the wounds. However, omission of the exact spectrographic results from the Commission's evidence and the subsequent refusal of the government to release the spectrographer's findings do not leave one at all confident that these tests support the official solution to the assassination.

4

The President's Wounds

There is evidence independent of the spectrographic analyses that reasonably, although not conclusively, disassociates Oswald's rifle from the wounds inflicted on President Kennedy. Certain aspects of the medical evidence strongly indicate that the President was *not* struck by bullets of the type recovered and traced back to the C2766 Mannlicher-Carcano purchased by Oswald. The implication of this evidence as well as the evidence relating to Governor Connally's wounds is that the identifiable bullet recovered at Parkland Hospital and the bullet fragments found in the limousine played no role in the wounding of either victim, and came to rest in their location of discovery by some means other than that alleged by the Commission. More precisely, the significance of the medical evidence is that it forces the conclusion that the items of physical evidence that implicate Oswald in the murder—his rifle, the spent cartridge cases, and the bullets—were deliberately "planted" for the purpose of implicating Oswald, although none played a role in the actual shooting.

We must recognize that the medical evidence in this case suffers severe limitations, to which almost infinite discussion could be and has been devoted.[1] Because the

107

scope of this study does not include an examination of the official investigation into the President's wounds, including the autopsy and other examinations, it must suffice here to say that most of the medical evidence available today is not credible and precludes a positive reconstruction of the exact manner in which President Kennedy was killed. There is currently enough solid information to say with some precision what did *not* happen to the President, and it may, in fact, never be possible to say more than that.

Respecting the limits of the medical evidence, I will make no effort to explain exactly how President Kennedy was shot, from which directions, by how many bullets, and so on. Instead, I will focus on one aspect of the wounds, namely, the type of ammunition that produced them. This is the only aspect of the medical evidence that relates to the question of Oswald's guilt, assuming, of course, that at least some of the assassination shots originated from the rear. The question to be answered is this: Could the President's wounds have been caused by bullets of the type recovered and traced to Oswald's rifle?

The Head Wounds

The wounds to President Kennedy's head can be briefly described as follows: There was a 15 by 6 mm. entrance wound situated at the rear top of the head. Most of the right half of the brain had been blasted away by a bullet. Numerous tiny metal fragments were depicted on X-rays as being located in the right-frontal portion of the head. Much of the skull and scalp in the right frontal area had also been blasted away, creating a large, irregular defect from which lacerated brain tissue oozed. Many lacerations of the scalp and severe fractures of the skull accompanied this large defect. It can be said with reasonable certainty that *a* bullet

struck the President's head from the rear. The evidence
does *not* establish that it was the rear-entering bullet
that produced the explosive wound to the right-front of
the head, nor is there currently any evidence to preclude the possibility that the head was in fact struck
by two separate bullets from different directions.

The Warren Commission made no serious effort to
establish the type of ammunition that produced the
head wounds, and it failed to establish *any* connection
between those wounds and the ammunition allegedly
used by Oswald. The Commission postulates that Oswald fired military ammunition. Such bullets are constructed of a lead core chemically hardened and in-
serted into a jacket of copper alloy.[2] The principal
reason for this type of construction is to insure good
penetrating ability by inhibiting bullet deformation.
Hard metal-jacketed military bullets can be deformed
upon striking resistant tissue such as bone. In such a
case, the bullet is liable to become mangled and distorted in shape. When such bullets undergo fragmentation, it is rarely extensive. Typically, the jacket may
separate from the core which, in turn, may break up
into relatively large chunks, depending on the nature
of the resistant tissue and the force with which it was
struck.[3]

The autopsy pathologists concluded that one bullet
struck the head, entering through the small rear entrance wound, and explosively exiting through the gaping defect in the right-frontal area of the head. The
conclusion that the rear wound was one of entrance
was justified on the basis of the information available.
However, the pathologists could present no evidence to
substantiate the "conclusion" that the gaping defect
was an exit wound. The unmistakable inference of the
testimony of Dr. James Humes, the chief autopsy
pathologist, is that the doctors "concluded" this was an

exit wound solely because the only other external head wound was one of entrance (2H352). This reasoning is in total disregard of any practicable medico-legal standards, and is worthless without tangible evidence to buttress it.

Given the unsupportable premise that one bullet caused all the head wounds, Assistant Counsel Arlen Specter was able to adduce worthless testimony from Dr. Humes about the type of ammunition involved. First he asked Dr. Humes whether a "dumdum" bullet struck the head:

> Dr. Humes: I believe these were not dumdum bullets, Mr. Specter. A dumdum is a term that has been used to describe various missiles which have a common characteristic of fragmenting extensively upon striking.
> . . .Had [the entrance wound on the head] been inflicted by a dumdum bullet, I would anticipate that it would not have anything near the regular contour and outline which it had. I would also anticipate that the skull would have been much more extensively disrupted, and not have, as was evident in this case, a defect which quite closely corresponded to the overlying skin defect because that type of missile would fragment on contact and be much more disruptive at this point. (2H356)

Thus, the clean characteristics of the entrance hole led Dr. Humes to conclude that it was not caused by a "dumdum" bullet. What such a bullet would produce upon striking the skull, according to Humes, is in essence what appeared on the right side of the President's head and was arbitrarily designated an exit wound. The Commission never raised the proper question: Was the gaping head defect really the "exit" wound or could it have been another entrance, caused by a "dumdum"?

The Commission members continued this line of

questioning. First Mr. McCloy queried about soft-nose ammunition having caused *only* the entrance wound:

> Dr. Humes: From the characteristics of this wound, Mr. McCloy, I would believe it must have had a very firm head rather than a soft head.
> Mr. McCloy: Steel jacketed, would you say, copper jacketed bullet?
> Dr. Humes: I believe more likely a jacketed bullet.

Allen Dulles joined in:

> Mr. Dulles: Believing that we know the type of bullet that was usable in this gun ["Oswald's" rifle], would this be the type of wound that might result from that kind of bullet?
> Dr. Humes: I believe so, sir. (2H357)

During his testimony, Col. Pierre Finck, who participated in the autopsy as a consultant to Dr. Humes, was asked about the nature of the bullet's fragmentation within the head. Commissioner Gerald Ford, apparently feeling that he had asked one question too many, cut Finck off at the vital point and did not permit him to elaborate:

> Mr. Ford: Is it typical to find only a limited number of fragments as you apparently did in this case?
> Dr. Finck: *This depends to a great deal on the type of ammunition used.* There are many types of bullets, jacketed, not-jacketed, pointed, hollow-nosed, hollow-points, flatnose, roundnose, all these different shapes will have a different influence on the pattern of the wound and the degree of fragmentation.
> Mr. Ford: That is all. (2H384; emphasis added)

The Report does not cite any of the above-quoted testimony. Instead, it discusses ballistics which, it asserts,

showed that the rifle and bullets identified above were
capable of producing the President's head wound. The
Wound Ballistics Branch...at Edgewood Arsenal, Md.,
conducted an extensive series of experiments to test the
effect of...the type [of bullet] found on Governor
Connally's stretcher and in the Presidential limousine,
fired from the C2766 Mannlicher-Carcano rifle found in
the Depository....One series of tests, performed on reconstructed inert human skulls, demonstrated that the
President's head wound could have been caused by the
rifle and bullets fired by the assassin from the sixth floor
window. (R87)

How could such tests "demonstrate that the
President's head wound could have been caused by"
bullets fired from a rifle traceable to Oswald? The tests,
in fact, do *not* suggest *any* correlation between the
head wounds and "Oswald's" rifle. When analyzed, they
prove to be nothing more than incompetent, meaningless, hence invalid simulations.

Used for these tests were old skulls, hard and brittle,
having long lost the natural moisteners of living bone.
These test skulls were filled and covered with a 20 percent gelatin solution, a standard simulant for body tissues (5H87). Not simulated in the experiments was a
vital determining factor—the scalp. As the "expert"
who conducted the tests admitted, the scalp of a living
person would serve to retain or hold together the bones
of the cranium upon impact of a missile (5H89). Obviously, this reconstructed "head" could not possibly respond to a bullet's strike as would a normal, living
head.

Ten skulls were fired upon with "Oswald's" rifle
under conditions duplicating only those under which
Oswald allegedly fired. Only one skull was subsequently shown to the Commission; the bullet that

struck it "blew out the right side of the reconstructed skull in a manner very similar to the head wound of the President" (R87). This persuaded the "expert" to conclude—contrary to his beliefs nurtured by prior experience—"that the type of head wounds that the President received could be done by this type of bullet" (R87).

The pictures of this test exhibit printed by the Commission show a gelatin-filled skull with the bone of the entire right side missing (17H854). However, the gelatin underlying this missing bone is completely intact, so utterly undisturbed that it still bears the various minute impresions of the skull that once covered it. This gelatin was supposed to simulate the tissues within the skull (5H87). Yet those tissues, according to the autopsy report, were "lacerated," "disrupted," and "extensively lacerated" (16H981, 983). Obviously, even upon its entering the bony vault of the skull, the test bullet was not capable of producing the extensive damage attributed to it by the Commission. As for the disruption of the skull on the test exhibit, almost *any* force could have dislodged pieces of the brittle skull not restrained by scalp. As forensic pathologist Dr. John Nichols confirmed to me, even a blow with a hammer could have produced the damage shown on the test skull.[4]

The Commission adds a further note, again unjustly incriminating Oswald. Two large fragments of the bullet that struck the test skull were recovered, a portion of the copper jacket near the base, and a sizable piece of the lead core. The Commission had its "expert" compare these fragments with the two similar fragments that were found in the front seat of the presidential limousine and identifiable with "Oswald's" rifle. The

result of this comparison, as presented in the Report, is
seemingly to associate these traceable fragments with
the head wounds. The expert is quoted as follows:

> the recovered fragments were very similar to the ones re-
> covered on the front seat and the floor of the car.
>   This to me, indicates that those fragments did come
> from the bullet that wounded the President in the head.
> (R87)

These are the last words of the Report's discussion of
the head wounds. Since no qualifying language follows,
the reader is left with the impression that the "expert
opinion" is valid in associating the identifiable fragments with the wounds. Nowhere in the Report do we
find the simple fact that the fragmentation of both the
test bullet and the found bullet pieces is not an exclusive occurrence, as implied. The break-up observed is
consistent with the normal fragmentation pattern of
full-jacketed military bullets. When such bullets break
apart, the core usually separates from the jacket.[5] The
Commission could have produced the same effect if it
fired the bullet through a piece of masonite.

Thus, for all its claims, the Commission was able to
present no credible evidence associating bullets from
"Oswald's" rifle, or even military bullets in general,
with the President's head wounds.

The nature of the bullet fragmentation within the
President's head actually disassociates military bullets
from the head wounds, and strongly suggests that some
type of sporting ammunition struck the head.

One essential fact about the entrance wound in the
head was omitted from both the autopsy report and the
pathologists' testimonies. It came to light in the following passage from a report released by Attorney
General Ramsey Clark in January 1969. (In February

1968, Clark secretly convened a panel of three forensic pathologists and a radiologist to study and report on the photographs and X rays taken of the President's body during the autopsy. [This photographic material has been withheld from the public for a variety of reasons.] Clark kept the report of his panel secret until January 1969, when he released it as part of the Justice Department's legal argument against New Orleans District Attorney Jim Garrison's attempt to have the pictures and X-rays produced at the conspiracy trial of Clay Shaw.) The passage reads:

> Also there is, embedded in the outer table of the skull close to the lower edge of the [entrance] hole, a large metallic fragment which. . .lies 25 mm. to the right of the midline. This fragment. . .is round and measures 6.5 mm. in diameter.[6]

The "Clark Panel" is describing a 6.5 mm. piece of metal that separated from the bullet upon entering the skull and became embedded in the skull at the bottom portion of the entrance wound. This, the key to the type of ammunition causing the wound, vitiates Dr. Humes's previously cited testimony that a "jacketed bullet" probably caused this entrance wound.

The bullet from which was shaved this substantial fragment upon entrance could *not* have been covered with a hard metal jacket such as copper alloy. Such a fragment is, in fact, a not infrequent occurrence from a *lead* bullet. Rowland Long, in his book *The Physician and the Law,* speaks of the penetration of lead bullets into the skull and asserts: "Not infrequently a collar shaped fragment of lead is shaved off around the wound of entrance and is found embedded in the surrounding scalp tissues."[7] Criminologist LeMoyne Snyder describes a similar phenomenon in his book

Homicide Investigation.[8] Forensic pathologist Halpert Fillinger explained to me the principles that rule out full-jacketed ammunition and suggest a lead bullet:

> You can appreciate the fact that a jacketed projectile is going to leave very little on the [bone] margins because it's basically a hardened jacket, and it's designed so that it will not scrape off when it goes through a steel barrel. One can appreciate the fact that going through bone, which is not as hard as steel, may etch or scratch it, but it's not going to peel off much metal. In contrast to this a softer projectile might very well leave little metallic residues around the margins.[9]

The Commission's case against Oswald requires full-jacketed ammunition to have been used to inflict the wounds of President Kennedy. The presence of the 6.5 mm. metallic fragment in the margin of the skull entrance wound eliminates the possibility that a full-jacketed bullet entered through this hole. Such a fragment located at that site is indicative of a lead or soft-nosed bullet.

Most of the right hemisphere of the President's brain had been shot away. The intact portions of the right side were extensively disrupted, with laceration and fragmentation (see 2H356; The "Clark Panel" Report, p. 8; R541, 544). However, when seen and photographed at the autopsy, the brain was missing more tissue than had been blown out directly from the force of the missile. The Zapruder film shows brain tissue oozing out of the gaping skull defect subsequent to the impact of the fatal bullet. Similarly, the Parkland doctors who viewed the President shortly after he suffered this wound reported that brain matter was slowly oozing out and becoming detached (R519, 521, 523, 530).

The loss of a substantial quantity of brain tissue becomes significant when we consider Dr. Humes's testimony that the X rays showed "30 or 40 tiny dustlike particle fragments" of metal in the President's head (2H353). Humes cautioned that the fragments that appeared to be "the size of dust particles" (2H359) on the X rays would actually have been smaller because "X ray pictures. . .have a tendency to magnify these minute fragments somewhat in size" (2H353). Secret Service Agent Roy Kellerman saw the X rays during the autopsy and provided a similar description: ". . .the whole head looked like a little mass of stars, there must have been 30, 40 lights where these little pieces were so minute that they couldn't be reached" (2H100).

The Clark Panel adds some details about the head fragments. It reports that the majority of these fragments were located "anteriorly and superiorly" (toward the front and top of the head), and that none were visible on the left side of the brain or below a horizontal plane through the anterior floor of the skull.[10] With such minute fragments scattered through the brain, we can infer that an indeterminable amount of metal was evacuated from the head as brain tissue oozed out subsequent to the President's head being struck. From this it follows that (a) there were originally more fragments in the head than are shown in the X rays and, (b) the pattern of distribution of these fragments as illustrated by the X rays may not precisely represent the original distribution except to indicate that the majority were situated toward the front of the head.

The only solid observation that can be made on the basis of fragmentation depicted in the head X rays is that *a* bullet striking the head fragmented extensively, leaving pieces of metal, for the most part "the size of dust particles," concentrated toward the frontal portion of the brain. This type of fragmentation is not consistent with the type of full-jacketed military ammunition

that the Commission says was used. The construction
and composition of full-jacketed bullets obviates any
such massive break-up. As noted previously, when
military ammunition fragments, it is usually in such a
manner that the core separates from the jacket. The
core may undergo further break-up, although its metallic composition does not permit the creation of numerous dustlike particles.[11] Dr. Fillinger tells me that the
fragments described in the President's brain were not
characteristic of a military round, and, while he makes
no absolute statement, he has expressed his skepticism
that they actually came from such a round. He feels
that the break-up of the bullet is more consistent with
a hunting round.[12]

In addition to this extensive brain damage and the
accompanying bullet fragmentation, a good deal of
scalp and skull in the right frontal and parietal area of
the President's head had been blasted away by the bullet, creating a large, irregular defect. Associated with
this gaping wound was fracturing and fragmentation of
the skull so extensive that the contours of the head
were "grossly distorted."[13] Dr. Humes reported that in
peeling the scalp away from the skull around the mar-
gins of the head defect, pieces of skull would come
"apart in our hands very easily" or fall to the table
(2H354). Dr. Humes stated also that "radiating at various points from the large defect were multiple
crisscrossing fractures of the skull which extended in
several directions" (2H351). The Clark Panel describes
multiple fractures of the skull "bilaterally"—on *both*
sides—extending into the base of the skull.[14] Information recorded in contemporary autopsy notes indicates
that the vomer (a bone in the nose) was crushed, and
that there was a fracture through the floor of the globe
of the right eye (17H46). Dr. J. Thornton Boswell, as-

sistant to Dr. Humes at the autopsy, has confirmed to a private researcher that a large area of skull damage was present in the mid- and low-temple region, although none of these fractures had broken the skin.[15]

The size and extent of the gaping defect, and the associated fracturing and fragmentation of the skull, are indicative of a high-velocity bullet's having struck the head to produce this damage. Dr. Fillinger has expressed to me his strong feeling that the extensive fragmentation of the skull is the consequence of a high-velocity round.[16] He stated that the presence of such massive fracturing means that "there is a tremendous amount of force applied to the skull to produce all these fractures. . . .This has been pretty well fragmented, as a matter of fact," he told me, "and again, it speaks for some sort of high-velocity round."[17]

The gaping defect and accompanying extensive fragmentation of the skull are not consistent with having been produced by the type of ammunition the Commission alleges was used which, despite contrary claims, was of "medium" velocity.

The Commission asserts that the fatal shot was fired at a distance of 270 feet (R585). Although the Report gives the average striking velocity of the bullets fired from "Oswald's" rifle at other distances as measured during the wound ballistics tests, it does not record the velocity for the head shot tests at the proper distance. At 210 feet, the average striking velocity was 1,858 feet per second (R584). Dr. Fillinger told me that he would consider an impact velocity of 2,000 f.p.s. "medium."[18] Even Dr. Malcolm Perry of Parkland Hospital testified that he considered the Mannlicher-Carcano "a medium velocity weapon" (3H389). FBI ballistics expert Robert Frazier called the velocity "low" (3H414), although this would appear more of a comparative evaluation than an absolute statement, since bullets can be fired as slowly as 800 f.p.s. or as fast as 4,100 f.p.s.

Because there was great damage to the head and extensive bullet fragmentation in the brain, Dr. Fillinger was doubtful that the Mannlicher-Carcano could have produced these wounds. "To produce this kind of effect," he told me, "you have to have a very high-velocity projectile, and the Carcano will not stand very high bolt pressures."[19] The massive defect corresponds perfectly to the characteristics that Humes described in reference to bullets that "have a common characteristic of fragmenting extensively upon striking," and that would have "extensively disrupted" the skull at the point of impact (2H356). Such a bullet would most likely be that which is used for "varminting." Bullets used in varmint hunting must be fired at very high velocities ranging upward from 2,700 f.p.s., and are designed so that they will smash apart immediately on impact. They commonly leave pinhead-sized fragments scattered throughout the tissues.[20]

Without consideration of the question of whether the damage to the President's head was the consequence of a strike by one or two bullets, it can be said with a reasonable degree of certainty that in no instance are any of the head wounds associable with full-jacketed military ammunition of the type attributed to Oswald. The medical evidence relating to the head wounds is thus exculpatory of Oswald, for his guilt hinges on the assumption that he fired full-jacketed military bullets from the Mannlicher-Carcano rifle found in the Depository and linked to him.

The Neck and Upper Thorax Wounds

The autopsy report concludes that a bullet struck the

President in the upper thoracic region of his back and penetrated his body on a slightly downward angle, exiting through the lower part of the anterior neck. This theory has long been rendered incredible in numerous critical analyses.[21] However, one piece of information in particular prevents anyone, whether or not he believes the Warren Report, from asserting that a bullet went through the neck in the manner described in the autopsy report. In order to substantiate the assumption of a continuous bullet track, that track must be dissected at the autopsy. According to Drs. Fillinger and Wecht, there is no way to positively identify a bullet path other than by dissecting it—taking it apart and following it through every fraction of an inch of the tissue it penetrates.[22] In his New Orleans testimony, Colonel Finck stated explicitly, under oath, that the putative bullet track in the President's neck was *not* dissected.[23] This failure to dissect is, according to Dr. Fillinger, "the most critical thing of the whole autopsy."[24] Without such dissection, *no one,* including the autopsy pathologists, can be in a position to assert that one bullet made a continuous path through the President's neck.

There is one piece of information concerning the neck and upper thorax wounds that establishes beyond any doubt that (1) the particular bullet traced to Oswald's rifle and alleged by the Commission to have penetrated the President's neck could not have produced the damage attributed to it, and (2) military ammunition of the general type attributed to Oswald could not have caused these wounds. This information came to light in the report of the Clark Panel.

Describing antero-posterior X-ray views of the lower neck region, the Panel Report declared, "Also several small metallic fragments are present in this region."[25]

This observation by the Panel vitiates Dr. Humes's sworn testimony to the Commission that the X rays revealed no metallic fragments in the neck region (2H361).

Detailed information concerning these fragments is scant. Of their number, the Clark Panel says only that there are "several"; of their size, that they are "small." My requests to the Panel for more specific designations have gone unanswered. The radiologist on the Panel, Dr. Russell Morgan, has told me that the exact "region" in which these fragments appeared on the films was just lateral to the tip of the right transverse process of the seventh cervical vertebra, which is located at the very base of the neck.[26] However, the back-to-front (or front-to-back) distribution of these fragments cannot be determined because the inventory of X rays includes no lateral views of the neck. As I learned from Dr. Fillinger, antero-posterior X-ray views can be very deceiving in depicting the front-to-back distribution of X-ray densities. As a case in point, he showed me X rays of a boy shot in the chest with shotgun pellets. The "A-P" view seemed to show the tiny "shot" particles in the same plane within the chest. A lateral X ray, however, revealed that the particles were actually scattered throughout the chest at various levels from front to back.[27] Thus, all we can know about the distribution of the fragments in the President's neck is that they were at the level of the seventh cervical vertebra.

Nevertheless, the knowledge that there were metallic fragments in the neck, regardless of their number, size, or distribution, is sufficient to eliminate the possibility that military ammunition of the type attributed to Oswald was responsible for the neck wounds.

As previously noted, full-jacketed military bullets are constructed so that they will not fragment in soft tissue. Even if a bone in the neck region were struck (the official story is that *no* bone in President Kennedy's neck region was struck), it is unlikely that this military ammunition of medium velocity could have produced "several small" fragments and no large ones. (There was no point on the body from which a large fragment could have exited. The 5 mm. wound on the anterior neck, alleged by the autopsy pathologists and the Commission to have been an exit wound, was entirely too small and regular to have been caused by a large section of a bullet that had become deformed as a result of fragmenting.)

That neither the head nor the neck wounds are attributable to the ammunition Oswald allegedly used would seem to provide persuasive evidence that Oswald played no part in the shooting of the President. In fact, the evidence of the neck fragments is clearly exculpatory, as is illustrated in an actual case presented by LeMoyne Snyder in *Homicide Investigation*.[28] Snyder relates the story of a hunter found dead from a rifle wound in the chest. Investigation disclosed only two persons who could have shot the man—one armed with a military rifle firing jacketed ammunition, the other with a .30-calibre Winchester firing soft-nosed hunting bullets. According to Snyder, "The problem was to try to determine whether the victim had been killed by jacketed ammunition or a soft-nosed bullet." In reference to an X ray of the victim's chest, Snyder writes: "Notice the numerous flecks of lead scattered through the tissues, strongly indicating that the wound was caused by soft-nosed ammunition." The parallel to the assassination is striking, for the fragments scattered in the President's neck must "strongly indicate . . .soft-nosed ammunition," although the government's suspect allegedly fired jacketed bullets.

Snyder's case ends justly; the guilty person is identified by the medical evidence, the innocent is exculpated. Tests using the two suspect weapons demonstrated that the military ammunition would have left
no metal in the chest, while the soft-nosed bullet would
have scattered numerous tiny fragments, proving "that
it was soft-nosed ammunition and not a jacketed bullet
which killed the man." In denying the Commission
knowledge of the neck fragments, Dr. Humes denied
Oswald the possible proof of his innocence.

The presence of these fragments in the President's
neck further disassociates Oswald from the crime because it establishes beyond any doubt that the specific
bullet alleged by the Commission to have penetrated
the neck could *not* have produced the damage attributed to it. The Report never directly identifies a particular bullet as having caused the neck wounds. However, it clearly implies that the bullet that wounded
Governor Connally had first penetrated the President's
neck. It asserts that a whole bullet traceable to the
Mannlicher-Carcano was found on Governor Connally's
stretcher at Parkland Hospital (R79, 81), and expresses
the belief that this bullet caused the Governor's
wounds. Obviously, according to the theory that one
bullet produced all the nonfatal wounds to both men, it
must be the Commission's belief that the President's
neck was penetrated by the "stretcher bullet," Commission Exhibit 399.

CE 399 could not have produced the President's neck
wounds, for the simple reason that it is unfragmented.
Several factors destroy the possibility that the bullet
merely brushed some fragments from its surface in
passing through the neck, thereby leaving the metallic
pieces observed on X rays. The loss of fragments that
might almost insignificantly have reduced the bullet's

mass would certainly have created some irregularity of its surface. Yet an irregular missile of substantial size could not have produced the small round wound in the throat upon exiting (see 6H5, 15).

In his testimony at the New Orleans conspiracy trial, FBI ballistics expert Robert Frazier described the condition of CE 399 and the circumstances under which it could have deposited metal fragments:

> Mr. Frazier: In my opinion there was no jacketing missing, no discernible amount of jacket missing [from the bullet].
> Mr. Oser: ...If such a pellet as Exhibit 399 is shot...during its travel what could possibly remove the copper jacketing in order for the lead contained therein to be deposited into a particular target?
> Mr. Frazier: The bullet would have to strike some object with sufficient force to rupture the jacket either from striking head-on or if it were tumbling the striking of the side, or the other alternative would be if the bullet tumbled in flight and wound up in a base-first attitude, then the lead would be exposed at the point of impact.
> Mr. Oser: In Commission Exhibit 399, you found the copper jacketing intact, I believe you said?
> Mr. Frazier: Yes.[29]

Because none of CE 399's jacket was missing, the neck fragments could not possibly have come from that area of the bullet. The only other means by which 399 could have lost fragments (since the jacket was not ruptured) is if it somehow began tumbling in the neck, presenting its base to some hard surface and scraping off fragments. Had 399 been tumbling in this manner, it would have produced a massive and lacerated exit wound, which certainly did not occur on the President's neck.

Thus, there is no conceivable way in which 399 could

have deposited metallic fragments in the President's neck.

Although the putative bullet track through the neck was never dissected, on the night of the autopsy the pathologists were able to insert metal "probes" into the back wound to a depth of about two inches.[30] No path could be probed beyond this point and the pathologists speculated that the bullet that entered the back might somehow have stopped short after this modest penetration and fallen out of the wound prior to the autopsy.[31] Although the pathologists abandoned this theory when they were confronted with the anterior neck wound to be accounted for, others, including the FBI and some critics of the Warren Report, have suggested that the "stretcher" bullet, CE399, penetrated the President's back a very short distance and dropped out of the wound at Parkland Hospital.[32] This theory seems to offer an alternative by which a bullet fired from Oswald's rifle might be connected with the President's wounds. However, to postulate that CE 399 or any other bullet of the type allegedly fired by Oswald penetrated two inches of flesh and suddenly stopped short is to beg for the ludicrous; as a theory, it is unworthy of serious consideration. I base this assertion on the following considerations brought out to me by Richard Bernabei, a fellow researcher who has made substantial contributions to the medical-ballistics aspects of this case.

General Principles. A cartridge, or round of ammunition, is composed of a primer, a cartridge case, powder, and a bullet. The primer, a metal cup containing a detonatable mixture, fits into the base of the cartridge case, which is loaded with the powder. The bullet fits into the neck of the cartridge case. To fire the bullet, the cartridge is placed in the chamber of the firearm, immediately behind the barrel, with its base resting against a solid support which, in a bolt-operated weapon, is called the bolt face. When the trigger is pulled a firing pin strikes a swift, hard blow into the primer, detonating the primer mixture. The flames from the resulting explosion ignite the powder, causing a rapid combustion whose force propels the bullet forward through the barrel (R547).

Because the bullet is propelled by the pressure of the expanding gases in the cartridge case, the bullet's velocity will vary with the amount of pressure generated. This pressure not only expands the sides of the case, but also drives the base back against the bolt face.[33] The latter action flattens out the base, and the degree of flattening plus the resultant depth of the firing-pin indentation provide a very fair means of estimating whether the pressure was normal, high, or low, and thus whether the bullet was fired at its standard velocity.[34]

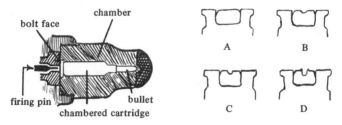

Fig. 3. Cross sections of cartridge-case bases showing firing-pin indentation in primer: A) unfired case B) feeble pressure C) normal pressure D) high pressure

Background. According to the Warren Report, three empty cartridge cases were found near the alleged "assassin's window," all of which were traceable to "Oswald's" rifle owing to the microscopic marks left on the bases (R79, 84-85). The presence of these expended cases weighed heavily in the Commission's conclusion that three shots were fired. The Report states: "The most convincing evidence relating to the number of shots was provided by the presence...of three spent cartridges" (R110). Without making comment as to the soundness of this reasoning and assuming for argument's sake that the Carcano was used, I claim that it logically follows that bullet 399, if it is a legitimate assassination bullet, was fired from one of the spent cases.

Drawback. Bullets fired from "Oswald's" rifle into flesh simulants exhibited good penetrating power, passing easily through more than 72 cm. of gelatin. These bullets struck a simulated neck from a distance of 180 feet, traveling at approximately 1,904 f.p.s. and exiting from the simulant at 1,779 f.p.s. (R581-82). As ballistics expert Charles Dickey confirmed to me, bullets moving at such speeds would not stop short in muscle, as is demanded by the theory placing CE 399 in the President's back.[35]

The only way a bullet such as CE 399 could have made a short penetration into muscle at a distance of 50 yards is if its velocity had somehow been significantly retarded. Owing to the lack of physical mitigants, the only explanation for such a tremendous slowing down is a "short-charge" cartridge, whose explosive power is far less than standard.[36] Dickey told me that this would be an extremely unusual occurrence and that, despite the age of the alleged ammunition, the propellants should have remained stable.[37] In all the many times this ammunition has been test-fired subsequent to the assassination, not one "short charge" has been reported.[38]

Disproof. As mentioned previously, a key indication of the velocity at which a bullet was fired is found by the degree of flattening of the cartridge base and the depth of the primer indentation. Dick Bernabei had told me that, from his own examination of the three found cartridge cases and two others fired from the rifle for comparison purposes, the primer indentations on all the cases were identical, proving that they had all been fired at the same velocity. To check this, I had the National Archives prepare a photo illustrating the five bases all under similar lighting. This picture confirmed Dick's observations, indicating that the bullets fired from the suspect cases were fired at their normal velocity.

Thus, from the unlikely to the impossible, neither bullet 399 nor any other bullet of that type fired at standard velocity from the Mannlicher-Carcano could have lodged in the soft tissues of the President's back.

Conclusion

Throughout this chapter, I have endeavored to answer the question: Could the President's wounds have been caused by bullets of the type recovered and traced to Oswald's rifle? The answer to that question, to the most reasonably certain degree allowed by the limitations of the medical evidence, is No. The nature of the bullet fragmentation observed within the President's wounds strongly indicates that he was *not* struck by military ammunition of the type attributed to Oswald's rifle. In every case, it is likely that the President's wounds were produced by some type of sporting ammunition. It is possible to conclude beyond a reasonable doubt that a specific bullet, CE 399, traced to Oswald's rifle, did *not* penetrate the President's neck, for there is no way in which that bullet could have deposited the metallic fragments located in the neck region. Before

any conclusions can be drawn concerning whether CE
399 played any role in the shooting, we must first ask
whether it is possible for CE 399 to have produced the
wounds of Governor Connally.

5

The Governor's Wounds and the Validity of the Essential Conclusions

In the case of Governor Connally, it is not possible to determine the type of ammunition that produced his wounds. Three bones in his body were struck by a bullet, two of them seriously broken and fractured, and flecks of metal were observed in, and in one case removed from, his injuries. The presence of these metallic fragments in the Governor's wounds, however, does not specifically indicate that he was struck by a type of sporting ammunition, because the force with which the bone tissue was struck was sufficient for military ammunition to have deposited the fragments observed. It is the Warren Commission's belief that the Governor's wounds were caused by the almost pristine bullet, CE 399, fired from Oswald's rifle (R95). Therefore, in this chapter I will deal not with the general question of the type of ammunition, but with a specific bullet, CE 399.

131

The question to be answered is this: Did bullet 399 produce the wounds sustained by Governor Connally?

A bullet entered the back of the Governor's chest to the left of his right armpit. This bullet struck the fifth rib and shattered it, actually stripping away about 10 cm. of bone starting immediately below the armpit (4H105; 6H86). The right lung was severely lacerated (6H88). The bullet exited from the anterior chest, causing a large sucking wound about 5 cm. in diameter just below the right nipple (6H85). There was an atypical entrance wound on the dorsal (back of the hand) side of the Governor's wrist and an atypical exit wound on the volar (palm) side (6H07; R93). The radius (wrist bone) had been broken into about seven or eight pieces from the passage of the bullet (4H120). There was a 1 cm. puncture wound located on the Governor's left thigh some five to six inches above the knee (R93). X rays revealed a small metallic fragment embedded in the left thigh bone, the femur (6H106). This fragment was not surgically removed and still remains in Mr. Connally's femur.

It is probable that one bullet caused all of Connally's injuries. In support of this hypothesis, the Report paraphrases the Parkland doctors as follows:

> In their testimony, the three doctors who attended Governor Connally expressed independently their opinion that a single bullet had passed through his chest; tumbled through his wrist with very little exit velocity, leaving small metallic fragments from the rear portion of the bullet; punctured his left thigh after the bullet had lost virtually all of its velocity; and had fallen out of the thigh wound. (R95)

A footnote to this statement cites portions of the doctors' depositions taken in Dallas on March 23, before two of them were brought to Washington to testify for the Commission a month later. At this time, they had not seen bullet 399 and spoke on a strictly hypothetical basis.

Dr. Tom Shires, who was involved in the Governor's medical treatment, explained that, from the discussion among Connally's surgeons, "everyone was under the impression this was one missile—through and through the chest, through and through the arm and the thigh." When asked if any of the doctors had dissented from this consensus he replied, "Not that I remember" (6H110).

Dr. Charles Gregory, who attended to the Governor's wrist wound, best explained the reasoning behind the theory that one bullet caused Connally's wounds:

> Mr. Specter: Would you consider it possible, in your professional opinion, for the same bullet to have inflicted all of the wounds which you have described on Governor Connally?
>
> Dr. Gregory: Yes; I believe it is very possible, for a number of reasons. One of these—is the apparent loss of energy manifested at each of the various body surfaces, which I transected, the greatest energy being at the point of entry on the posterior aspect of the chest and of the fifth rib, where considerable destruction was done and the least destruction having been done in the medial aspect of the thigh where the bullet apparently expended itself.
>
> . . .We know that high velocity bullets striking bone have a strong tendency to shatter bones and the degree to which the fifth rib was shattered was considerably in excess of the amount of shattering which occurred in the radius—the forearm.
>
> . . .I think that the missile was continually losing velocity with each set of tissues which it encountered and transected, and the amount of damage done is progressively less from first entrance to the thorax to the last entrance in the thigh. (6H101-2)

The Report is entirely misleading, however, when it

asserts that the doctors felt that the wrist fragments were left "from the rear portion of the bullet" and that this *bullet* subsequently punctured the thigh. In their original testimonies, the doctors did not postulate from what part of the bullet the fragments had come. The intent of the Report is obvious, when we consider that the only possible surface from which CE 399 could have lost fragments is its rear, or base, where the lead core was naturally exposed. The thinking of the doctors, however, tended to rule out the possibility of CE 399's having gone into the wrist at all, because they felt that this wound was the result of an irregular or fragmented missile (6H90-91, 98-99, 102). Dr. Robert Shaw, who conducted the operation on the Governor's chest, was puzzled as to how the wrist wounds could have appeared as they did if a whole bullet had caused them (6H91).

According to Dr. Shaw, it is not exactly correct to assert that a whole bullet entered the thigh. In the portion of his original testimony cited by the Report, Dr. Shaw explained the theory of one bullet's causing all the Governor's wounds in this way: "I have always felt that the wounds of Governor Connally could be explained by the passage of one missile through his chest, striking his wrist and *a fragment of it* going on into his left thigh" (6H91; emphasis added).

What the Report does not reflect is the substantial change in Drs. Shaw's and Gregory's opinions when shown the bullet that allegedly produced the Governor's wounds. The first indication of varied opinions came through this exchange between Dr. Shaw and Commissioners Cooper, Dulles, and McCloy. Dr. Shaw had been asked about the possibility that one bullet had caused the Governor's wounds:

Dr. Shaw: ...this is still a possibility. But I don't feel that it is the only possibility.

Sen. Cooper: Why do you say you don't think it is the only possibility? What causes you *now* to say that it is the location—

Dr. Shaw: This is again the testimony that I believe Dr. Gregory will be giving, too. It is a matter of whether the wrist wound could be caused by the same bullet, and we felt that it could *but we had not seen the bullets until today,* and we still do not know which bullet actually inflicted the wound on Governor Connally.

Mr. Dulles: Or whether it was one or two rounds?

Dr. Shaw: Yes.

Mr. Dulles: Or two bullets?

Dr. Shaw: Yes; or three.

Mr. McCloy: You have no firm opinion that all these three wounds were caused by one bullet?

Dr. Shaw: I have no firm opinion....Asking me now if it was true. *If you had asked me a month ago I would have* [had].

Mr. McCloy: Could they have been caused by one bullet, in your opinion?

Dr. Shaw: They could.

Mr. McCloy: I gather that what the witness is saying is that it is possible that they might have been caused by one bullet. But that he has no firm opinion *now* that they were.

Mr. Dulles: As I understand it too. Is our understanding correct?

Dr. Shaw: That is correct. (4H109; emphasis added)

It might be regarded as highly culpable that Commissioners Dulles and McCloy, who professed such a clear understanding of Dr. Shaw's position, signed a report stating the opposite of what Dr. Shaw had testified to, with a footnote referring to prior statements withdrawn by Shaw in their presence. Dr. Shaw's testimony is explicit that, prior to seeing the bullet in evidence, he felt that all the Governor's wounds were caused by one bullet; when shown the bullet, CE 399, which allegedly did this damage, he retracted his original opinion. What was it about this bullet that caused such a change of judgment?

Under questioning by Arlen Specter, Dr. Shaw summed up the indications that CE 399 did not produce the Governor's wounds. He had first been asked to comment on the possibility of *a* bullet's having caused the wounds:

> Mr. Specter: When you started to comment about it not being possible, was that in reference to the existing mass and shape of bullet 399?
> Dr. Shaw: I thought you were referring directly to the bullet shown as Exhibit 399.
> Mr. Specter: What is your opinion as to whether bullet 399 could have inflicted all the wounds on the Governor, then, without respect at this point to the wound of the President's neck?
> Dr. Shaw: I feel that there would be some difficulty in explaining all of the wounds as being inflicted by bullet Exhibit 399 without causing more in the way of loss of substance to the bullet or deformation of the bullet. (4H114)

CE 399 is a virtually undistorted, intact bullet. Its weight is approximately two grains below the average weight of an unfired bullet of that type. As was mentioned in the previous chapter, none of the copper jacket of 399 is missing. The nose and sides of this bullet—as shown in photographs and as I saw in a personal examination—are without gross deformity. The base of 399 has been slightly squeezed so that, in contrast to its rounded shaft, the tail end is slightly elliptical in shape. A small amount of lead, which apparently has flowed from the open base, creates a slight irregularity of the base.

Given the almost pristine condition of CE 399, it is understandable that Drs. Shaw and Gregory were puzzled at the inference that this bullet had caused the Governor's wounds. Before having seen 399, they imagined the bullet that penetrated Connally as being irregular or distorted, the natural consequence of powerful impacts with two substantial bones. Dr. Shaw did not think the bullet could even have remained intact (6H91). On the basis of the nature of the wrist wound, Dr. Gregory thought that "the missile that struck it could be virtually intact, insofar as mass was concerned, but probably was *distorted*" (6H99).

According to Dr. Gregory, the wrist wound showed characteristics of suffering the impact of an *irregular* missile (6H98, 102). In his testimony before the Commission, Dr. Gregory expounded on the nature of this "irregular" missile:

> Dr. Gregory: The wound of entrance (on the wrist) is characteristic in my view of an irregular missile in this case, an irregular missile which has tipped itself off as being irregular by the nature of itself.
> Mr. Dulles: What do you mean by irregular?
> Dr. Gregory: I mean one that has been distorted. It is in some way angular, it has sharp edges or something of this sort It is not rounded or pointed in the fashion of an ordinary missile. (4H124)

Obviously, the condition of the bullet that produced the wrist wound, as described by Dr. Gregory, does not match that of bullet 399, which is not "distorted" or "irregular." There is only one surface on CE 399 that is the least bit "irregular," the base end where the lead core is naturally exposed. When Arlen Specter asked

Dr. Gregory about a possible correlation between CE 399 and the wrist wound, the latter responded:

> the only. . .deformity which I can find is at the base of the missile. . . .The only way that this missile could have produced this wound, in my view, was to have entered the wrist backward. . . .That is the only possible explanation I could offer to correlate this missile with this particular wound. (4H121)

Dr. Gregory admitted, in response to a hypothetical question from Counsel Specter, that the slight irregularity in the base of CE 399 "could have" been sufficient to produce the lacerated wounds observed on the Governor's wrist (4H122).

Yet, Dr. Gregory's only correlation of CE 399 to the wrist wound is not applicable to the circumstances of the shooting. Dr. Gregory examined 399 in its spent state, long after it had been fired and incurred its slight amount of damage. He related the bullet in *this* state to a bullet in flight that had not suffered the full extent of its damage. The irregularity of 399's base would have occurred *after* it hit the wrist, as the Commission postulates. Certainly a base-first strike on the radius would not have left the base in the same condition as it was *prior* to impact. Dr. Gregory's answer to Specter's hypothetical question could not apply to the actual shooting.

Specter knew independently from wound ballistics experts that the condition of CE 399 was not at all consistent with having struck a wrist. Two conferences that Specter attended were held during the week prior to Dr. Gregory's Commission testimony. The consensus of the first meeting was, in part, that "the bullet recovered from the Governor's stretcher does not appear to have penetrated a wrist."[1] The expert opinion was more explicit at the next meeting, held the day of the Shaw-Gregory testimony and attended by those doctors, the wound ballistics experts, Specter, McCloy, and others. A memorandum of this conference reports that

> in a discussion after the conference Drs. Light and Dolce (two wound ballistics experts from Edgewood Arsenal) expressed themselves as being very strongly of the opinion that Connally had been hit by two different bullets, principally on the ground that the bullet recovered from Connally's stretcher could not have broken his radius without having suffered more distortion. Dr. Olivier (another wound ballistics expert) withheld a conclusion until he has had the opportunity to make tests on animal tissue and bone with the actual rifle.[2]

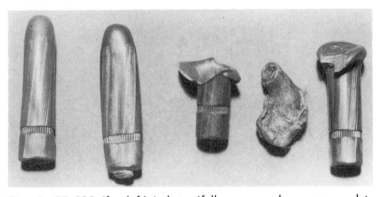

Fig. 4. CE 399 (far left) is beautifully preserved as compared to similar bullets fired from the Carcano: (from left to right) CE 853, fired through a goat's chest, CE 857 (in two pieces), fired into a human skull, and CE 856, fired into a human wrist. Not one of the three, each of which did less damage than the Commission attributes to 399, emerged as undistorted as 399. It is preposterous to assume that 399 could have struck so many obstructions and remained so undamaged. (This photograph was taken for Harold Weisberg by the National Archives.)

Dr. Olivier's tests, despite their shortcomings, demonstrated a very common ballistics principle—that a bullet striking bone will usually suffer some form of distortion.

As is apparent from Figure 4, none of Dr. Olivier's test bullets admitted into evidence matched 399, since all were grossly deformed by extreme flattening, indenting, or separation of jacket from core (see also 17H849-51).

Although Dr. Olivier's tests included shots through ten cadaver wrists, only one of the bullets recovered from this series was admitted into evidence, CE 856 (see Fig. 4). The other bullets are not in the National Archives, and until recently no researchers had seen them. On March 27, 1973, the Archives declassified a once-"Confidential" report written in March 1965 by Dr. Olivier and his associate, Dr. Arthur J. Dziemian. This report is entitled "Wound Ballistics of 6.5-MM Mannlicher-Carcano Ammunition," and represents the final report of the research conducted for the Commission at Edgewood Arsenal. This report includes photographs of four of the test bullets fired through human wrists, published here for the first time ever (Fig. 5). The bullet marked "B" in Figure 5 is apparently CE 856. However, the other three bullets, which produced damage similar to that suffered by Governor Connally's wrist, are even more mutilated than the one bullet that was preserved for the record. These newly released photographs graphically reveal the degree of mutilation that might be found on Mannlicher-Carcano bullets that had struck human wrists, and make even more preposterous the Commission's assertion that near-pristine 399 penetrated Connally's wrist.

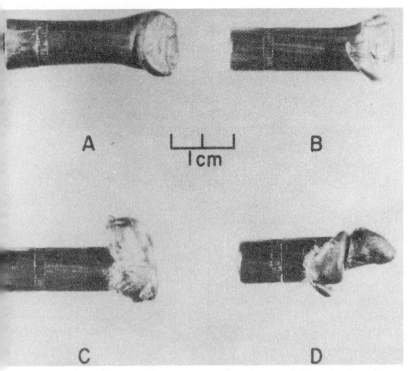

Fig. 5. This photograph was considered "Confidential" by the government and withheld from researchers for eight years. It depicts "6.5-MM Mannlicher-Carcano Bullets Recovered after being Fired Through Distal Ends of Radii of Cadaver Wrists."

The obvious conclusion dictated by the nature of the Governor's wounds is that CE 399 could not have caused them. This is contrary to the Report's assertion that "all the evidence indicated that the bullet found on the Governor's stretcher could have caused all his wounds" (R95). The substantiating argument of the Report is that the total weight of the bullet fragments in the Governor's body does not exceed the weight lost by 399. This argument is nonsensical, for it ignores the thoroughly nonstatistical nature of ballistics and the expected consequences of bullets striking bone; such a line of reasoning attempts to replace imprecision with pseudo-exactness and inapplicable mathematics.

It is therefore, in light of the well-preserved state of that bullet, preposterous to postulate that CE 399 caused Governor Connally's wounds. Drs. Shaw and Gregory, barraged by the official contention that 399 was discovered on the Governor's stretcher and thus must have caused his wounds, were reserved in expressing themselves on the unlikelihood of such a proposition. Other experts have been more free in voicing their opinions. I have yet to find one expert who will concede the likelihood of an occurrence such as the Commission assumes. When I spoke with ballistics expert Charles Dickey at Frankford Arsenal, he cautioned me that he could not speak out directly against the validity of the government's beliefs relating to the assassination. Even he found it hard to accept that 399 caused the Governor's wounds.[3] Among the many forensic pathologists who have scoffed at this theory are William Enos,[4] Halpert Fillinger,[5] Milton Helpern,[6] John Nichols,[7] and Cyril Wecht.[8]

The absence of gross deformity in bullet 399 contradicts the career of massive bone-smashing attributed to it. However, as I learned from Dr. Fillinger and as Harold Weisberg pointed out several years ago in a copyrighted study of the medical evidence, the most crucial aspect of 399's state is its absence of significant distortion detectable through microscopic examination.[9]

The barrels of modern firearms are "rifled," that is, several spiral grooves are cut into the barrel from end to end. As the bullet is propelled through the barrel, these spiral grooves and lands (the raised portions of the barrel between the grooves) set the bullet spinning around its axis, giving it rotational as well as forward movement, thus increasing its stability in flight. The

lands and grooves consequently etch a pattern of very
fine striated lines along the sides of the bullet, which
will vary from one weapon to another just as fingerprints vary from one person to another. Like fingerprints, the lands and grooves scratched onto the surface
of the bullet can be microscopically identified with a
particular weapon to the exclusion of all others, provided that they remain sufficiently intact subsequent
to impact (R547-48).

The very fine lands and grooves along the copper
sides of CE 399 allowed the conclusive determination
that the bullet had been fired from "Oswald's" rifle.
FBI agent Frazier provided vital testimony about the
defacement of these microscopic markings on 399:

> Mr. Eisenberg: Were the markings of the bullet at all
> defaced?
> Mr. Frazier: Yes; they were, in that the bullet is dis-
> torted by having been slightly flattened or twisted.
> Mr. Eisenberg: How material would you call that de-
> facement?
> Mr. Frazier: It is hardly visible unless you look at the
> base of the bullet and notice it is not round.
> Mr. Eisenberg: How far does it affect your examination
> for purposes of identification?
> Mr. Frazier: It had no effect at all. . .because it did not
> mutilate or distort the microscopic marks beyond the
> point where you could recognize the pattern and find the
> same pattern of marks on one bullet as were present on
> the other. (3H430)

From Frazier's testimony it is apparent that the very
slight "defacement" of 399's lands and grooves could be
better termed a "displacement," for the microscopic
marks were distorted only by an almost insignificant
change in the *contour* of the bullet as opposed to a disruption in the continuity of the surface.

After closely examining 399 at a magnification of

five diameters, I was convinced of the veracity of Frazier's testimony. I followed each set of lands and grooves on the bullet and saw that all were continuous and without disruption, beginning just below the rounded nose and running smoothly down to the tail end.

Dr. Fillinger emphasized to me that a jacketed bullet such as 399 could strike one bone and leave its lands and grooves intact so far as visible *to the naked eye*. When I assured him that Agent Frazier had found these marks still to be intact even through microscopic examination, Fillinger seemed somewhat taken aback. "Well, this is unlikely," he said. "It's very unlikely, as a matter of fact. Even our own ballistics people here don't get that kind of good luck."[10] One can readily appreciate that forceful contact with firm bone tissue is bound to disrupt the fine striations on a bullet's surface, even with a jacketed projectile.

If 399 wounded Governor Connally, then it was necessarily immune to the conditions that distort and deform other bullets of its kind. If it smashed through two substantial bones and rammed into another one, it failed to manifest the normal indications of such a flight, those which marked other bullets under even less stress. The theory that 399 wounded the Governor is valid only on the premise that it was a magic bullet capable of feats never before performed in the history of ballistics.

Bullet 399 is not magic. It is just the typical mass of copper and lead that constitutes other bullets of its kind. Governor Connally was likewise not magic. His flesh and bones would deform bullets as would anyone else's; his wounds showed very strong indications that the bullet causing them had, in fact, become distorted and irregular.

The only tenable conclusion warranted by the evidence of the Governor's wounds, the condition of 399, and the laws of physics is that 399 did not wound Governor Connally.

The Search for Legitimacy

Did 399 figure in the assassination shots?

As we have seen, there is no possible way by which bullet 399 can be related to the President's wounds. The extensive fragmentation involving the fatal wounds rules out a missile left intact. The presence of fragments in the President's neck likewise rules out 399, for there is no possible circumstance under which it could have deposited fragments in the neck and still account for the other wounds, such as the tiny hole in the throat. Had the President sustained a back wound of short penetration, it could not have been caused by a bullet whose penetrating power was as great as 399's.

Governor Connally, to judge from the nature of his wounds and the predictable consequences of a strike such as he endured, was hit by a missile that did not leave behind a very large percentage of its substance but ended its flight in a distorted or mangled condition.

Thus, CE 399 can not be related to any of the wounds inflicted on either victim during the assassination. From this it follows that 399 must have turned up at Parkland Hospital in a manner not related to the victims and their treatment. It had to have been placed on the stretcher at some time, manually and intentionally.

It can not be a legitimate assassination bullet.

The situation at Parkland on the afternoon of the assassination would have enabled almost anyone to gain access to the area where 399 was discovered on the stretcher. A man identifying himself as an FBI agent tried to enter the room in which the dead President lay at the hospital. The Secret Servicemen who witnessed this incident and had to restrain the man with force reported that he "appeared to be *determined* to enter the President's room" (18H798-99 and 795-96). The Commission apparently made no efforts to determine the identity of this man and sought no further details from other witnesses.

Two witnesses were positive that they saw Jack Ruby at Parkland Hospital at about the time the President's death was announced (15H80; 25H216).

Harold Weisberg, in his book *Oswald in New Orleans,* reveals that a Cuban refugee of "disruptive influence" was employed at Parkland at the time of the assassination. Pointing out that the Commission's best evidence indicated that 399 was a "plant," Weisberg finds it extremely suspicious that no effort was made to identify this "political Cuban" when his existence was known to both the Secret Service and the Commission.[11] Such a man would have had access to the stretcher on which 399 was found and would not have attracted the least suspicion, since he was an employee of the hospital.

Nurse Margaret Henchcliffe related an incident that illustrates how almost *anyone* could have made his way to the area of the stretcher. She reported that a 16-year-old boy *carrying a camera* had gotten into the Emergency Area, seeking to take pictures of the room in which the President had died less than an hour before (21H240).

There is currently no evidence against the possibility that the two bullet fragments found in the front seat of the limousine and traced to "Oswald's" rifle were likewise "planted" after the victims were taken to the hospital. We should recall from the discussion of the President's head wounds that the fatal damage was, in no instance, consistent with the damage produced by military ammunition of the type attributed to Oswald. Photographs taken outside the hospital show substantial crowds in proximity to the unguarded limousine.[12] As in the case of the stretcher bullet, the circumstances *did* permit incriminating evidence to be planted.

It cannot be said, and indeed I make no pretense of saying, that a phony FBI man, a "disruptive Cuban," Jack Ruby, or a young boy with a camera planted bullet 399 at Parkland Hospital. The thrust of this discussion has been that anyone could have gained access to the locations in which evidence pointing to Oswald was found. This point may also be applied to the Book Depository, where Oswald's rifle and three spent shells were discovered. Within fifteen minutes of the assassination, the Depository was swarming with unidentified people.[13] The medical evidence, as the discussion in this and the previous chapter demonstrates, disassociates military bullets from the President's wounds and proves that a specific bullet traced to Oswald's rifle and found at Parkland could *not* have wounded either victim in the assassination. The spectrographic analyses, the only evidence that could correlate Oswald's rifle with the wounds, was conspicuously avoided by the Commission, and has been suppressed by the government so that no one to this day may know the spectrographer's findings. It is therefore not unreasonable to postulate, in accordance with the only scientific evidence currently available, that the tangible evidence that implicates Oswald was deliberately "planted," and did not figure in the actual shooting. The unmistakable inference from the medical evidence is that the rifle, the cartridge cases, and the bullets *had* to have been planted. The circumstances at the Book Depository and at Parkland Hospital indisputably could have enabled a "conspirator" to plant evidence pointing to Oswald. The Commission has produced no evidence that precludes the possibility of a "plant."

The discussion in this section has removed the very foundation of the official case against Oswald by demonstrating, to the degree of certainty possible, that Oswald's rifle was not responsible for the wounds of President Kennedy and Governor Connally. The medical/ballistics evidence thus exculpates Oswald and presents several unmistakable conspiratorial implications.

The Warren Commission claimed to have much evidence, apart from the medical/ballistics findings, that proved or indicated that Oswald was the assassin. This additional evidence, and the Commission's treatment of it, I will consider in Part III.

PART III:

THE ACCUSED

6

The Rifle in the Building

The Mannlicher-Carcano C2766 rifle was brought into the Book Depository and taken to the sixth floor in some way at some time prior to 1:30 P.M., November 22, when it was found hidden in a stack of boxes near the sixth-floor stair landing. For the "lone assassin-no conspiracy" theory to be valid, the only man who could have brought the rifle into the building is Lee Harvey Oswald.

The Commission's conclusion that Oswald brought the rifle into the Depository demands premeditation of the murder. According to the Report, Oswald deliberately lied to co-worker Frazier about his reason for returning to Irving the day before the assassination and constructed a paper sack on or before Thursday, November 21, for the purpose of carrying his rifle into the building (R137).

The prerequisite of premeditation in this case is prior knowledge of the motorcade route. If Oswald did not

151

know by Tuesday morning that President Kennedy would pass his building, he obviously could not have planned to shoot the President. The closest the Commission came to considering the question of prior knowledge was to assert that Oswald could have known the motorcade route as early as November 19, when it appeared in the Dallas papers (R40, 642). It never established whether Oswald *did* know the route.

Despite the Commission's assurances, on the basis of newspaper accounts neither Oswald nor any Dallas resident could have known the *exact* motorcade route, for conflicting accounts were published. The problem, as stated by the Report in its "Speculations and Rumors" appendix, is this:

> *Speculation.* —The route shown in the newspaper took the motorcade through the Triple Underpass via Main Street, a block away from the Depository. Therefore, Oswald could not have known that the motorcade would pass directly by the. . .Depository Building. (R643).

The Report appears to dispel this speculation by asserting that the published route clearly indicated a turn-off from Main onto Houston, and Houston onto Elm, taking the President directly in front of the Depository as the procession approached the underpass. In dispelling this rumor, the Report quotes incompletely and dishonestly from the relevant Dallas papers.

On November 16, the *Dallas Times Herald* reported that while the route had not yet been determined, "the presidential party apparently will loop through the downtown area, probably on Main Street" (22H613). Both the *Dallas Morning News* and the *Times Herald* carried the release of the motorcade route on November 19, including the information about the turn onto Elm (22H614-15). The next day, the *Morning News* carried another description of the route, saying the motorcade "will travel on Mockingbird Lane, Lemmon Avenue, Turtle Creek Boulevard, Cedar Springs, Harwood, Main and Stemmons Freeway," with mention of the Houston-to-Elm stretch omitted (22H616). Not included in the Commission's evidence but discovered and printed by Harold Weisberg, is a map of the motorcade route that appeared on the front page of the *Morning News* of November 22, the day of the President's visit. The map shows the route as taking Main down to Stemmons Freeway again, avoiding the cut-over to Elm.[1]

The Report never quotes those press accounts which did not include the Elm Street stretch, leaving the impression that Oswald, in his premeditation, knew previously that the President would pass directly before him, and therefore present an easy target (R40). The distinction is not major, because either published route would have put the President within shooting range of the Depository. It should be noted, however, that the Commission, in making its case, quoted selectively from the record.

Before it can be stated that Oswald knew of *any* motorcade route, it must first be established that he had access to a medium by which he could have been so informed. Roy Truly and Bonnie Ray Williams thought that Oswald occasionally read newspapers in the Depository (3H218, 164). Mrs. Robert Reid saw Oswald in the building some five to ten times and recalled that "he was usually reading," although she did not specify what he read (3H279). Charles Givens provided the best detail on Oswald's reading habits during work. He testified that Oswald would generally read the previous day's paper: "Like if the day was Tuesday, he would read Monday's paper in the morning." Givens was certain that the editions of the paper Oswald read, the *Dallas Morning News,* were dated, for he usually looked at them after Oswald finished (6H352).

Oswald's sufficient access to the electronic media is not definitely established. Mrs. Earlene Roberts, the woman who rented Oswald his small room on North Beckley, testified that he rarely watched television: "If someone in the other rooms had it on, maybe he would come and stand at the back of the couch—not over 5 minutes and go to his room and shut the door" (6H437). The police inventory of materials confiscated from Oswald's room reveals he had a "brown and yellow gold Russian make portable radio" (24H343), although there is no information as to whether the radio was usable, or used.

Although the evidence of Oswald's accessibility to information relating to the motorcade route does not establish whether he *could* have known *anything* about the exact route, there are indications that he was, in fact, totally uninformed about and uninterested in the procession. The narrative written by Marina Oswald when she was first put under protective custody leads one to believe that Oswald knew nothing of the President's trip. "Only when I told him that Kennedy was coming the next day to Dallas and asked how I could see him—on television, of course—he answered that he did now know," Marina wrote of the night before the assassination (18H638).[2]

More important information was provided by co-worker James Jarman, who met Oswald on the first floor of the Depository between 9:30 and 10:00 on the morning of November 22. According to Jarman, Oswald

was standing up in the window and I went to the window also, and he asked me what were the people gathering around the corner for, and I told him that the President was supposed to pass that morning, and he asked me did I know which way he was coming, and I told him, yes; he probably come down Main and turn on Houston and then back again on Elm.

Then he said, "Oh, I see," and that was all. (3H201)

Jarman first reported this incident on November 23, 1963, in his affidavit for the Dallas Police (24H213).

Jarman's story is subject to two interpretations. If Oswald spoke honestly, then he clearly revealed his ignorance of the day's events, knowing neither the reason for the crowds gathering around the building nor the route of the motorcade. If Oswald knew the answers to the questions he posed to Jarman, it would seem that he was deliberately trying to "plant" false information to indicate his lack of interest in the motorcade, a good defense in case he was later apprehended in connection with the assassination. However, as Sylvia Meagher has pointed out, if Oswald deliberately dropped exculpatory hints to Jarman, why did he not later offer this to the police as part of the evidence in his favor?[3] In all the pages of reports and testimony relating to Oswald's interrogation sessions, there is no indication that Oswald ever mentioned the early morning meeting with Jarman.

Thus there is no basis for asserting that Oswald knew the exact motorcade route as of Thursday morning, November 21. The newspapers, including the one Oswald normally saw a day late, carried conflicting versions of the route, varying at the crucial juncture —the turn-off on Houston Street. While there is no way of knowing whether Oswald had seen any of the published information relevant to the motorcade, his actions indicate a total unawareness of the events surrounding the procession through Dallas.

During October and November of 1963, Oswald lived

in a Dallas roominghouse while his wife, Marina, and
two children lived in Irving at the home of Ruth Paine,
some 15 miles from the Depository. In the words of the
Report, "Oswald traveled between Dallas and Irving on
weekends in a car driven by a neighbor of the Paines,
Buell Wesley Frazier, who also worked at the Depository. Oswald generally would go to Irving on Friday afternoon and return to Dallas Monday morning" (R129).
On November 21, the day before the assassination,
Oswald asked Frazier whether he could ride home with
him that afternoon to obtain "some curtain rods" for
"an apartment." Sinister implications are attached to
this visit to Irving, which the Report would have us believe was unprecedented. Assuring us that the
curtain-rod story was a fabrication, and asserting that
"Oswald's" rifle was stored in the Paine garage, the
Report lays ground for the ultimate assertion that Oswald returned to Irving to pick up his rifle and bring it
to work the next day.

The Report's explanation of Oswald's return to Irving
hinges on the assumption that the C2766 rifle was
stored in the Paine garage. Of this there is not a single
shred of evidence. The Commission had one tenuous
item that could indicate the presence of *a* rifle wrapped
in a blanket in the Paine garage; Marina testified she
once peeked into this blanket and saw the *stock* of a
rifle (R128). The other evidence indicates only that a
bulky object was stored in the blanket. Certainly no
one saw the *specific* C2766 rifle in the garage. As
Liebeler has pointed out, "that fact is that not one person alive today ever saw that rifle in the Paine garage
in such a way that it could be identified as that rifle."[4]

The Report recounts in dramatic detail the police
search of the Paine garage on the afternoon of the assassination. When asked that day if her husband

owned a rifle, Marina pointed to the rolled-up blanket, which the officers proceeded to lift. The blanket hung limp in an officer's hand; it was empty (R131). Although there was no evidence that the rifle had ever been stored there, the Commission found the presence of the empty blanket on November 22 evidence that Oswald "removed the rifle from the blanket in the Paines' garage on Thursday evening" (R137). Had the rifle been stored where the Commission assumed, *anyone* could have removed it at almost *any* time prior to the afternoon of the shooting. The Paines apparently were not preoccupied with the security of their home, as indicated on Saturday, November 23. While the police were searching the Paine house that day, Mr. and Mrs. Paine drove off, leaving the officers completely alone (7H193).

With no evidence that Oswald ever removed the rifle from the Paine garage or that the rifle was even stored there, the Commission's case loses much of its substance, however circumstantial. Further reducing the suspicion evoked by Oswald's return to Irving is the fact that this trip was *not* particularly unusual. Despite the Commission's statement that he generally went home only on weekends, Oswald kept to no exact pattern for visiting his wife during the short time he was estranged from her. On the contrary, Oswald frequently violated the assumed "pattern" of weekend visits. He began his employment at the Depository on October 16. That Friday, the 18th, he came to Irving but did not return to Dallas the following Monday because his wife had given birth to a second daughter that Sunday; he visited Marina on Monday and spent the night at the Paines's. The next weekend was "normal." However, there are strong indications that Oswald returned to Irving the next *Thursday,* October 31. Dur-

ing the weekend of November 8, Oswald again spent
Monday with his wife in Irving, this time because it
was Veteran's Day. Furthermore, Oswald did not return at all the following weekend, and he fought over
the telephone with his wife that Sunday about his use
of an assumed name in registering at the roominghouse. The following Thursday, the 21st, he returned to
Irving (see R737-40).

The Report does not include mention of a visit by
Oswald to Irving on any Thursday other than
November 21. But there is strong evidence of another
such return, as was brought out by Sylvia Meagher:

> It does not appear that Oswald's visit on Thursday
> evening without notice or invitation was unusual. But it
> is not clear that it was unprecedented. An FBI report
> dealing with quite another matter—Oswald's income and
> expenditures—strongly suggests that Oswald had cashed a
> check in a grocery store in Irving on Thursday evening,
> October 31, 1963 [CE 1165, p. 6]; the Warren Commission
> decided arbitrarily that the transaction took place on Fri-
> day, November 1 [R331]. Neither Oswald's wife nor Mrs.
> Ruth Paine, both of whom were questioned closely about
> the dates and times of Oswald's visits to Irving during Oc-
> tober and November, suggested that he had ever come
> there—with or without prior notice—on a Thursday. It is
> possible, though implausible, that Oswald came to Irving
> on Thursday, October 31, 1963 solely to cash a check and
> then returned to Dallas without contacting his wife or vis-
> iting the Paine residence. More likely, Marina and Mrs.
> Paine forgot that visit or, for reasons of their own, prefer-
> red not to mention it. Either way, it is clear that Oswald's
> visit to Irving on Thursday night, November 21, may not
> have been unprecedented.[5]

Oswald's excuse for his return to Irving Thursday
was that he intended to pick up curtain rods for "an
apartment." The Report attempts to vitiate this excuse
by noting that (a) Oswald spoke with neither his wife,

nor his landlady, nor Mrs. Paine about curtain rods, (b) Oswald's landlady testified that his room on North Beckley Avenue had curtains and rods, and (c) "No curtain rods were known to have been discovered in the Depository Building after the assassination" (R130).

The source cited for the assertion that no curtain rods were found in the Depository after the assassination is CE 2640. The Report neglects to mention that CE 2640 details an investigation conducted on September 21, 1964, ten months after the assassination, when only one person, Roy Truly, was questioned about curtain rods (25H899). Truly was "certain" that no curtain rods had been found because "it would be customary for any discovery of curtain rods to immediately be called to his attention." Aside from the ludicrous implication that the Depository had rules governing the discovery of curtain rods, this "inquiry" was too limited and too late to be of any significance.

Apparently, the Commission's request for this inquiry calculated its worthlessness. Rankin made this request of Hoover in a letter dated August 31, 1964. The letter, which I obtained from the National Archives, leaves little doubt that the result of the inquiry was preconceived to be against Oswald. Rankin ordered that Truly be interviewed "in order to establish that no curtain rods were found in the [Depository] following the assassination."[6] This phraseology seems to instruct Hoover *not* to conduct an objective investigation; otherwise, the letter would have read "in order to establish *whether any* curtain rods were found."

The Commission accepted without question the landlady's assurance that Oswald's room had curtain rods. Had it conducted the least investigation, it could easily have determined that the room *did* need rods. Black Star photographer Gene Daniels followed many

of the events in Dallas on the weekend of the assassination. On Saturday morning, November 23, he went
to Oswald's rooming house and obtained a fascinating
set of pictures. Daniels explained the circumstances to
me:

> I went to the rooming house the following morning and
> requested permission to make the photograph from the
> landlady. I'm not sure of her name but I don't think she
> was the owner. We went into the room and she told me
> she preferred not to have me take any pictures until she
> put "the curtains back up." She said that newsmen the
> evening before had disturbed the room and she didn't
> want anyone to see it messed up. I agreed and stood in the
> room as she and her husband stood on the bed and ham-
> mered the curtain rods back into position. While she did
> this, I photographed them or possibly just her I forget
> right now, up on the bed with the curtain rods etc.[7]

It seems doubtful in the extreme that the activity of
newsmen the night before could physically have removed curtain rods from the wall in Oswald's room. A
more reasonable possibility is that the rods had not
been up at all until November 23, when Daniels witnessed and photographed the landlady and her husband hammering the rods into the wall.

This renovating of Oswald's cubicle could not have
come at a better time in the development of the Dallas
police case against Oswald. On the day of the assassination, Wesley Frazier filed an affadavit for the police
that included information about the curtain-rod story
(24H209). At 10:30 on the morning of November 23,
police Captain Will Fritz asked Oswald if he had carried curtain rods to work the previous day. According
to Fritz, Oswald denied having told the curtain-rod
story to Frazier (R604). (This denial, in light of opposing testimony from Frazier and his sister, was apparently a falsehood.)

Thus, the Commission is on shaky ground when it assumes Oswald's excuse for returning to Irving to have been false. The inferences drawn from the premise of a spurious excuse are likewise weakened or disproved. This Commission, which seems to have become a panel of amateur psychiatrists in conjuring up "motives" for Oswald, showed an appalling lack of sympathy and understanding in "evaluating" the "false excuse."

> In deciding whether Oswald carried a rifle to work in a long paper bag on November 22, the Commission gave weight to the fact that Oswald gave a false reason for returning home on November 21, and one which provided an excuse for the carrying of a bulky package the following morning. (R130)

> The preponderance of the evidence supports the conclusion that Lee Harvey Oswald...told the curtain rod story to Frazier to explain both the return to Irving on a Thursday and the obvious bulk of the package which he intended to bring to work the next day. (R137)

The curtain-rod story may not have been false. However, there are several possible explanations for Oswald's Irving visit other than the one that had such appeal to the Commission—that Oswald came to pick up his rifle. As Leo Sauvage has pointed out, Ruth Paine and Marina had their own theory about Oswald's return.[8] In the words of the Report:

> The women thought he had come to Irving because he felt badly about arguing with his wife about the use of the fictitious name. He said that he was lonely, because he had not come the previous weekend, and told Marina that he "wanted to make his peace" with her. (R740)

Sylvia Meagher, more understanding than the Com-

mission, finds nothing suspicious in a man's trying to
"make his peace" with his wife or visiting his two
young daughters after not having seen them for two
weeks. She points out that if this were the reason for
Oswald's visit, it is unlikely that he would have admitted it to Frazier, with whom he was not close. Oswald
could very innocently have lied about the curtain rods
to Frazier to cover up a personal excuse, bringing a
package the next morning to substantiate his story and
avoid embarrassing questions.[9] (The Paine garage,
stuffed almost beyond capacity with the paraphernalia
of two families, contained many packages that Oswald
could have taken on the spur of the moment.)

As the record now stands, Oswald's actions on
November 21 could well have been perfectly innocent.
The fact is that we do not know why Lee Oswald returned to Irving that Thursday, but the trip is no more
an indictment of Oswald than it is an element of his
defense. However, official misrepresentations allowed
unnecessary and unfair implications to become associated with the return. There is no reason to believe
that Oswald knew anything about the November 22
motorcade. His visit to Irving on a Thursday probably
was not unprecedented. Since there is no proof that the
C2766 rifle was ever stored in the Paine garage, there
is no basis for the theory that Oswald's return was for
the purpose of obtaining that rifle. A number of innocent explanations for the visit present themselves as
far more plausible than the incriminating and unsubstantiated notion of the Commission.

The Long and Bulky Package

At about 7:15 on the morning of the assassination,
Oswald left the Paine home to walk to the residence of
Mrs. Linnie Mae Randle, Buell Wesley Frazier's sister.

Mrs. Randle and Frazier were the only two people to see Oswald that morning before he arrived at the Depository; they were likewise the only two people who saw the long package that Oswald had brought with him to work. Their accounts are critical in the whole case and deserve close scrutiny.

Standing at the kitchen window of her house, Mrs. Randle saw Oswald approaching. In his right hand he carried "a package in a sort of heavy brown bag," the top of which was folded down. Mrs. Randle specified that Oswald gripped the package at the very top and that the bottom almost touched the ground (2H248). When Commission Counsel Joseph Ball had Mrs. Randle demonstrate how Oswald held the package, he apparently tried to lead her into providing a false description for the record; she corrected him:

> Mr. Ball: And where was his hand gripping the *middle* of the package?
> Mrs. Randle: No, sir; the *top* with just a little bit sticking up. You know just like you grab something like that.
> Mr. Ball: And he was grabbing it with his right hand at the top of the package and the package almost touched the ground?
> Mrs. Randle: Yes, sir.[10] (2H248; emphasis added)

Mrs. Randle estimated the length of this package as "a little more" than two feet. When shown the 38-inch paper sack found near the alleged "assassin's" window, she was sure this was too long to have been the one carried by Oswald unless it had been folded down. In fact, she volunteered to fold the bag to its proper length; the result was a 28½-inch sack (2H249-50). Furthermore, the FBI, in one of its interviews with Mrs. Randle, staged a "reconstruction" of Oswald's movements in which a replica sack was used and folded

according to Mrs. Randle's memory. "When the proper
length of the sack was reached according to Mrs.
Randle's estimate," states the FBI report of this interview, "it was measured and found to be 27 inches long"
(24H408).

We must admire Mrs. Randle's consistency in estimating the length of Oswald's package despite severe
questioning before the Commission. Her recollection of
the sack's length varied by only one and half inches in
at least two reconstructions and one verbal estimate. If
we recall her specific description of the manner in
which Oswald carried the sack (gripped at the *top* with
the bottom almost touching the ground), it is obvious
that the package *could not* have exceeded 29 inches in
maximum length. (Oswald was 5 feet, 9 inches [24H7].)

Frazier first noticed the package on the back seat of
his car as he was about to leave for the Depository. He
estimated its length as "roughly about two feet long"
(2H226). From the parking lot at work, Oswald walked
some 50 feet ahead of Frazier. He held the package
parallel to his body, one end under his right armpit,
the other cupped in his right hand (2H228). During his
testimony before the Commission, Frazier, slightly over
6 feet tall compared to Oswald's 5 feet, 9 inches, held a
package that contained the disassembled Carcano. He
cupped one end in his right hand; the other end protruded over his shoulder to the level of his ear. Had this
been the case with Oswald's package, Frazier is sure he
would have noticed the extra length (2H243). Frazier's
Commission testimony is buttressed by the original
sworn affidavit he filed on November 22, 1963. Here he
estimated the length of the sack as "about two feet
long," adding "I noticed that Lee had the package in
his right hand under his arm. . .straight up and down"
(24H209). Furthermore, during another "reconstruc-

tion," Frazier indicated for FBI agents the length occupied by the package on the back seat of his car; that distance was measured to be 27 inches (24H409). Again, if we take Frazier's description of how Oswald held the package in walking toward the Depository, the maximum length is fixed at 27 to 28 inches.

Frazier and Mrs. Randle proved to be consistent, reliable witnesses. Under rigorous questioning, through many reconstructions, their stories emerged unaltered and reinforced: the package carried by Oswald was 27 to 28 inches long. Both witnesses provided ample means for verifying their estimates of length; on each occasion their recollections proved accurate. Frazier and Mrs. Randle both independently described the package as slightly more than two feet long; they both physically estimated the length of the package at what turned out to be from 27 to 28½ inches; they both recalled Oswald's having carried his sack in a manner that would set the maximum length at about 28 inches. One could hardly expect more credible testimony. Perhaps it is true that the combined stories of Frazier and Mrs. Randle, persuasive as they are, do not *prove* that Oswald's package was 27 to 28 inches long. However, no evidence has been put forth challenging their stories, and until such evidence can be produced, establishing a valid basis for doubt, we are forced to accept the 28-inch estimate as accurate.

Not even the Commission could produce a single piece of evidence disputing Frazier and Mrs. Randle. It merely believed what it wanted to believe and quoted what it wanted to quote, even to the point of self-contradiction. Without comment as to the remarkably accurate aspects of Mrs. Randle's testimony, the Report dismisses her story entirely by asserting with no substantiation that she "saw the bag fleetingly." It then quotes Frazier as saying he did not pay much attention to Oswald's package (R134). This, however, was not the full extent of what Frazier had said, as the self-contradictory Report had previously quoted. "Like I said, I remember I didn't look at the package very much," warned Frazier, ". . .*but when I did look at it he did have his hands on the package like that*" (R133-34).

Accepting Frazier's and Mrs. Randle's stories would have aborted in its early stages the theory that Oswald killed the President unassisted. The longest component of the Mannlicher-Carcano rifle *when disassembled* is 34.8-inches long (3H395). The Commission's best and, in fact, *only* evidence on this point said the package carried to work by Oswald was too short to have contained the rifle in its shortest possible form, disassembled. Obviously, a 35-inch package strains the limits imposed by the recollections of Frazier and Mrs. Randle. Such a sack would have dragged on the ground when grasped at the top, protruded over Oswald's shoulder when cupped in his hand (as Frazier himself demonstrated), occupied more space on the back seat of Frazier's car, and been perceptibly longer than was consistently described by the two people who saw it. There is just no reason to believe that the package was over 28 inches long, and every reason to believe that 28 inches was very close to its proper length. The Commission could give no valid reason for rejecting that estimate; it merely chose to disregard the stories of its only two witnesses. Any alternative would have entailed admitting that Oswald did not carry the "assassination weapon" to work with him that morning.

The Report plays up its rejection of the Frazier-Randle testimony as if, virtually torn between witness accounts and cold, hard, scientific fact, it gave in to the latter. In the words of the Report:

The Commission has weighed the visual recollection of Frazier and Mrs. Randle against the evidence here presented that the bag Oswald carried contained the assassination weapon and has concluded that Frazier and Randle are mistaken as to the length of the bag. (R134)

What evidence was "presented that the bag... contained the assassination weapon"?

"A [38-inch long] handmade bag of paper and tape was found in the southeast corner of the sixth floor alongside the window from which the shots were fired. It was not a standard type bag which could be obtained in a store and it was presumably made for a particular purpose," says the Report (R134). Before *any* evidence relevant to this bag is presented, the Report draws an important inference from its location; "The presence of the bag in this corner is cogent evidence that it was used as the container for the rifle" (R135). The Commission was unequivocal; the evidence meant only what the Commission wanted it to mean—nothing more, nothing less. To take issue with the inference read into the evidence: the presence of that bag in that corner is "cogent evidence" *only* that someone placed the bag in the corner. Its location of discovery can not tell who made the bag, when it was made, or what it contained. The Commission wanted it to have contained the rifle; therefore, it must have.

Having attached a significance to this bag (CE 142) "cogent" only for the Commission's predisposition toward Oswald's sole guilt, the Report presents what it labels "Scientific Evidence Linking Rifle and Oswald to Paper Bag." There was no difficulty in linking Oswald to the bag; his right palmprint and left index fingerprint were on it, proving that at some time, in some way, he had handled it. Again, the Commission reads an improper inference into this evidence. Because the

168 PRESUMED GUILTY

palmprint was found at the bottom of the paper bag, says the Report, "it was consistent with the bag having contained a heavy or bulky object when [Oswald] handled it since a light object is usually held by the fingers" (R135). Not mentioned is the fact that, as Oswald walked to Frazier's home, he grasped his package at the *top,* allowing it to hang freely, almost touching the ground. According to the Commission's analysis of how people hold packages, it would seem unlikely that Oswald's bag contained anything "heavy or bulky." Nor is there any proof that Oswald was holding CE 142 when he left prints on it. Had it been lying on a hard, flat surface, Oswald could have leaned against or on it and left prints.

The Report quotes questioned-documents experts to show that CE 142 had been constructed from paper and tape taken from the Depository's shipping room, probably within three days of November 22 (R135-36). Here the Report explicitly states what it had been implying all along: "One cannot estimate when, prior to November 22, *Oswald* made the paper bag." The bag was made from Depository materials; at some time it was touched by Oswald. This does not prove or so much as indicate that *Oswald* constructed the bag. The Commission *assumed* Oswald made it, offering no evidence in support of its notion. It *could not* provide substantiation, for the evidence proves Oswald did *not* make CE 142.

Troy Eugene West, a full-time mail wrapper at the Depository, worked at the same bench from which the materials for the paper sack were taken. As Harold Weisberg points out in *Whitewash,* "West had been employed by the Book Depository for 16 years and was so attached to his place of work that he never left his bench, even to eat lunch. His only separation from it, aside from the necessary functions of life [and this is presumed; it is not in his testimony], was on arrival before work, to get water for coffee."[11]

Although West was the one man who could know if Oswald had taken the materials used in constructing CE 142, he was never mentioned in the Report. In his deposition, he virtually obviated the possibility that Oswald made the bag:

Mr. Belin: Did Lee Harvey Oswald ever help you wrap mail?

Mr. West: No, sir; he never did.

Mr. Belin: Do you know whether or not he ever borrowed or used any wrapping paper for himself?

Mr. West: No, sir; I don't.

Mr. Belin: You don't know?

Mr. West: No; I don't.

Mr. Belin: Did you ever see him around these wrapper rolls or wrapper roll machine, or not?

Mr. West: No, sir; I never noticed him being around. (6H360)

West brought out another important piece of information. Expert examination showed that one long strip of tape had been drawn from the Depository's dispenser and then torn into smaller pieces to assemble the bag (R579-80). West told Counsel Belin that the dispensing machine was constructed so that the dried mucilage on the tape would be automatically moistened as tape was pulled out for use. The only way one could obtain dry tape, he added, was if he removed the roll of tape from the machine and tore off the desired length (6H361). However, the tape on CE 142 possessed marks that conclusively showed that it had been pulled through the dispenser (R580). Thus, the tape used in making

CE 142 was wet as soon as it left the dispenser; it had to be used at that moment, demanding that the entire sack be constructed at West's bench.

The fabricator of CE 142 had to remain at or near the bench long enough to assemble the entire bag. West never saw Oswald around the dispensing machines, which indicates that Oswald did not make the bag. This contention is supported by those who observed Oswald during his return to Irving on Thursday evening. Frazier never saw Oswald take anything with him from work (2H141), despite the fact that, even folded, CE 142 would have been awkward to conceal. Likewise, neither Ruth Paine nor Marina ever saw Oswald with such a sack on or before November 21 (1H120; 3H49; 22H751).

The Report thus far has done some rather fancy footwork with the paper sack, asserting without basis that Oswald was its fabricator when the evidence allows the conclusion only that Oswald once touched the bag. Next in line was the "scientific evidence" that the Commission promised would link the "rifle. . .to paper bag."

When FBI hair-and-fiber expert Paul Stombaugh examined CE 142 on November 23, he found that it contained a single, brown, delustered viscose fiber and "several" light-green cotton fibers (R136). The Report does not mention Stombaugh's qualification of the word "several" as indicating only two or three fibers (4H80). It seems that these few fibers matched some composing the blanket in which the rifle was allegedly stored, although Stombaugh could render no opinion as to whether the fibers had in fact come from that blanket (R136-37). How does this relate the *rifle* to the paper bag when it does not conclusively relate even the *blanket* to the bag? The Commission's theory is "that the rifle could have picked up fibers from the blanket and transferred them to the paper bag" (R137).

Had the Commission not been such a victim of its bias, it could have seen that this fiber evidence had no value in relating anything. The reason is simple: the evidence indicates that the Dallas Police took no precautions to prevent the various articles of evidence from contacting each other *prior* to laboratory examination. On Saturday morning, November 23, physical items such as the rifle, the blanket, the bag, and Oswald's shirt arrived in Washington, on loan from the police for FBI scrutiny. It was then that Stombaugh found fibers in the bag (4H75). Prior to Oswald's death, this evidence was returned to the police. However, on November 26, the items remaining in police custody were again turned over to the FBI. Before the second return, some of the items were photographed together on a table (4H273-74). This photograph, CE 738, shows the open end of the paper bag to be in contact with the blanket. Such overt carelessness by the police ruined the bag for any subsequent fiber examinations. If this was any indication of how the evidence was handled by the police when *first* turned over to the FBI, *all* the fiber evidence becomes meaningless because the various specimens could have come in contact with each other *after* they were confiscated.

There is ample evidence that CE 142 never contained the Mannlicher-Carcano. James Cadigan, FBI questioned-documents expert, disclosed an important piece of information in his testimony concerning his examination of the paper sack:

I was also requested. . .to examine the bag to determine

PRESUMED GUILTY

rasions or *anything* by which it could be associated with
the rifle, Commission Exhibit 139, that is, could I find *any*
markings that I could tie to that rifle....And I couldn't
find *any* such markings. (4H97; emphasis added)

Cadigan added that he could not know the significance
of the absence of marks (4H97-98).

There is, however, great significance, due to circumstances unknown to Cadigan. If Oswald placed the rifle
into CE 142, he could have done so only between 8 and
9 P.M. on November 21; he simply did not have time to
do it the following morning before going to work.[12] Had
he removed the rifle immediately upon arriving at the
Depository at 8 A.M., it would still have remained in
the bag for at least 12 hours. The bag likewise would
have been handled by Oswald during a half-block walk
to Frazier's house and a two-block walk from the parking lot to the Depository. It is stretching the limits of
credibility to assume that a rifle in *two* bulky parts
(the 40-inch Carcano could have fit into the 38-inch
bag *only* if disassembled) in a single layer of paper
would fail to produce obvious marks after over 12
hours of storage and handling through two-and-a-half
blocks of walking. More significantly, Cadigan made no
mention of oil stains having been found on the bag, but
the rifle was described by FBI Director Hoover as
"well-oiled" (26H455). It is reasonable to conclude from
the condition of CE 142 that this sack, even if Oswald
had made it, never held "Oswald's" rifle.

CE 142 may be significant in two ways. Judging
from the immediate impression received that this sack
had been used to transport the rifle (despite the lack of
evidence that it did), it is not impossible that it was
made and left by the window with exactly that effect in
mind, even for the purpose of incriminating Oswald.

Fig. 6. The Commission says that all these pieces of the disassembled Carcano were carried in this bag without leaving any identifiable marks or oil stains. There is no crease in the bag where it would have been folded over had it contained the disassembled rifle. Oswald's careless handling of his package is not consistent with its having contained so many loose parts.

However, with all the trash scattered about the storage spaces in the building, it is conceivable that CE 142 had been made for some unknown purpose entirely unrelated to the shooting and merely discarded on the sixth floor. The evidence that Oswald neither made 142 nor carried it home the evening of November 21 leads to the inference that the bag he *did* carry on the 22nd has never come to light subsequent to the assassination. Likewise, it follows that the contents of Oswald's package may never have been found. (There is evidence suggesting that Oswald, before entering the Depository, may actually have discarded his package in rubbish bins located in an enclosed loading dock at the rear of the building. Employee Jack Dougherty saw

Oswald arrive for work, entering through a back door. At that time, Dougherty saw nothing in Oswald's hands [6H377].)

There is not the slightest suggestion in any of the evidence that Oswald carried his rifle to work the morning of November 22. The indications are persuasive and consistent that Oswald carried almost anything *but* his rifle. Oswald took little care with his package, hardly treating it as if it contained the apparatus with which he later intended efficiently to commit murder. As he approached Frazier's house, he held the package at the top, "much like a right handed batter would pick up a baseball bat when approaching the plate" (24H408), certainly a peculiar and dangerous way for one to transport a package containing a rifle in two bulky parts. Every indication of the length of Oswald's sack consistently precludes its having contained the disassembled rifle. Interestingly enough, Frazier had once worked in a department store uncrating packaged curtain rods. Having seen the appearance of these, Frazier found nothing suspicious about Oswald's package which, he was informed, contained curtain rods (2H229).

It is no longer sufficient to say, as I did in the first chapter, that there is no evidence that Oswald carried his rifle to work on the morning of the assassination. There is, as the evidence indicates, no reason even to suspect that he did (based on the descriptions of the package he carried), that he would have (based on the indications that he knew nothing of the motorcade route), or that he could have (based on the total lack of proof that the C2766 rifle had been stored in the Paine garage). The most reasonable conclusion—if any is to be drawn—is that Oswald did not carry his rifle to work that morning.

7

Oswald at Window?

Hard as the Commission tried to make tenable that Oswald carried his rifle to work on November 22, it tried even harder to place him at the southeast corner window of the Depository's sixth floor, the putative source of the shots. This was the location at which a man with a gun had been seen, and to which Oswald had unlimited access. In accordance with the official story, Oswald's guilt hinges on this one point; he had to have been at the window to have fired some or all of the shots.

The first evidence discussed in this section of the Report concerns the fingerprints left by Oswald on two cartons located next to the "assassin's" window. As was noted in chapter 2, the Commission used this evidence to place Oswald at the window at some time. In doing this, it read an unfair and improper meaning into limited data. The presence of Oswald's prints on these objects indicates *only* that he handled them and does not disclose exactly when or *where* he did so. I noted that Oswald could have touched the cartons *prior* to the time they were moved to the southeast corner window. The fingerprints were the only "physical evidence" the Commission could offer to relate Oswald to that specific window (R140-41). Since the fingerprint evidence in fact does *not* relate Oswald to the window, it is important to note that *no* physical evidence placed Oswald at the window at any time.

Oswald's Actions Prior to the Shooting

On the morning of the assassination, a number of Depository employees had been putting down flooring on the sixth floor. About 15 minutes before noon, these employees decided to break for lunch. Going to the northeast corner of the building, they began to "race" the elevators down to the first floor. On their way down, they noticed Oswald standing at the elevator gate on the fifth floor (6H349), where he was shouting for an elevator to descend (3H168; 6H337).

One of the floor-laying crew, Charles Givens, told the Commission that upon returning to the sixth floor at 11:55, to get his cigarettes, he saw Oswald on that floor (6H349). The Report attaches great significance to Givens's story by calling it "additional testimony linking Oswald with the point from which the shots were fired" (R143). No testimony was needed to link Oswald with the sixth floor; he worked there. However, the Report adds that Givens "was the last known employee to see Oswald inside the building prior to the assassination," unfairly precipitating a bias against Oswald by implying that he remained where Givens saw him for the 35 minutes until the assassination.

It is necessary to note, although admittedly it is not central to Oswald's possible involvement in the shooting, that there are many aspects of Givens's story that cast an unfavorable light on its veracity.[1] It seems illogical that Oswald would have gone *up* to the sixth floor after yelling for an elevator *down* from the fifth; even at that, such "jumping" between floors is consistent with the type of work Oswald did: order filling. In addition, police Lieutenant Jack Revill and Inspector Herbert Sawyer both testified that Givens was taken to city hall on the afternoon of the shooting to make a statement about seeing Oswald on the sixth floor (5H35-36; 6H321-22). However, the police radio log indicates that Givens was picked up because he had a police record (narcotics charges) and was missing from the Depository (23H873). Givens himself told the Commission he was picked up and asked to make a statement, but not in reference to having seen Oswald (6H355). Indeed, the affidavit he filed on November 22, 1963, makes no mention of either his return to the sixth floor or his having seen Oswald there (24H210).

The previous information forms a basis for doubting Givens's story. There is one other consideration that strongly suggests this entire episode to be a fabrication: it was physically impossible for Givens to have seen Oswald as he swore he had done. From Givens's testimony, it is clear that his position on the sixth floor when he claimed to have seen Oswald was somewhere between the elevators at the northwest corner of the building to about midway between the north and south walls. Either way, he would have been along the far west side of the sixth floor (6H349-50). However, Givens said he observed Oswald walking along the *east* wall of the building, walking *away* from the southeast corner in the direction of the elevators (6H349-50). Dallas Police photographs of the sixth floor (CEs 725, 726, 727, 728) show that such a view would have been obscured by columns and stacks of cartons as high as a

man. If Givens saw Oswald, then there *must* be a
major flaw in his description of the event. As the record stands, Givens *could not* have seen Oswald on the
sixth floor at 11:55.

We should recall that when Oswald was seen on the
fifth floor at about 11:45, he was shouting for an
elevator to take him *down*. Apparently this is exactly
the course Oswald pursued, if not by elevator, then by
the stairs. Bill Shelley was part of the floor-laying crew
that left the sixth floor around 11:45. He testified un-
ambiguously that after coming down for lunch he saw
Oswald on the first floor near the telephones (7H390).
Mention of this fact is entirely absent from the Report.

The Commission seized upon Givens's story because,
according to the Report, he was the last person known
to have seen Oswald prior to the shots. The Report
strongly implies that Oswald must have remained on
the sixth floor, since no one subsequently saw him
elsewhere. But Oswald was both inconspicuous and
generally unknown at the Depository; he always kept
to himself. Likewise, most of the other employees had
left the building during this time. It would have been
unremarkable if no one noticed his presence, especially
then. However, if someone *had* noticed Oswald in a location other than the sixth floor after 11:55, his story
would have been all the more important by virtue of
Oswald's inconspicuousness.

The Report makes two separate assurances that no
one saw Oswald after 11:55 and before the shots, first
stating "None of the Depository employees is known to
have seen Oswald again until after the shooting"
(R143), and later concluding, "Oswald was seen in the
vicinity of the southeast corner of the sixth floor approximately 35 minutes before the assassination and
no one could be found who saw Oswald anywhere else

in the building until after the shooting" (R156). A footnote to the first statement lists "CE 1381" as the source of information that no employee saw Oswald between 11:55 and 12:30 that day.

CE 1381 consists of 73 statements obtained by the FBI from all employees present at the Depository on November 22, 1963. In almost every instance, the particular employee is quoted as saying he did not see Oswald at the time of the shots. A few people stated they either had never seen Oswald at all or had not seen him that day (see 22H632-86). This collection of statements does not support the Report's assertion that no employee saw Oswald between 11:55 and 12:30, for it almost never addresses that time period, usually referring only to 12:30, the time of the shots.

I have learned that General Counsel Rankin, in requesting these statements from the FBI, deliberately sought information relating to Oswald's whereabouts at 12:30 *only,* never considering the 11:55 to 12:30 period. The Report then falsely and wrongly applied this information to the question of Oswald's whereabouts between 11:55 and 12:30.

I obtained from the National Archives a letter from J. Lee Rankin to Hoover dated March 16, 1964, in which Rankin requested that the FBI "obtain a signed statement from each person known to have been in the Texas School Book Depository Building on the assassination date reflecting the following information:" Rankin then listed six items to be included in each statement: "1. His name. . .[etc.], 2. Where he was at the time the President was shot, 3. Was he alone or with someone else. . . ?, 4. If he saw Lee Harvey Oswald *at that time?,*" plus two other pieces of information.[2] Clearly, Rankin desired to know whether any employee had seen Oswald *at the time of the shots.* There is no reason to expect that the agents who obtained the statements would have sought any further detail, and the final reports reveal that indeed none was sought. Even Hoover, in the letter by which he transmitted CE 1381 to the Commission, reported, "Every effort was made to comply with your request that six *specific* items be incorporated in each statement" (22H632).

Why did Rankin, when he had the FBI go to such extensive efforts in contacting all 73 employees present that day, fail to request the added information about the time between 11:55 and 12:30, the period that could hold the key to Oswald's innocence had he been observed then in a location other than the sixth floor?

The Commission knew of at least two employees who *had* seen Oswald on the first floor between 12:00 and 12:30. It suppressed this information from the Report, lied in saying that no one had seen Oswald during this time, and cited an incomplete and irrelevant inquiry in support of this drastic misstatement.

Depository employee Eddie Piper was questioned twice by Assistant Counsel Joseph Ball. During one of his appearances, Piper echoed the information he had recorded in an affidavit for the Dallas Police on November 23, 1963, namely, that he saw and spoke with Oswald on the first floor at 12:00 noon (6H383; 19H499). Piper seemed certain of this, and he was consistent in reporting the circumstances around his brief encounter with Oswald. Clearly, this is a direct contradiction of the Report's statement that no one saw Oswald between 11:55 and 12:30. The Report, never mentioning this vital piece of testimony, calls Piper a "confused witness" (R153). This too was the opposite of the truth. Piper was able to describe events after the shooting in a way that closely paralleled the known sequence of events (6H385). There was, in fact, no aspec of Piper's testimony that indicated he was less than a credible witness.

While Piper's having seen Oswald on the first floor at 12:00 does not preclude Oswald's having been at the window at 12:30, it is significant that this information was suppressed from the Report, which makes an assertion contrary to the evidence. One aspect of Piper's story could have weighed heavily in Oswald's defense. In his November 23 affidavit, Piper recalled Oswald as having said "I'm going up to eat" during the short time the two men met (19H499). In his testimony, Piper modified this quotation, expressing his uncertainty whether Oswald had said "up" or "out" to eat (6H386). Despite the confusion over the exact adverb Oswald used, the significant observation is that he apparently intended to eat at 12:00. He would most likely have done this on the first floor in the "domino" room or in the second-floor lunchroom. *Oswald consistently told the police that he had been eating his lunch at the time the President was shot* (R600, 613). The suppression of Piper's story was, in effect, the suppression of an aspect of Oswald's defense.

The Commission had other corroborative evidence of a probative nature. Oswald's account of his whereabouts and actions at and around the time of the shooting cannot be fully known, for no transcripts of his police interrogations were kept—a significant departure from the most basic criminal proceedings (see 4H232; R200). Our only information concerning Oswald's interrogation sessions during the weekend of the assassination is found in contradictory and ambiguous reports written by the various participants in the interrogations —police, FBI, and Secret Service (R598-636).

The interrogation reports are generally consistent in relating that Oswald said that he had been eating his

lunch at the time of the shots. In three of these reports
a significant detail is added, in three partially contradictory versions. Captain Fritz thought Oswald "said
he ate lunch with some of the colored boys who worked
with him. One of them was called 'Junior' and the
other was a little short man whose name he didn't
know" (R605). FBI Agent James Bookhout wrote that
"Oswald had eaten lunch in the lunchroom...alone,
but recalled possibly two Negro employees walking
through the room during this period. He stated possibly
one of these employees was called 'Junior' and the
other was a short individual whose name he could not
recall but whom he would be able to recognize" (R622).
Secret Service Inspector Thomas Kelley recalled that
Oswald "Said he ate lunch with the colored boys who
worked with him. He described one of them as 'Junior,'
a colored boy, and the other was a little short negro
[*sic*] boy" (R626).

These versions are consistent in reporting that Oswald had been eating lunch (probably on the first floor)
when he saw or was with two Negro employees, one
called "Junior," the other a short man. It is possible
that Oswald was in a lunchroom (the domino room)
during this time, although we cannot be certain that
Oswald directly stated so to the police. Likewise, it is
possible that Agent Bookhout correctly reported that
Oswald ate alone and merely observed the two Negro
employees, while Fritz and Kelley misconstrued
Oswald's remarks as indicating that he ate his lunch
with these two men.

James Jarman was a Negro employed at the Depository; his nickname was "Junior" (3H189; 6H365).
On November 22, Jarman quit for lunch at about
11:55, washed up, picked up his sandwich, bought a
coke, and went to the first floor to eat. He ate some of

his lunch along the front windows on the first floor, near two rows of bins; walking alone across the floor toward the domino room, he finished his sandwich. After depositing his refuse, Jarman left the building with employees Harold Norman and Danny Arce through the main entrance (3H201-2).

Harold Norman, another Negro employee, was of rather modest height, fitting the description of the man Oswald thought had been with Jarman on the first floor (see CE 491). On November 22, Norman ate his lunch in the domino room and "got with James Jarman, he and I got together on the first floor." According to Norman, Jarman was "somewhere in the vicinity of the telephone" near the bins when the two men "got together." This would define a location toward the front of the building. Norman confirmed Jarman's testimony that the two subsequently left the building through the main entrance (3H189).

There is no firm evidence pinpointing the exact time Jarman and Norman left the Depository. Their estimates, as well as those of the people who left at the same time or who were already standing outside, are not at all precise, apparently because few workers had been paying much attention to the time. The estimates varied from 12:00 as the earliest time to 12:15 as the latest (see 3H189, 219; 6H365; 22H638, 662; 24H199, 213, 227). Twelve o'clock seems a bit early for Jarman and Norman to have finished eating and to be out on the street; the time was probably closer to 12:15. It was most likely within five minutes prior to 12:15 that Jarman and Norman "got together" near the front or south side of the first floor and walked out the main entrance together.

Jarman and Norman appeared together on the first floor again, about ten minutes after stepping outside.

Because the crowds in front of the Depository were so
large, the two men went up to the fifth floor at 12:20 or
12:25. To do this, they walked around to the back of
the building, entering on the first floor through the
rear door and taking the elevator up five stories
(3H202).

Obviously, Oswald could not have told the police that
"Junior" and a short Negro employee were together on
the first floor unless he had seen this himself.[3] For
Oswald to have witnessed Jarman and Norman in this
manner, he had to have been on the first floor between
either 12:10 and 12:15 or 12:20 and 12:25. The fact
that Oswald was able to relate this incident is cogent
evidence that he was in fact on the first floor at one or
both of these times. If he was on the *sixth* floor, as the
Commission believes, then it was indeed a remarkable
coincidence that out of all the employees, Oswald
picked the two who were on the first floor at the time
he said, and together as he described. Since this is a
remote possibility that warrants little serious consideration, I am persuaded to conclude that Oswald was on
the first floor at some time between 12:10 and 12:25,
which is consistent with the previously cited testimony
of Eddie Piper.[4]

Buttressing the above-discussed evidence is the story
of another employee, who claimed to have seen Oswald
on the first floor around 12:15. Mrs. Carolyn Arnold, a
secretary at the Depository, was the crucial witness.
Her story was omitted not only from the Report but
also from the Commission's printed evidence. It was
only through the diligent searching of Harold Weisberg
that an FBI report of an early interview with her came
to light.[5] She spoke with FBI agents on November 26,
1963, only three days after the assassination. The brief
report of the interview states that

she was in her office on the second floor of the building on November 22, 1963, and left that office between 12:00 and 12:15 PM, to go downstairs and stand in front of the building to view the Presidential Motorcade. As she was standing in front of the building, she stated that she thought she caught a fleeting glimpse of LEE HARVEY OSWALD standing in the hallway between the front door and the double doors leading into the warehouse, located on the first floor. She could not be sure this was OSWALD, but said she felt it was and believed the time to be a few minutes before 12:15 PM. (CD5:41)

As Weisberg cautioned in his book *Photographic Whitewash,* where he presents this FBI report, "This is the FBI retailing of what Mrs. Arnold said, not her actual words."[6]

Mrs. Arnold was never called as a witness before the Commission; absolutely no effort was made to check her accuracy or obtain further details of her story. If what she related was true, she provided the proof that Oswald could not have shot at the President. The Commission's failure to pursue her vital story was a failure to follow up evidence of Oswald's innocence.

Mrs. Arnold was reinterviewed by the FBI on March 18, 1964, in compliance with Rankin's request to Hoover for statements from all Depository employees present at work November 22 (22H634). In accordance with the deliberate wording of Rankin's items to be included in the statements as discussed earlier, Mrs. Arnold was not asked about seeing Oswald *before* the shooting, as she earlier said she did. Instead, she provided the specific information requested in item (4) of Rankin's letter: "I did not see Lee Harvey Oswald at the time President Kennedy was shot." "At the time" of the assassination obviously is not the same as "before" the assassination. If Rankin for some specific reason avoided asking about any employee who had seen Os-

wald right before the shots, he could have had no better witness in mind than Mrs. Arnold.

In her March 18 statement, Mrs. Arnold wrote: "I
left the Texas School Book Depository at about 12:25
PM." The report of her first interview states that she
left her office on the second floor between 12:00 and
12:15 and saw Oswald from outside the building at "a
few minutes before 12:15." The important distinction
between these two estimates is that one is in Mrs.
Arnold's words, the other but a paraphrase. Of the people who left the Depository with Mrs. Arnold, Mrs.
Donald Baker recalled having left at about 12:15
(22H635), Miss Judy Johnson at about 12:15 (22H656),
Bonnie Rachey also at 12:15 (22H671), and Mrs. Betty
Dragoo at 12:20 (22H645).

It is perfectly reasonable to assert that Mrs. Arnold
saw a man whom "she felt" was Oswald on the first
floor anywhere between a few minutes before 12:15
and, at the latest, 12:25. The actual time probably
tended toward the 12:15 to 12:20 period. The significance of this one piece of information is startling; the
"gunman" on the sixth floor was there from 12:15 on. If
Mrs. Arnold really did see Oswald on the first floor at
this time, he could not have been a sixth-floor assassin.

Arnold Rowland is the first person known to have
spotted a man with a rifle on the sixth floor of the Depository. The time of this observation was, according to
Rowland, who had noted the large "Hertz" clock atop
the Depository, 12:15 (2H169-72). Rowland provided an
even more accurate means for checking his time estimate:

> there was a motorcycle parked just on the street, not in
> front of us, just a little past us, and the radio was on it
> giving details of the motorcade, where it was positioned,

and right *after* the time I noticed him (the man on the sixth floor) and when my wife was pointing this other thing to me...the dispatcher came on and gave the position of the motorcade as being on Cedar Springs. This would be in the area of Turtle Creek, down in that area....And this was the position of the motorcade and it was about 15 or 16 after 12. (2H172-73; emphasis added)

Rowland could not have had access to the police radio logs. However, every version of these logs in the Commission's evidence shows that the location of the motorcade described by Rowland was in fact broadcast between 12:15 and 12:16 PM (17H460; 21H390; 23H911). We must note also that while Rowland first noticed this man *before* hearing the broadcast at 12:15, it is possible that he had been there for some period of time prior to that.

The difference between Mrs. Arnold's earliest estimate of the time she possibly saw Oswald on the first floor and the time Rowland saw the sixth-floor gunman is but a few minutes, hardly enough time for Oswald to have picked up his rifle, made his way to the sixth floor, assembled the rifle, and appeared at the appropriate window. If Mrs. Arnold's later estimates are accurate, then Oswald was, in fact, on the first floor while the "assassin" was on the sixth.

Without elaboration from Mrs. Arnold, we can draw no conclusions based on the brief FBI report of her first interview. At this late date, I feel that Mrs. Arnold can not honestly clarify the information reported by the FBI, either through fear of challenging the official story or through knowledge of the implication of what she knows. It was the duty of the Warren Commission to seek out Mrs. Arnold to obtain her full story and test her accuracy, if not in the interest of truth, certainly so as not posthumously to deny Oswald the possible proof of his innocence.

The Commission failed in its obligation to the truth for the simple reason that it (meaning its staff and General Counsel) never sought the truth. The truth, according to *all* the relevant evidence in the Commission's files, is that Oswald was on the first floor at a time that eliminates the possibility of his having been the sixth-floor gunman, just as he told the police during his interrogations.

Identity of the Gunman

The Commission relied solely on the testimony of eyewitnesses to identify the source of the shots as a specific Depository window. The presence of three cartridge cases by this window seemed to buttress the witnesses' testimony. The medical findings, although not worth credence, indicated that some shots were fired from above and behind; still, that evidence, even if correct, cannot pinpoint the *precise* source "above and behind" from which certain shots originated. It was the people who said they saw a man with a gun in this window who provided the evidence most welcome to the Commission.

The Commission's crew of witnesses consisted of Howard Brennan and Amos Euins, both of whom said they saw the man fire a rifle; Robert Jackson and Malcolm Couch, two photographers riding in the motorcade, who saw the barrel of a rifle being drawn slowly back into the window after the shots (although neither saw a man in the window); Mrs. Earle Cabell, wife of the city's mayor, who, also riding in the procession, saw "a projection" from a Depository window (although she could not tell if this was a mechanical object or someone's arm); and James Crawford, who saw a "movement" in the window after the shots but could not say for sure whether it was a person whom he had seen (R63-68). Two additional witnesses are added in the Report's chapter "The Assassin." They are Ronald Fischer and Robert Edwards, both of whom saw a man without a rifle in the window shortly before the motorcade arrived.

Two other "sixth-floor gunman" witnesses didn't quite make it into the relevant sections of the Report —one, in fact, never made the Report at all. Arnold Rowland saw the gunman 15 minutes before the motorcade arrived at the plaza. However, at this time, the man was in the far south*west* (left) window. Rowland told the Commission that another man then occupied the southeast corner (right) window. The Commission, whose legal eminences knew that another man on the sixth floor at this time satisfied the legal definition of conspiracy, sought only to discredit Rowland, rejecting his story under a section entitled "Accomplices at the Scene of the Assassination" (R250-52). Mrs. Carolyn Walther saw the gunman in the right window, shortly before the procession arrived. However, she too saw a second man on the sixth floor, although the "accomplice" she described was obviously different from Rowland's (24H522). Rowland sprang his information on the Commission by surprise, none of the various reports on him having ever mentioned the second man. Mrs. Walther told of a second man from the beginning and was totally ignored by the Commission.

While the testimony indicates the presence of a man *holding* a rifle in the southeast-corner sixth-floor window, there is *no* evidence that this rifle was *fired* during the assassination. Under questioning by Arlen Specter, Amos Euins, a 16-year-old whose inarticulateness inhibited the effectiveness with which he conveyed his observations, said he saw the Depository gunman fire the second shot (2H209). However, Specter never

asked Euins what caused him to conclude that the gun
he saw had actually discharged, that is, that the gunman was not merely performing the *motions* of firing
that gave the impression of actual discharge when
combined with the noises of other shots, but was fully
pulling the trigger and shooting bullets.

The Report cites the testimony of three employees
who were positioned on the fifth floor directly below
the "assassin's" window, one of whom claimed to have
heard empty cartridge cases hitting the floor above
him, with the accompanying noises of a rifle bolt (R70).
However, there is nothing about the testimony of any
of these men to indicate that the *shots* came from
directly above them on the sixth floor. As Mark Lane
points out in *Rush to Judgement,* the actions of these
men subsequent to the shooting were not consistent
with their believing that any shots came from the sixth
floor; one of the men even denied making such a
statement to the Secret Service[7] (3H194). The stories of
the fifth-floor witnesses, if valid, indicate no more than
the presence of someone on the sixth floor operating
the bolt of a rifle and ejecting spent shells.

Howard Brennan was the Commission's star witness
among those present in the plaza during the assassination. His testimony is cited in many instances, including passages to establish the source of the shots and
the identity of the "assassin." Brennan was the only
person other than Euins who claimed to have seen a
gun fired from the Depository window (R63). Yet, in
spite of Brennan's testimony that he saw the sixth-floor
gunman take aim and *fire* a last shot, there is reason
to believe that the man Brennan saw never discharged
a firearm. Brennan was asked the vital questions that
Euins was spared.

Mr. McCloy: Did you see the rifle explode? Did you see the flash of what was either the second or the third shot?

Mr. Brennan: No.

Mr. McCloy: Could you see that he had discharged the rifle?

Mr. Brennan: No...

Mr. McCloy: Yes. But you saw him aim?

Mr. Brennan: Yes.

Mr. McCloy: Did you see the rifle discharge, did you see the recoil or the flash?

Mr. Brennan: No.

Mr. McCloy: But you heard the last shot?

Mr. Brennan: The report; yes, sir. (3H154)

If Brennan looked up at the window as he said, his testimony would strongly indicate that he saw a man aim a gun *without firing it*. When the Carcano is fired, it emits a small amount of smoke (26H811) and manifests a recoil (3H451), as do most rifles. That Brennan failed to see such things upon observing the rifle and hearing a shot is cogent evidence that the rifle Brennan saw did not fire the shot.

Thus, the Commission's evidence—taken at face value—indicates only that a *gunman* was present at the sixth-floor window, not an *assassin*. This distinction is an important one. A mere gunman (one armed with a gun) cannot be accused of murder; an assassin is one who has committed murder. A gunman present at the sixth-floor window could have served as a decoy to divert attention from real shooters at other vantage points.[8] While we cannot know surely just what the man in the sixth-floor window was doing, it is vital to note that evidence is entirely lacking that this gunman was, in fact, an assassin.

To the Commission, the gunman was *the* assassin, no questions asked. The limitations of the evidence could

not be respected when the conclusions were prefabri-
cated. By arbitrarily calling a gunman the "assassin,"
the Commission, in effect, made the charge of murder
through circumstances, without substantiation.

As was discussed in chapter 1, the Commission had
no witness identification of the "assassin" worthy of
credence. Of the few who observed the gunman, only
Brennan made any sort of identification, saying both
that Lee Harvey Oswald *was* the gunman and that he
merely *resembled* the gunman. The Commission rejected Brennan's "positive identification" of Oswald,
expressed its confidence that the man Brennan saw at
least looked like Oswald, and evaluated Brennan as an
"accurate observer" (R145).

Many critics have challenged the Report's evaluation
of Brennan as "accurate."[9] Evidence that I have recently discovered indicates that Brennan was not even
an "observer," let alone an accurate one.

One of the main indications of Brennan's inaccuracy
is his description of the gunman's position. Brennan
contended that in the six-to-eight-minute-period prior
to the motorcade's arrival, he saw a man "leave and return to the window 'a couple of times.' " After hearing
the first shot, he glanced up at this Depository window
and saw this man taking deliberate aim with a rifle
(R144). The Report immediately begins apologizing for
Brennan:

> Although Brennan testified that the man in the window
> was standing when he fired the shots, most probably he
> was either sitting or kneeling. . . .It is understandable,
> however, for Brennan to have believed that the man with
> the rifle was standing. . . .Since the window ledges in the
> Depository building are lower than in most buildings [one
> foot high], a person squatting or kneeling exposes more of
> his body than would normally be the case. From the
> street, this creates the impression that the person is
> standing. (R144-45)

The Report's explanation is vitiated by the fact that Brennan claimed to have seen the gunman standing *and sitting.* "At one time he came to the window and he sat sideways on the window sill," swore Brennan. "That was previous to President Kennedy getting there. And I could see practically his whole body, from his hips up" (3H144). Thus, Brennan should have known the difference between a man standing and sitting at the window, despite the low window sill. Had the gunman been standing, he would have been aiming his rifle through a double thickness of glass, only his legs visible to witness Brennan. Had he assumed a sitting position—on the sill or on nearby boxes—he would have had to bend his head down *below* his knees to fire the rifle out the window (see photographs taken from inside the window, at 22H484-85).

From November 22 until the time of his Commission testimony, Brennan said he was looking at the sixth floor at the time of the last shot. His November 22 affidavit states this explicitly (24H203) and it can be inferred from his later interviews. In observing the Depository, Brennan contended that he stopped looking at the President's car immediately after the first shot (3H143-44). Obviously, then, he could not have seen the impact of the fatal bullet on the President's head, which came late, probably last, in the sequence of shots. However, Brennan's observations were suddenly augmented when he was interviewed by CBS News in August 1964 for a coast-to-coast broadcast. As was aired on September 27, 1964, Brennan told CBS "The President's head just exploded."[10] Unless Brennan lied to either CBS or the federal and local authorities, it must now be believed that he saw the sixth-floor gunman fire the last shot, then turned his head faster than the speeding bullet to have seen the impact of that bullet on the President's head, then turned back toward

the window with equal alacrity so as to have seen the
gunman slowly withdraw his weapon and marvel at his
apparent success. Unless, of course, Brennan had eyes
in the back of his head—which is far more credible
than any aspect of his "witness account."

Brennan's identification of Oswald as the man he
saw (or said he saw?) in the sixth-floor window
weighed heavily in the Commission's "evaluation" of
the "evidence." As was discussed in chapter 1, the
Commission first rejected Brennan's positive identification in discussing the evidence, and subsequently accepted it in drawing the conclusion that Oswald was at
the window. Without Brennan, there would have been
not even the slightest suggestion in any of the evidence
that Oswald was at the window during the shots. No
one else even made a pretense of being able to identify
the sixth-floor gunman.

On November 22, 1963, Brennan was unable to identify Oswald as the man he saw in the window, but
picked Oswald as the person in a police line-up who
bore the closest resemblance to the gunman. Months
later, when he appeared before the Commission, Brennan said he could have made a positive identification
at the November 22 lineup,

> but did not do so because he felt that the assassination
> was "a Communist activity, and I felt like there hadn't
> been more than one eyewitness, and if it got to be a
> known fact that I was an eyewitness, my family or I,
> either one, might not be safe." (R145)

The Report continued that, because Brennan had originally failed to make a positive identification, the
Commission did "not base its conclusion concerning the
identity of the assassin on Brennan's subsequent cer-

tain identification of Lee Harvey Oswald as the man he saw fire the rifle." Through the Report, the Commission expressed its confidence that "Brennan saw a man in the window who closely resembled Lee Harvey Oswald, and that Brennan believes the man he saw was in fact. . .Oswald" (R146).

The Commission accepted Brennan's observations and assurances without question. However, the excuse Brennan offered for not originally making a positive identification was falsely and deliberately contrived, as the evidence reveals. As Brennan is quoted, he felt that he had been the only eyewitness and feared for his family's security should his identity become known. Contrary to this sworn statement, Brennan immediately knew of at least one other witness who had seen the sixth-floor gunman. Secret Service Agent Forrest Sorrels spoke with Brennan in Dealey Plaza within twenty minutes after the shooting, at which time he asked Brennan "if he had seen anyone else, and he pointed to a young colored boy there, by the name of Euins" (7H349). Sorrels testified that Brennan also expressed his willingness to identify the gunman. On the afternoon of the assassination, *before* he attended the line-up, Brennan filed an affidavit with the police (3H145; 7H349) in which he again made it known that he could identify the man if he were to see him once more (24H203). This contradicts Brennan's testimony that he could have identified Oswald on November 22 but declined to do so for fear of its becoming known.

Thus, Brennan originally indicated a willingness to identify the gunman, saw Oswald in a line-up and declined to make a positive identification, and subsequently admitted lying to the police by saying that he *could* have made the identification but was afraid to.

However, even Brennan's identification of Oswald as the man who most closely resembled the gunman is invalid, since prior to the line-up, Brennan twice viewed Oswald's picture on television (3H148). Brennan again contradicted himself in speaking of the effect that seeing Oswald's picture had on his later identification of Oswald.

On December 17, 1963, Brennan spoke with an FBI Agent to whom he confided "that he can now say that he is sure that LEE HARVEY OSWALD was the person he saw in the window." At this time, Brennan began offering his many excuses for not having originally made a positive identification. One of these

> was that prior to appearing at the police line-up on November 22, 1963, he had observed a picture of OSWALD on his television set at home when his daughter asked him to watch it. He said he felt that since he had seen OSWALD on television before picking OSWALD out of the line-up at the police station that it tended to "cloud" any identification of OSWALD at that time. (CD5:15)

On January 7, 1964, Brennan's "clouded identification" was further lessened, for he told another FBI Agent that seeing Oswald's picture on television "of course, did not help him retain the original impression of the man in the window with the rifle" (24H406). Finally, on March 24, Brennan could no longer tell just what seeing Oswald prior to the line-up had done. On this date, Brennan testified before the Commission:

> Mr. Belin: What is the fact as to whether or not your having seen Oswald on television would have affected your identification of him one way or the other?
> Mr. Brennan: That is something I do not know. (3H148)

As his earlier interviews demonstrate, Brennan "knew" but was not saying. It seems obvious that seeing Oswald's picture on television prior to the line-up not only would have "clouded" and "not helped" the identification, but would also have prejudiced it.

The best that can be said of Howard Brennan is that he provided a dishonest account that warrants not the slightest credence. He contradicted himself on many crucial points to such a degree that it is hard to believe that his untruths were urintentional. He was warmly welcomed by the unquestioning Commission as he constantly changed his story in support of the theory that Oswald was guilty. This man, so fearful of exposure as to "lie" to the police and possibly hinder justice, consented to talk with CBS News for a coast-to-coast broadcast *before* the Warren Report was released,[11] and allowed himself to be photographed for the October 2, 1964, issue of *Life* magazine, where he was called by Commissioner Ford "the most important witness to appear before the Warren Commission."[12] His identification of Oswald, incredible as it was through each of his different versions of it, was worthless, if for no other reason than that he saw Oswald on television prior to the police line-up.

Through twenty pages of repetitious testimony, Howard Brennan rambled on about the man he saw and who he looked like, interjecting apologies, and inaccurately marking various pictures. The Commission could not get enough of Brennan's words, for he spoke the official language: "Oswald did it." Yet, when Brennan offered one meaningful and determinative fact, he was suddenly shown the door. Commission Counsel David Belin had been showing Brennan some of Oswald's clothing when Brennan interjected:

Mr. Brennan: And that was another thing that I called their [the police's] attention to at the lineup.

Mr. Belin: What do you mean by that?

Mr. Brennan: That he [Oswald] was not dressed in the same clothes that I saw the man in the window.

Mr. Belin: You mean with reference to the trousers or the shirt?

Mr. Brennan: Well, not particularly either. In other words, he just didn't have the same clothes on.

Mr. Belin: All right.

Mr. Brennan: I don't know whether you have that in the record or not. I am sure you do.

Mr. Dulles: Any further questions? I guess there are no more questions, Mr. Belin.

Mr. Belin: Well, sir, we want to thank you for your cooperation with the Commission.

Mr. Dulles: Thank you very much for coming here. (3H161)

The Commission had no witness-identification-by-appearance that placed Oswald in the window at the time of the shots. No one, including Brennan, could identify the sixth-floor gunman. However, Brennan's statement that the gunman wore clothes different from those that Oswald wore on that day might indicate the presence of someone other than Oswald in the window.

If there is anything consistent in the testimonies of those who observed a man on the sixth floor, it is the clothing descriptions. Rowland recalled that the man wore "a very light-colored shirt, white or a light blue. . .open at the collar. . .unbuttoned about halfway" with a "regular T-shirt, a polo shirt" underneath (2H171). Brennan described light-colored, possibly khaki clothes (3H145). Ronald Fisher and Bob Edwards described "an open-neck. . .sport shirt or a T-shirt. . .light in color; probably white" (6H194), and a "light colored shirt, short sleeve and open neck" (6H203), respectively. Mrs. Carolyn Walther saw a gunman "wearing a white shirt" (24H522).

In each case, these witnesses have described a shirt completely different from that worn by Oswald on November 22. That day Oswald wore a long-sleeved rust-brown shirt open at the neck with a polo shirt underneath. At least two witnesses described such attire on Oswald *before* he went to his rooming house within a half hour after the shots (see 2H250; 3H257), and a third provided a similar but less-complete description (R159). From the time of his arrest until sometime after midnight that Friday, Oswald was still wearing this shirt, as is shown in many widely printed photographs.[13] Although it seems likely that he wore the same shirt all day long, Oswald told police he changed his shirt during a stop at his rooming house at 1:00 P.M. that afternoon, having originally been wearing a red long-sleeved buttondown (see R605, 613, 622, 626). However, Oswald did not possess a shirt of this description (see CEs 150-64).

The Commission never sought to determine if Oswald had worn the same shirt continually that day or if he had changed prior to his arrest. Apparently it was not going to risk the implications of Brennan's testimony that the clothing worn by Oswald in the line-up (Oswald wore the rust-brown shirt during the line-ups on November 22 [7H127-29, 169-70]) differed from that of the sixth-floor gunman. Indeed, when shown the shirt in question, CE 150, Brennan said the gunman's shirt was lighter (3H161).

The testimony of Marrion Baker, a police officer who encountered Oswald right after the shots, is somewhat illuminating on this point. When Baker later saw Oswald in the homicide office at police headquarters, "he looked like he did not have the same [clothes] on" (3H263). However, the reason for Baker's confusion (and Baker was not nearly so positive about the disparity as was Brennan) was that the shirt Oswald wore when seen in the Depository was "a little bit *darker*" than the one he had on at the police station (3H257; emphasis added).

The crux of the matter is whether Oswald was wearing his rust-brown shirt all day November 22, or if he changed into it subsequent to the assassination. While there is testimony indicating that he wore the same shirt all along, the nature of the existing evidence does not permit a positive determination. Had Oswald been wearing CE 150 at the time of the shots, it would seem that he was not the sixth-floor gunman, who wore a white or very light shirt, probably short sleeved. While it can be argued that Oswald may have appeared at the window in only his white polo shirt, he was seen within 90 seconds after the shots wearing the brown shirt.[14] As will be discussed in the next chapter, there was not enough time, had Oswald been at the window, for him to have put on his shirt within the 90-second limit.

The Commission had no evidence in any form that Oswald was at the sixth-floor window during the shots; its only reliable evidence placed Oswald on the first floor shortly before this time. The Commission concluded that Oswald was at this window because it wanted, indeed needed, to have him there. To do this, it put false meaning into the meaningless—the fingerprint evidence and Givens's story—and believed the incredible—Brennan's testimony. Through its General Counsel, it suppressed the exculpatory evidence, and claimed to know of no evidence placing Oswald in a location other than the sixth floor when its *only* evidence did exactly that. The conclusion that Oswald was at the window is simply without foundation. It demands only the presumption of Oswald's guilt for acceptance. It cannot stand under the weight of the evidence.

8

The Alibi: Oswald's Actions after the Shots

The first person to see Oswald after the assassination was Dallas Patrolman Marrion Baker, who had been riding a motorcycle behind the last camera car in the motorcade. As he reached a position some 60 to 80 feet past the turn from Main Street onto Houston, Baker heard the first shot (3H246). Immediately after the last shot, he "revved up that motorcycle" and drove it to a point near a signal light on the northwest corner of Elm and Houston (3H247). From here Baker ran 45 feet to the main entrance of the Book Depository, pushing through people and quickly scanning the area. At the main entrance, Baker's shouts for the stairs were spontaneously answered by building manager Roy Truly as both men continued across the first floor to the northwest corner, where Truly hollered up twice for an elevator. When an elevator failed to descend, Truly led Baker up the adjacent steps to the second floor.

From the second floor, Truly continued up the steps to the third; Baker, however, did not. The Report describes the situation:

> On the second floor landing there is a small open area with a door at the east end. This door leads into a small vestibule, and another door leads from the vestibule into the second-floor lunchroom. The lunchroom door is usually open, but the first door is kept shut by a closing mechanism on the door. This vestibule door is solid except for a small glass window in the upper part of the door. As Baker reached the second floor, he was about 20 feet from the vestibule door. He intended to continue around to his left toward the stairway going up but through the window in the door he caught a fleeting glimpse of a man walking in the vestibule toward the lunchroom. (R151)

Baker ran into the vestibule with his pistol drawn and stopped the man, who turned out to be Lee Harvey Oswald. Truly, realizing that Baker was no longer following him, came down to the second floor and identified Oswald as one of his employees. The two men then continued up the stairs toward the Depository roof.

"In an effort to determine whether Oswald could have descended to the lunchroom from the sixth floor by the time Baker and Truly arrived," the Commission staged a timed reconstruction of events. The Commission knew that this encounter in the lunchroom such a short time after the shots could have provided Oswald with an alibi, thus exculpating him from involvement in the shooting. The reconstruction could not establish whether Oswald was at the sixth-floor window; it could, however, tell whether he was *not*. In the interest of determining the truth, it was vital that this reenactment be faithfully conducted, simulating the proper actions to the most accurate degree possible.

From beginning to end, the execution of the reconstruction was in disregard of the known actions of the participants, stretching—if not by intent, certainly in effect—the time consumed for Baker to have arrived on the second floor and shrinking the time for the "assassin's" descent.[1]

To begin with, the reconstruction of Baker's movements started at the wrong time. Baker testified that he revved up his motorcycle immediately after the *last* shot (3H247). However, Baker's time was clocked from a simulated *first* shot (3H252). To compare the time of the assassin's descent with that of Baker's ascent, the reconstruction obviously had to start after the last shot. Since the time span of the shots was, according to the Report, from 4.8 to over 7 seconds, the times obtained for Baker's movements are between *4.8 and 7 seconds in excess.*

Although Baker testified that he was flanking the last "press" car in the motorcade (3H245), the record indicates that he was, in fact, flanking the last *camera* car—the last of the convertibles carrying the various photographers, closer to the front of the procession than the vehicles carrying other press representatives. Baker said he was some 60 to 80 feet along Houston Street north of Main when he heard the first shot (3H246). Those in the last camera car were also in this general location at the time of the first shot (Jackson: 2H158; Couch: 6H156; Dillard: 6H163-64; Underwood: 6H169;). During the reconstruction, Baker drove his motorcycle from his location at the time of the *first* shot a distance of 180 to 200 feet to the point in front of the Depository at which he dismounted (3H247). However, since Baker had revved up his cycle immediately after the *last* shot on November 22, the distance he traveled in the reenactment was entirely too

long. Since the motorcade advanced about 116 feet during the time span of the shots, the distance Baker
should have driven in the reconstruction was no greater than 84 feet (200 − 116 = 84). This would have
placed Baker near the intersection of Elm and Houston
at the time he revved up his cycle, not 180 feet from it
as was reconstructed. Likewise, the men in the last
camera car recalled being in proximity to the intersection at the time of the last shot (Underwood: 6H169;
Couch: 6H158; Jackson: 2H159).

With 116 feet extra to travel in a corresponding
added time of 4.8 to 7 seconds, Baker was able to reach
the front entrance of the Depository in only 15 seconds
during the reconstruction (7H593). Had the reenactment properly started at the time of the last shot, it
follows that Baker could have reached the main entrance in 8 to 10 seconds. Did Baker actually consume so
little time in getting to the Depository on November 22?

The Commission made no effort to answer this question, leaving an incomplete and unreliable record. Billy
Lovelady, Bill Shelley, Joe Molina, and several other
employees were standing on the steps of the
Depository's main entrance during the assassination.
Lovelady and Shelley testified that another employee,
Gloria Calvery, ran up to them and stated that the
President had been shot; the three of them began to
run west toward the parking lot, at which time they
saw Truly and a police officer run into the Depository
(6H329-31, 339). This story is contradicted by Molina
who contended that Truly (he did not notice Baker) ran
into the main entrance before Gloria Calvery arrived
(6H372). Mrs. Calvery was not called to testify, and the
one statement by her to the FBI does not address this
issue. From her position just east of the Stemmons
Freeway sign on the north side of Elm (22H638), i

does not seem likely that she could have made the 150-foot run to the main entrance in only 15 seconds. Yet, adding to this confusion is an affidavit that Shelly executed for the Dallas Police on November 22, 1963. Here he stated that *he* ran down to the "park" on Elm Street and met Gloria Calvery *there* (24H226). Obviously, the issue cannot be resolved through these witnesses.

While Molina felt that Truly ran into the Depository some 20 to 30 seconds after the shots (6H372), Lovelady and Shelley estimated that as much as three minutes had elapsed (6H329, 339). When Counsel Joe Ball cautioned Lovelady that "three minutes is a long time," Lovelady partially retracted because he did not have a watch then and could not be exact (6H339). Supporting Molina's estimate, Roy Truly told the Secret Service in December 1963 that Baker made his way to the front entrance "almost immediately" (CD87, Secret Service Control No. 491); almost a year later Truly said on a CBS News Special that Baker's arrival "was just a matter of seconds after the third shot."[2]

I was able to resolve the issue concerning Baker's arrival at the Depository through evidence strangely absent from the Commission's record. Malcolm Couch, riding in the last camera car (Camera Car 3), took some very important motion-picture footage immediately after the shots. Couch, whose car was almost at the intersection of Elm and Houston when the last shot sounded, immediately picked up his camera, made the proper adjustments, and began filming (6H158). Others in Camera Car 3 related how their car came to a stop or hesitated in the middle of the turn into Elm to let some of the photographers out (2H162; 6H165, 169). Couch's film begins slightly before the stop, just as the car was making the turn (6H158). From Couch's testimony and the scenes depicted in his film, in addition to the testimony of others in the same car, it can be determined that Couch began filming no more than 10 seconds after the last shot.[3]

The first portion of the Couch film depicts the crowds dispersing along the island at the northwest corner of Elm and Houston. The camera pans in a westerly direction as the grassy knoll and Elm Street come into view. In these beginning sequences, a motorcycle is visible, parked next to the north curb of Elm, very slightly west of a traffic light at the head of the island. Baker testified that he parked his cycle 10 feet *east* of this signal light (3H247-48). The position of the motorcycle in the Couch film is not in great conflict with the position at which Baker recalled having dismounted; it is doubtful that Baker paid much attention to the exact position of his motorcycle in those confused moments. It would appear that this cycle, identical with the others driven in the motorcade, *must* have been Baker's, for it is not visible in any photographs taken *during* the shots, including footage of that area by David Weigman,[4] and no other motorcycle officer arrived at that location in so short a time after the shots. No policeman appears on or around the cycle depicted in the Couch film.

Thus, photographic evidence known to, but never sought by, the Commission proves that Officer Baker had parked and dismounted his motorcycle *within 10 seconds after the shots*. Corroborative evidence is found in the testimony of Bob Jackson, also riding in Camera Car 3. Jackson told the Commission that after the last shot, as his car hesitated through the turn into Elm, he saw a policeman run up the Depository steps, toward the front door (2H164). This is entirely consistent with Baker's abandoned motorcycle's appearing at this same time in the Couch film.

During the Baker-Truly reconstructions, Baker reached the second floor in one minute and 30 seconds on the first attempt and one minute, 15 seconds on the second (3H252). Since Baker's simulated movements up to the time he reached the main entrance consumed 15 seconds (7H593), the actions subsequent to that must have been reenacted in a span of one minute to about 75 seconds. However, since Baker actually reached the main entrance within 10 seconds on November 22, the reconstructed time is cut by at least five seconds. Further reductions are in order.

Officer Baker described the manner in which he simulated his movements subsequent to dismounting his motorcycle:

> From the time I got off the motorcycle we walked the first time and then we kind of run the second time from the motorcycle on into the building. (3H253)

Baker neither walked nor "kind of" ran to the Depository entrance on November 22. From his own description, he surveyed the scene as he was parking his cycle, and then "*ran* straight to" the main entrance (3H248-249). Billy Lovelady also swore that Baker was *running* (6H339). However, Truly provided the most graphic description of Baker's apparent "mad dash" to the building:

> I saw a young motorcycle policeman *run* up to the building, up the steps to the entrance of our building. He *ran* right by me. And he was pushing people out of the way. He pushed a number of people out of the way before he got to me. I saw him coming through, I believe. As he *ran* up the stairway—I mean up the steps, I was almost to the steps, and I *ran* up and caught up with him. (3H221; emphasis added)

Thus, walking through this part of the reconstruction

was, as Harold Weisberg aptly termed it, pure fakery, unnecessarily and unfaithfully burdening Baker's time.[5] The Report, on the other hand, assures us that the time on November 22 would actually have been *longer,* because "no allowance was made for the special conditions which existed on the day of the assassination—possible delayed reaction to the shot, jostling with the crowd of people on the steps and scanning the area along Elm Street and the Parkway" (R152-53). Had the Commission directed any significant effort to obtaining as many contemporaneous pictures as possible—including those taken by Couch—it could not have engaged in such excuse-making. Even at that, how could the Commission dare go to all the efforts of staging a reconstruction and then admit—to its own advantage—that it deliberately failed to simulate actions? As was discussed in chapter 1, this child's play was inexcusable as an effort bearing such weight in deciding Oswald's guilt. The Couch film eliminates the possibility that the factors mentioned in the Report could have slowed Baker down. As for "jostling with the crowd of people on the steps," the Report neglected to mention other disproof of this as a slowing factor. As Truly testified,

> when the officer and I ran in, we were shouldering people aside in front of the building, so we possibly were slowed a little bit more coming in than we were when he and I came in on March 20 (date of the reconstruction). *I don't believe so. But it wouldn't be enough to matter there.* (3H228; emphasis added)

Once in the building during the reconstruction, the two men proceded to the elevators "at a kind of trot. . .it wasn't a real fast run, an open run. It was more of a trot, kind of" (3H253). This, again, was not an accurate simulation of the real actions. While Truly admitted that the reconstruction pace across the first floor was "about" the same as that of November 22, he described the former as a trot and the latter as "a little more than a trot" (3H228). Baker himself said that once through the door, he and Truly "kind of ran, not real fast but, you know, *a good trot*" (3H249), not the "kind of trot" he described during the reconstruction. A swinging door at the end of the lobby in the main entrance was jammed because the bolt had been stuck. Apparently, the pace on November 22 was of sufficient speed for Truly to bang right into this door and Baker to subsequently collide with Truly in the instant before the door was forced open (3H222). Likewise, Eddie Piper, a first-floor witness, had seen the two men *run* into the building, yell up for an elevator, and "take off" up the stairs (6H385).

In walking through part of the reconstruction, which should have been conducted running and was begun at least five seconds early, Baker and Truly managed to arrive on the second floor in one minute, 30 seconds. In the reconstruction, equally begun too early but staged at a pace closer to, though not simulating that of November 22, the time narrowed to a minute and 15 seconds. While Baker and Truly felt that the reconstructed times were minimums (3H228, 253), it would seem that the opposite was true. Subtracting the extra seconds tacked on by including the time span of the shots reduces even the maximum time to one minute, 25 seconds. The understandably hurried pace of November 22 as manifested in all the evidence would indicate that Truly and Baker reached the second floor in under 85 seconds, and the Couch film introduces the possibility that it may have taken as little as 70 seconds, since Baker parked and abandoned his motorcycle within ten seconds of the last shot.

The second part of the reconstruction was supposed to have simulated the "assassin's" movements from the sixth-floor window down to the second-floor lunchroom. Here the figurative lead weights tied to Baker and Truly during the reconstruction of their movements are exchanged for figurative roller skates, to shorten the time of the "assassin's" descent.

Secret Service Agent John Howlett stood in for the "assassin." He executed an affidavit for the Commission in which he described his actions:

> I carried a rifle from the southeast corner of the sixth floor northernly along the east aisle to the northern corner, then westernly [sic] along the north wall past the elevators to the northwest corner. There I placed the rifle on the floor. I then entered the stairwell, walked down the stairway to the second floor landing, and then into the lunchroom. (7H592)

This test was done twice. At a "normal walk" it took one minute and 18 seconds; at a "fast walk," one minute, 14 seconds (3H254). This reconstruction also suffered from most serious ommissions.

The "assassin" could not just have walked away from his window as Howlett apparently did. If the gunman fired the last shot from the Carcano as the official theory demands, a minimum time of 2.3 seconds after the last shot must be added to the reconstructed time since the cartridge case from that shot had to be ejected—an operation that involves working the rifle bolt. Furthermore, witnesses recalled that the gunman had been in no hurry to leave his window (2H159; 3H144).

There were also physical obstructions that prevented immediate evacuation of the area. Commission Exhibit 734 shows that some stacks of boxes nearest to the "assassin's" window did not extend far enough toward the east wall of the building to have blocked off the window there completely. However, as Commission Exhibits 723 and 726 clearly show, other columns of

boxes were situated behind the first stacks; these
formed a wall that had no openings large enough for a
man to penetrate without contortion. Deputy Sheriff
Luke Mooney discovered three cartridge cases by this
window. He had to squeeze "between these two stacks
of boxes, I had to turn myself sideways to get in there"
(3H285). The gunman would have had to squeeze
through these stacks of boxes while carrying a 40-inch,
8-pound rifle. Considering these details, we must add
at least six or seven seconds to the Commission's time
to allow for the various necessary factors that would
slow departure from the window.

Fig. 7. CE 723 shows the "barricade" of boxes through which
Luke Mooney had to squeeze in order to gain access to the
"assassin's window." The gunman likewise must have squeezed
through these boxes to leave the window.

To simulate the hiding of the rifle, Howlett "leaned over as if he were putting a rifle there [near the stair landing at the northwest corner of the sixth floor]" (3H253). The Commission did not do justice to its putative assassin who, as the photographs reveal, took meticulous care in concealing his weapon. The mere act of gaining access to the immediate area in which the rifle was hidden required time. This is what Deputy Sheriff Eugene Boone went through before he discovered the rifle:

> As I got to the west wall, there were a row of windows there, and a slight space between some boxes and the wall. I squeezed through them. . . .I caught a glimpse of the rifle, stuffed down between two rows of boxes with another box or so pulled over the top of it. (3H293)

Luke Mooney "had to get around to the right angle" before he could see the rifle (3H298). Likewise, Deputy Constable Seymour Weitzman reported that "it was covered with boxes. It was very well protected as far as the naked eye" (7H107). Another Deputy Sheriff, Roger Craig, recalled that the ends of the rows between which the rifle had been pushed were closed off by boxes, so that one could not see through them (6H269).

Photographs of the area in which the rifle was found (e.g., CE 719), and a bird's-eye view of the hidden rifle itself (e.g., CE 517), corroborate what these men have described and add other information. CE 719 shows that the rifle was found amid clusters of boxes that did not permit easy access. CE 517, in particular, is very revealing. It shows that the rifle had been pushed upright on its side between two rows of boxes that partially overlapped on top, thus eliminating the possibility that the rifle had merely been dropped down between the stacks. CE 517 also demonstrates that both ends of the rows of boxes were partially sealed off by other boxes, indicating a possibility never pursued by the Commission—namely, that boxes had to be moved to gain access to the weapon. When interviewed by CBS News, Seymour Weitzman inadvertently admitted this fact:

> I'll be very frank with you. I stumbled over it two times, not knowing it was there. ...And Mr. Bone [sic] was climbing on top, and I was down on my knees looking, and *I moved a box, and he moved a carton, and there it was.* And he in turn hollered that we had found a rifle.[6]

Hence, the concealment of the rifle required much maneuvering. In addition to squeezing in between boxes, the gunman had to move certain cartons filled with books. The rifle itself had been very carefully placed in position. Doubtless this would have added *at least* 15, perhaps 20, seconds to the reconstructed time *even if the hiding place had been chosen in advance* (of which there is no evidence either way).

If we take the Commission's minimum time of one minute, 14 seconds (giving the advantage to the official story) and add the additional six or seven seconds needed just to evacuate the immediate area of the window, plus the 15 to 20 seconds more for hiding the rifle, we find that it would have taken *at least* a minute and 35 seconds to a minute and 41 seconds for a sixth-floor gunman to have reached the second-floor lunchroom, *had all his maneuvers been planned in advance.* Had Oswald been the assassin, he would have arrived in the lunchroom *at least* five to eleven seconds *after* Baker reached the second floor, even if Baker took the *longest* time obtainable for his ascent—a minute, 30 seconds. Had Baker ascended in 70 seconds—as he easily could have—he would have arrived at least 25 seconds before

Oswald. Either case removes the possibility that Oswald descended from the sixth floor, for on November 22 he had unquestionably arrived in the lunchroom *before* Baker.

The circumstances surrounding the lunchroom encounter indicate that Oswald entered the lunchroom *not* by the vestibule door from without, as he would have had he descended from the sixth floor, but through a hallway leading into the vestibule. The outer vestibule door is closed automatically by a closing mechanism on the door (7H591). When Truly arrived on the second floor, he did not see Oswald entering the vestibule (R151). For the Commission's case to be valid, Oswald must have entered the vestibule through the first door before Truly arrived. Baker reached the second floor immediately after Truly and caught a fleeting glimpse of Oswald in the vestibule through a small window in the outer door. Although Baker said the vestibule door "might have been, you know, closing and almost shut at that time" (3H255), it is dubious that he could have distinguished whether the door was fully or "almost" closed.

Baker's and Truly's observations are not at all consistent with Oswald's having entered the vestibule through the first door. Had Oswald done this, he could have been inside the lunchroom well before the automatic mechanism closed the vestibule door. Truly's testimony that he saw no one entering the vestibule indicates either that Oswald was already in the vestibule at this time or was approaching it from another source. However, had Oswald already entered the vestibule when Truly arrived on the second floor, it is doubtful that he would have remained there long enough for Baker to see him seconds later. Likewise, the fact that neither man saw the mechanically closed

Fig. 8. CE 719 (above) shows that the Mannlicher-Carcano was found amid the clusters of boxes that did not permit easy access. (To provide a point of orientation, a box showing the hiding place of the rifle has been marked "A.")

Fig. 9. CE 517, an overhead view, reveals how carefully the rifle (arrow) was concealed amid clusters of boxes. This must have been a time-consuming effort.

door in motion is cogent evidence that Oswald did not enter the vestibule through that door.

One of the crucial aspects of Baker's story is his position at the time he caught a "fleeting glimpse" of a man in the vestibule. Baker marked this position during his testimony as having been immediately adjacent to the stairs at the northwest corner of the building (3H256; CE 497). "I was just stepping out on to the second floor when I caught this glimpse of this man through this doorway," said Baker.

It should be noted that the Report never mentions Baker's position at the time he saw Oswald in the *vestibule* (R149-51). Instead, it prints a floor plan of the second floor and notes Baker's position "when he observed Oswald in *lunchroom*" (R150). This location, as indicated in the Report, was immediately outside the vestibule door (see CE 1118). The reader of the Report is left with the impression that Baker saw Oswald in the vestibule as well from this position. However, Baker testified explicitly that he first caught a glimpse of the man in the vestibule from the stairs and, upon running to the vestibule door, saw Oswald in the lunchroom (3H256). The Report's failure to point out Baker's position is significant.

Had Oswald descended from the sixth floor, his path through the vestibule into the lunchroom would have been confined to the north wall of the vestibule. Yet the line of sight from Baker's position at the steps does not include any area near the north wall. From the steps, Baker could have seen only one area in the vestibule—the southeast portion. The only way Oswald could have been in this area on his way to the lunchroom is if he entered the vestibule through the southernmost door, as the previously cited testimony indicates he did.

TEXAS SCHOOL BOOK DEPOSITORY
DIAGRAM OF SECOND FLOOR
SHOWING ROUTE OF OSWALD

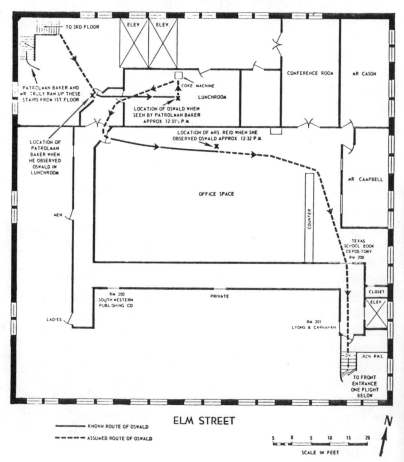

COMMISSION EXHIBIT No. 1118

Fig. 10. This is the diagram of the second floor as printed in the Report (R150). Note the failure to indicate Baker's position at the time he saw Oswald in the vestibule. Instead, the only notation is Baker's position "when he observed Oswald in lunchroom." This was not the same position as when he caught a fleeting glimpse of a man in the vestibule.

TEXAS SCHOOL BOOK DEPOSITORY
DIAGRAM OF SECOND FLOOR

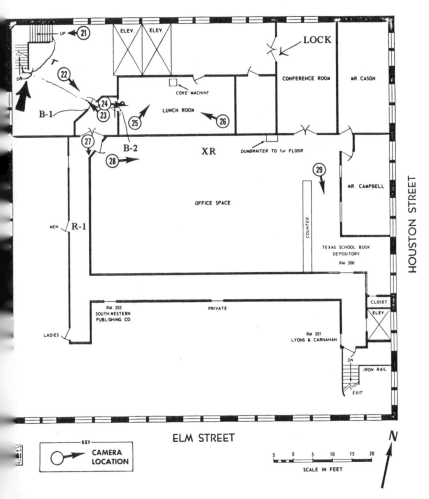

Fig. 11. This second-floor diagram, CE 497, was marked by Baker during his Commission testimony. On this he "marked. . .point 'B' where [he] thought [he was] at about the time [he] caught a glimpse of something. . .through the window in the door marked 23" (3H256). (I have drawn an arrow to Baker's notation.)

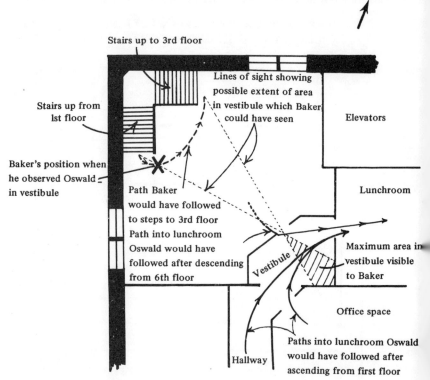

Fig. 12. Shown above is a detail of the northwest portion of the second floor. The line of sight from Baker's position at the stairs through the window in the vestibule door shows that he could not have seen a significant portion or the north area of the vestibule. Had Baker continued to the third-floor stairs before looking into the vestibule (i.e., he did not catch a glimpse of Oswals as soon as he arrived on the second floor), his field of view in the vestibule would have moved further south.

Had Oswald entered the vestibule after descending from the sixth floor, he would have followed a path into the lunchroom that would have put him out of Baker's view. The only way Oswald could have been in the area of the vestibule visible to Baker is if he entered through the south door, accessible to him only had he come up from the first floor. To do this, he would have gone the reverse of his "escape route" as illustrated in CE 1118.

Oswald could not have entered the vestibule in this manner had he just descended from the sixth floor. The only way he could have gotten to the southern door is from the first floor up through either a large office space or an adjacent corridor. As the Report concedes, Oswald told police he had eaten his lunch on the first floor and gone up to the second to purchase a coke when he encountered an officer (R182).

Thus, Oswald had an alibi. Had he been the sixth-floor gunman, he would have arrived at the lunchroom *at least* 5 seconds *after* Baker did, probably more. It is extremely doubtful that he could have entered the vestibule through the first door without Baker's or Truly's having seen the door in motion. Oswald's position in the vestibule when seen by Baker was consistent only with his having come up from the first floor as he told the police.

Oswald *could not* have been the assassin.

The Commission had great difficulty with facts, for none supported the ultimate conclusions. Instead, it found comfort and security in intangibles that usually had no bearing on the actual evidence. Amateur psychology seems to have been one of the Commission's favorite sciences, approached with the predisposition that Oswald was a murderer. This was manifested in the Report's lengthy chapter, "Lee Harvey Oswald: Background and Possible Motives" (R375-424).

To lend credibility to its otherwise incredible conclusion that Oswald was the assassin, the Commission accused Oswald of yet another assassination attempt—a shot fired at right-wing Maj. Gen. Edwin Walker on April 10, 1963 (R183-87). Thus, Oswald officially was not a newcomer to the "game" of political assassination. Although I am not in accord with the conclusion that Oswald shot at Walker, I find it illuminating that the Commission did not follow its inclination for psychology in its comparison of Oswald as the Walker assailant to Oswald as the Kennedy assailant.

Having just torn open the head of the President of the United States, as the Commission asserts, how did Oswald react when stopped by a policeman with a drawn gun? Roy Truly was first asked about Oswald's reaction to the encounter with Baker:

> Mr. Belin: Did you see any expression on his face? Or weren't you paying attention?
>
> Mr. Truly: He didn't seem to be excited or overly afraid or anything. He might have been a little startled, like I might have been if someone confronted me. But I cannot recall any change in expression of any kind on his face. (3H225)

Officer Baker was more explicit under similar questioning:

> Rep. Boggs: When you saw him [Oswald. . ., was he out of breath, did he appear to have been running or what?
>
> Mr. Baker: It didn't appear that to me. He appeared normal you know.
>
> Rep. Boggs: Was he calm and collected?
>
> Mr. Baker: Yes, sir. He never did say a word or nothing. In fact, he didn't change his expression one bit.
>
> Mr. Belin: Did he flinch in anyway when you put the gun up. . .?
>
> Mr. Baker: No, sir. (3H252)

> Sen. Cooper: He did not show any evidence of any emotion?
>
> Mr. Baker: No, sir. (3H263)

This "calm and collected" "assassin" proceeded to buy himself a coke and at his normal "very slow pace," was then observed by Depository employee Mrs. Robert Reid walking through the office space on the second floor on his way down to the first floor (3H279). Presumably he finished his coke on the first floor. Documents in the Commission's files (but omitted from the Report, which assumes Oswald made an immediate get-away) indicate very strongly that, at the main entrance after the shots, Oswald directed two newsmen to the Depository phones (CD354).

According to the evidence credited by the Commission, Oswald was not such a cool cucumber after his first assassination attempt. Here the source of the Commission's information was Oswald's wife, Marina, and his once close "friends," George and Jeanne De Mohrenschildt. The incident in question is described in the Report as follows:

The De Mohrenschildts came to Oswald's apartment on Neely Street for the first time on the evening of April 13, 1963 (three days after the Walker incident), apparently to bring an Easter gift for the Oswald child. Mrs. De Mohrenschildt then told her husband, in the presence of the Oswalds, that there was a rifle in the closet. Mrs. De Mohrenschildt testified that "George, of course, with his sense of humor—Walker was shot at a few days ago, within that time. He said, 'Did you take a pot shot at Walker by any chance?' " At that point, Mr. De Mohrenschildt testified, Oswald "sort of shriveled, you see, when I asked this question. . .made a peculiar face. . .(and) changed the expression on his face" and remarked that he did target-shooting. Marina Oswald testified that the De Mohrenschildts came to visit a few days after the Walker incident and that when De Mohrenschildt made his reference to Oswald's possibly shooting at Walker, Oswald's "face changed,. . .he almost became speechless." According to the De Mohrenschildts, Mr. De Mohrenschildt's remark was intended as a joke, and he had no knowledge of Oswald's involvement in the attack on Walker. Nonetheless, the remark appears to have created an uncomfortable silence, and the De Mohrenschildts left "very soon afterwards." (R282-83)

De Mohrenschildt further testified that his "joking" remark "had an effect on" Oswald, making him "very, very uncomfortable" (9H249-50). In another section, the Report adds that Oswald "was visibly shaken" by the remark (R274).

The Commission certainly chose a paradoxical assassin. We are asked to believe, according to the Commission, that Oswald was guilty of attacking both Walker and Kennedy. Yet, this man who officially became markedly upset when jokingly confronted with his attempt to kill Walker did not even flinch when a policeman put a gun to his stomach immediately after he murdered the President!

The Commission begged for the charge of being ludicrous in drawing its conclusions relevant to Oswald and the assassination; it insulted common sense and intelligence when it asked that those conclusions be accepted and believed.

9

Oswald's Rifle Capability

The lunchroom encounter was Oswald's alibi; it proved that he *could not* have been at the sixth-floor window during the shots. The Warren Commission falsely pronounced Oswald the assassin. In so doing, it alleged that Oswald had the proficiency with his rifle to have fired the assassination shots. Obviously, in light of the evidence that proves Oswald innocent, his rifle capability has no legitimate bearing on the question of his involvement in the shooting. In this chapter I will examine the Commission's handling of the evidence related to Oswald's rifle capability. It will be demonstrated that the Commission consistently misrepresented the record in an effort to make feasible the assertion that Oswald was the assassin.[1]

The first consideration germane to this topic is the nature of the shots, assuming theoretically that all originated from the sixth-floor window by a gunman using the Mannlicher-Carcano. For such a rifleman, "the shots were at a slow-moving target proceeding on a downgrade in virtually a straight line with the alignment of the assassin's rifle, at a range of 177 to 266 feet" (R189). According to the Commission, three shots were fired, the first and last strikes occurring within a span of 4.8 to 5.6 seconds; one shot allegedly missed, although the Commission did not decide whether it was the first, second, or third. While the current analysis ignores evidence of more than three shots from more than one location, I can make only a limited departure from reality in working under the Commission's postulations. My analysis of the wounds proved beyond doubt that the President and the Governor were wounded nonfatally by two separate bullets. This demands, in line with the Commission's three-shot-theory, that all shots hit in the car. The Zapruder film reveals that the first two hits occurred within a very brief time, probably shorter than the very minimum time needed to fire two successive shots with the Carcano, 2.3 to 3 seconds. The fatal shot came about four seconds after the one that wounded Connally.

The Report repeatedly characterizes the shots as "very easy" and "easy." However, the experts who made these evaluations for the Commission did not consider two essential factors that cannot be excluded from any hypothesizing: 1) the President was a living, moving target, and 2) the shots had to be fired in a very short period of time. First quoted in the Report is FBI ballistics expert Frazier:

> From my own experience in shooting over the years, when you shoot at 175 feet or 260 feet, which is less than 100 yards, with a telescopic sight, you should not have any difficulty hitting your target. (R190)

Frazier testified at the New Orleans trial of Clay

Shaw, where he modified his previous Commission testimony. How would the added consideration of a moving target affect his previous assessment?

> it would be a relatively easy shot, slightly complicated, however, if the target were moving at the time, it would make it a little more difficult.[2]

The next "expert" quoted is Marine Sgt. James A. Zahm, who was involved in marksmanship training in the Marine Corps:

> Using the scope, rapidly working the bolt and using the scope to relocate your target quickly and at the same time when you locate that target you identify and the cross-hairs are in close relationship to the point you want to shoot at, it just takes a minor move in aiming to bring the crosshairs to bear, and then it is a quick squeeze. (R190)

Zahm never used the C2766 Carcano; his comments related to four-power scopes in general as aids in rapid shooting with a bolt-action rifle. Another expert, Ronald Simmons, was directly involved in tests employing the Carcano. Although this is not reflected in the Report, he told the Commission that, contrary to Zahm's generalization of a "minor move" necessary to relocate the target in the scope, such a great amount of effort was needed to work the rifle bolt that the weapon was actually moved *completely* off target (3H449). There is yet another factor qualifying Zahm's evaluation. This was brought our during Frazier's New Orleans testimony:

> Mr. Oser: ...when you shoot this rifle...can you tell us whether or not in rebolting the gun you had to move your eye away from the scope?
> Mr. Frazier: Yes, sir, that was necessary.
> Mr. Oser: Why was that necessary?

Mr. Frazier: To prevent the bolt of the rifle from striking me in the face as it came to the rear.[3]

At best, the Report drastically oversimplified the
true nature of the shots. It is true that shots fired at
ranges under 100 yards with a four-power scope are
generally easy. However, the assassination shots, in
accordance with the Commission's lone-assassin theory,
were fired in rapid succession (indeed the first two
would have occurred within the minimum time needed
to operate the bolt) and at a moving target. The difficulty of such shots becomes apparent when it is considered that operation of the bolt would have thrown the
weapon off target and caused the firer temporarily to
move his eye from the sight.

One is prompted to ask what caliber of shooter would
be required to commit the assassination alone as described above. Simulative tests conducted by the Commission, while deficient, are quite illuminating.

The Commission's test firers were all rated as "Master" by the National Rifle Association (NRA); they
were experts whose daily routines involved working
with and shooting firearms (3H445). In the tests, three
targets were set up at 175, 240, and 365 feet respectively from a 30-foot-high tower. Each shooter fired two
series of three shots, using the C2766 rifle. The men
took 8.25, 6.75, and 4.60 seconds respectively for the
first series and 7.00, 6.45, and 5.15 for the second
(3H446). In the first series, each man hit his first and
third targets but missed the second. Results varied on
the next series, although in all cases but one, two
targets were hit. Thus, in only two cases were the
Commission's experts able to fire three aimed shots in
under 5.6 seconds as Oswald allegedly did. *None* scored
three hits, as was demanded of a lone assassin on
November 22.

These tests would suggest that three hits within such a short time span, if not impossible, would certainly have taxed the proficiency of the most skilled marksman.[4] In his testimony before the Commission, Ronald Simmons spoke first of the caliber of shooter necessary to have fired the assassination shots on the basis that only two hits were achieved:

> Mr. Eisenberg: Do you think a marksman who is less than a highly skilled marksman under those conditions would be able to shoot within the range of 1.2 mil aiming error [as was done by the experts]?
> Mr. Simmons: Obviously, considerable experience would have to be in one's background to do so. And with this weapon, I think also considerable experience with this weapon, because of the amount of effort required to work the bolt. (3H449)

> Well, in order to achieve three hits, it would not be required that a man be an exceptional shot. A proficient man with this weapon, yes. But I think with the opportunity to use the weapon and to get familiar with it, we could probably have the results reproduced by more than one firer. (3H450)

Here arises the crucial question: Was Lee Harvey Oswald a "proficient man with this weapon," with "considerable experience" in his background?

While in the Marines between 1956 and 1959, Oswald was twice tested for his performance with a rifle. On a scale of expert-sharpshooter-marksman, Oswald scored two points above the minimum for sharpshooter on one occasion (December 1956) and only one point above the minimum requirement for marksman on another (May 1959)—his last recorded score. Colonel A. G. Folsom evaluated these scores for the Commission:

The Marine Corps consider that any reasonable application of the instructions given to Marines should permit them to become qualified at least as a marksman. To become qualified as a sharpshooter, the Marine Corps is of the opinion that most Marines with a reasonable amount of adaptability to weapons firing can become so qualified. Consequently, a low marksman qualification indicates a rather poor "shot" and a sharpshooter qualification indicates a fairly good "shot." (19H17-18)

There exists the possibility that Oswald's scores were either inaccurately or unfairly recorded, thus accounting for his obviously mediocre to horrendous performances with a rifle. However, there is other information independent of the scores to indicate that Oswald was in fact *not* a good shot. In his testimony, Colonel Folsom examined the Marine scorebook that Oswald himself had maintained, and elaborated on his previous evaluation:

> Mr. Ely: I just wonder, after having looked through the whole scorebook, if we could fairly say that all that it proves is that at this stage of his career he was not a particularly outstanding shot.
> Col. Folsom: No, no, he was not. His scorebook indicates. . .that he did well at one or two ranges in order to acheive the two points over the minimum score for sharpshooter.
> Mr. Ely: In other words, he had a good day the day he fired for qualification?
> Col. Folsom: I would say so. (8H311)

Thus, according to Folsom, Oswald's best recorded score was the result of having "a good day"; otherwise, Oswald "was not a particularly outstanding shot."

Folsom was not alone in his evaluation of Oswald as other than a good shot. The following is exerpted from the testimony of Nelson Delgado, one of Oswald's closest associates in the Marines:

Mr. Liebeler: Did you fire with Oswald?

Mr. Delgado: Right; I was in the same line. By that I mean we were on the same line together, the same time, but not firing at the same position. . .and I remember seeing his. It was a pretty big joke, because he got a lot of "maggie's drawers," you know, a lot of misses, but he didn't give a darn.

Mr. Liebeler: Missed the target completely?

Mr. Delgado: He just qualified, that's it. He wasn't as enthusiastic as the rest of us. (8H235)

The Report tried desperately to get around this unanimous body of credible evidence. First Marine Corps Major Eugene Anderson (who never had any association with Oswald) is quoted at length about how bad weather, poor coaching, and an inferior weapon might have accounted for Oswald's terrible performance in his second recorded test (R191). Here the Commission scraped the bottom of the barrel, offering this unsubstantiated, hypothetical excuse-making as apparent fact. Weather bureau records, which the Commission did not bother to check, show that perfect firing conditions existed at the time and place Oswald last fired for qualification—better conditions in fact, than those prevailing during the assassination.[5] As for the quality of the weapon fired in the test, it is probable that at its worst it would have been far superior to the virtual piece of junk Oswald allegedly owned and used in the assassination.[6] Perhaps Anderson guessed correctly in suggesting that Oswald may have had a poor instructor; yet, from the time of his departure from the Marines in 1959 to the time of the assassination in 1963, Oswald had *no* instructor.

For its final "evaluation," the Report again turned to Anderson and Zahm. Each man is quoted as rating Oswald a good shot, somewhat above average, as compared to other Marines, and an "excellent" shot as compared to the average male civilian (R192). That the Commission could even consider these evaluations is beyond comprehension. Oswald's Marine scores and their offical evaluation showed that he did not possess even "a reasonable amount of adaptability to weapons firing." If this is better than average for our Marines, pity the state of our national "defense"! The testimonies of Folsom and Delgado—people who had *direct* association with Oswald in the Marines—are not mentioned in the Report.

Thus, Oswald left the Marines in 1959 as a "rather poor shot." If he is to be credited with a feat such as the assassination, it must be demonstrated that he engaged in some activity between 1959 and 1963 that would have greatly developed his rifle capability and maintained it until the time of the shooting. The Report barely touched on the vital area of Oswald's rifle practice. In a brief two-paragraph section entitled "Oswald's Rifle Practice Outside the Marines," the Report painted a very sketchy picture, entirely inadequate in terms of the nature of the issue (R192-93). In all, Oswald is associated with a weapon eleven or twelve times, ending in May 1963.

Let us examine each of the Commission's assertions from this section of the Report:

1. During one of his leaves from the Marines, Oswald hunted with his brother Robert, using a .22 caliber bolt-action rifle belonging either to Robert or Robert's in-laws.

A footnote to this statement refers to Robert Oswald's testimony at 1H327, where essentially the same information is found.

2. After he left the Marines and before departing for Russia, Oswald, his brother, and a third companion went hunting for squirrels and rabbits. On that occasion Os-

wald again used a bolt-action .22 caliber rifle; and according to Robert, Lee Oswald exhibited an average amount of proficiency with that weapon.

Here again the Report cites Robert Oswald's testimony at 1H325-327. Although Robert did say that Lee showed "an average amount" of proficiency (1H326), his other descriptions of the occasion would indicate that none of the men showed any proficiency at all that day. This excursion took place in a "briar patch" that "was very thick with cottontails." Among the three men, eight rabbits were shot, "because it was the type of brush and thorns that didn't grow very high but we were able to see over them, so getting three of us out there it wasn't very hard to kill eight of them." Robert further illuminated the proficiency of the shooting when he revealed that it once took all three men firing to hit one rabbit.

3. While in Russia, Oswald obtained a hunting license, joined a hunting club and went hunting about six times.

As mentioned in chapter 1, Liebeler criticized the inclusion of this statement in the Report, for Oswald hunted with a shotgun in Russia. Wrote Liebeler, "Under what theory do we include activities concerning a *shotgun* under a heading relating to *rifle* practice, and then presume not to advise the reader of that?"[7] The sources given for the above-quoted statement are CEs 1042, 2007, and 1403 (which establish Oswald's membership in the club) and 1H96, 327-28, and 2H466. The latter references to the testimony do not support the Report's implication that Oswald's Russian hunting trips helped to further his marksmanship abilities.

In the portion of her testimony cited (1H96), Marina Oswald said that Oswald hunted only once during the time she knew him in the Soviet Union. This prompted a brief exchanged not complimentary to Oswald's performance with his weapon during the hunt:

> Mr. Rankin: Was that when he went hunting for squirrels?
> Mrs. Oswald: If he marked it down in his notebook that he went hunting for squirrels, he never did. Generally they wanted to kill a squirrel when we went there, or some sort of bird, in order to boast about it, but they didn't.

Robert Oswald testified that Lee hunted "about six times" in Russia (1H327-328). He too revealed the poor nature of Oswald's performance:

> We talked about hunting over there, and he said that he had only been hunting a half dozen times, and so forth, and that he had only used a shotgun, and a couple of times he did shoot a duck.

The third reference to testimony is most revealing. The source is Mrs. Ruth Paine, who related what Marina had told her:

> She quoted a proverb to the effect that you go hunting in the Soviet Union and you catch a bottle of Vodka, so I judge it was a social occasion more than shooting being the prime object. (2H466)

Information not mentioned or cited in the Report corroborates the informal nature of Oswald's hunting in Russia as well as his usual poor performance with his weapon. CD 344 contains the transcript of a Secret Service interview with Marina recorded Sunday night, November 24, 1963, at the Inn of the Six Flags Motel at Arlington, Texas. This was Marina's first interview conducted while she was in protective custody. When asked about Oswald's membership in the hunting club, she made this response through an interpreter:

> While he was a member of this hunting club, he never attended any meetings. He simply had a card that showed his membership. She said Lee enjoyed nature and as a member of the club he was entitled to free transportation in an automobile which enabled him to go out of town.[8]

Marina added that Lee owned a "hunting gun" in Russia but "he never used it."

Other information came from Yuri I. Nosenko, a Soviet KGB staff officer who defected in February 1964 and apparently participated in or knew of the KGB investigation of Oswald in Russia. CD 451 contains an interview with Nosenko, but it is currently withheld from research. Liebeler, who saw CD 451 during his Commission work, composed a staff memorandum on March 9, 1964, repeating some of the information obtained from Nosenko. According to the memorandum, "Oswald was an extremely poor shot and it was necessary for persons who accompanied him on hunts to provide him with game."[9]

4. Soon after Oswald returned from the Soviet Union he again went hunting with his brother, Robert, and used a borrowed .22 caliber bolt-action rifle.

Robert Oswald is again the source of this information. The hunting trip in question took place at the farm of Robert's in-laws. However, according to Robert, "we did just a very little bit [of hunting]. I believe this was on a Sunday afternoon and we didn't stay out very long" (1H327).

5. After Oswald purchased the Mannlicher-Carcano rifle, he told his wife that he practiced with it. Marina

Oswald testified that on one occasion she saw him take the rifle, concealed in a raincoat, from the house on Neely Street. Oswald told her he was going to practice with it.

Marina Oswald is the source of this above-quoted information. The footnote in the Report refers to 1H14-15; CE 1156, p. 442; CE 1404, pp. 446-48.

Marina's progression of statements relevant to Oswald's rifle practice is truly amazing. The Report quotes her incompletely and dishonestly, choosing only those statements which support the belief that Oswald practiced with the Carcano. The following is a chronological listing of Marina's relevant words:

12/3/63, FBI report of interview with Marina: "MARINA said she had never seen OSWALD practice with his rifle or any other firearm and he had never told her that he was going to practice." (22H763)

12/4/63, FBI report of interview with Marina: "She cannot recall ever hearing Oswald state that he was going to fire the rifle in practice or that he had fired it in practice." (22H785)

12/4/63, Secret Service report of interview with Marina: "The reporting agent interviewed Marina Oswald as to whether she knew of any place or of a rifle range where her husband could do some practicing with a rifle, and whether she ever saw her husband taking the rifle out of the house. She said that she never saw Lee going out or coming in to the house with a rifle and that he never mentioned to her doing any practice with a rifle." (23H393)

12/10/63, Secret Service report of interview with Marina: "Marina Oswald was asked if she ever saw her husband doing any dry practice with the rifle either in their

apartments or any place else, and she replied in the nega-
tive." (23H402)

12/16/63, FBI report of interview with Marina: "She
cannot recall that [Oswald] ever practiced firing the rifle
either in New Orleans or in Dallas." (22H778)

*2/3/64, Marina makes her first appearance before the
Commission:*

Mr. Rankin: Did you learn at any time that he had been
practicing with the rifle?

Mrs. Oswald: I think he went once or twice. I didn't actually see him take the rifle, but I knew he was practicing.

Mr. Rankin: Could you give us a little help on how you
knew?

Mrs. Oswald: He told me. And he would mention that in
passing. . .he would say, "Well, today I will take the rifle
along for practice." (1H14-15)

2/17/64, FBI report of interview with Marina: "MARINA
advised OSWALD had told her after the WALKER incident that he had practiced with his rifle in a field near
Dallas. She said further that in the beginning of January,
1963, at the Neely Street address, he on one occasion was
cleaning his rifle and he said he had been practicing that
day. [The rifle was not mailed until the end of March
1963.]

"MARINA was asked if she had ever seen OSWALD
take the rifle from the house and she replied that she had
not. She was asked if she had ever known the rifle to have
been gone from the house at the same time OSWALD was
gone from the house. She replied that she could not recall
any such incident. She was then asked if it were true then
that she had never seen OSWALD take the rifle from the
house nor knew any occasion when he might have had the
rifle at a place other than at home. She then admitted
that she did know of such an occasion. She said this occa-

sion occurred on an evening in March, 1963. On this evening, she and JUNE [their daughter] and OSWALD left the
house at about 6:00 PM. OSWALD had his rifle wrapped
up in a raincoat. . . .When OSWALD returned about 9:00
PM, he told her he had practiced with his rifle." (22H197)

2/18/64, FBI report of interview with Marina: "She advised she had been mistaken on February 17, 1964, when
she said she had recalled OSWALD cleaning his rifle at
Neely Street, at which time he made the statement he
had been practicing. She said she is now able to place the
date. . .as being shortly before the WALKER
incident. . . .At one of the four or five times that she observed OSWALD cleaning his rifle at their home on Neely
Street. . .he told her he had been practicing with the rifle
but he did not say when he had practiced. On the other
occasions of his cleaning the rifle. . .he did not say he had
been practicing. MARINA deduced that he might have
been practicing with the rifle." (22H785)

6/11/64, Marina again testifies before the Commission:

"Lee didn't tell me when he was going out to practice. I
only remember one time distinctly that he went out because he took the bus. I don't know if he went to Love
Field at that time. I don't—after all this testimony, after
all this testimony, when I was asked did he clean his gun
a lot, and I answered yes, I came to the conclusion that he
was practicing with his gun because he was cleaning it afterwards." (5H397)

Sen. Cooper: Did he ever tell you that he was practicing
with a rifle?
Mrs. Oswald: Only after I saw him take the gun that
one time. (5H398)

Thus Marina, until three months after the assassination, denied any knowledge whatsoever of Oswald's rifle practice; he never told her he practiced, and she knew of no practice. When she first appeared before the Commission, her story changed. She suddenly knew of one or two instances when Oswald mentioned he was going to practice, although she never saw him take the rifle from the house. Subsequent to her testimony, she changed her story again. After telling the FBI she saw Oswald clean the rifle before he even ordered it, she "admitted" an incident in which she saw Oswald remove the rifle *concealed in a raincoat* to practice *at night*. The following day her memory conveniently improved as she retracted her statement that she had seen Oswald with the rifle as early as January 1963. She added at this time that although Oswald had actually admitted practicing only once, she "deduced" he had practiced other times. This, essentially, was the final version of her story.

Marina was an entirely incredible witness. No honest jury could have believed any of her statements; for everything she said, there almost always existed a contradictory statement that she had made earlier. The Commission merely chose her most "juicy" descriptions of rifle practice and cited them, ignoring completely the other statements. The official use of Marina's testimony could best be described in Aldous Huxley's words, "You pays your money and you takes your choice."

6. According to George De Mohrenschildt, Oswald said he went target shooting with that rifle.

The footnote to this assertion refers to portions of the testimonies of George De Mohrenschildt, the Oswalds' "friend" in Dallas, and his wife, Jeanne. The combined

stories of the De Mohrenschildts are so ridiculous as to
make Marina's appear reliable and consistent.

In his testimony, George De Mohrenschildt had been
relating the incident in which he and his wife paid a
late-night visit to the Oswalds shortly after the Walker
incident (as described in the previous chapter). De
Mohrenschildt described how his wife had seen a rifle
in the closet and offered "facts" unsubstantiated by any
of the Commission's evidence:

> Mr. De Mohrenschildt: And Marina said "That crazy
> idiot is target shooting all the time." So frankly I thought
> it was ridiculous to shoot target shooting in Dallas, you
> see, right in town. I asked him "Why do you do that?"
> Mr. Jenner: What did he say?
> Mr. De Mohrenschildt: He said, "I go out and do target
> shooting. I like target shooting." (9H249)

Despite the lack of corroborative evidence, De
Mohrenschildt's story might have remained plausible
had his wife not attempted to substantiate it. In the
portion of her testimony cited but *not* quoted in the
Report, she revealed—to the exasperation of staff
member Jenner—the details of the incident *ad absur-
dium:*

> Mrs. De Mohrenschildt: I just asked what on earth is he
> doing with a rifle?
> Mr. Jenner: What did she [Marina] say?
> Mrs. De Mohrenschildt: She said, "Oh, he just loves to
> shoot." I said, "Where on earth does he shoot? Where can
> he shoot?" when they lived in a little house. "Oh, he goes
> in the park and shoots at leaves and things like that." But
> it didn't strike me too funny, because I personally love
> skeet shooting. I never kill anything. But I adore to shoot
> at a target, target shooting.
> Mr. Jenner: Skeet?
> Mrs. De Mohrenschildt: I just love it.

Mr. Jenner: Didn't you think it was strange to have someone say he is going in a public park and shooting leaves?

Mrs. De Mohrenschildt: But he was taking the baby out. He goes with her, and that was his amusement.

Mr. Jenner: Did she say that?

Mrs. De Mohrenschildt: Yes; that was his amusement, practicing in the park, shooting leaves. That wasn't strange to me, because any time I go to an amusement park I go to the rifles and start shooting. So I didn't find anything strange.

Mr. Jenner: But you shot at the rifle range in these amusement parks?

Mrs. De Mohrenschildt: Yes.

Mr. Jenner: Little .22?

Mrs. De Mohrenschildt: I don't know what it was.

Mr. Jenner: Didn't you think it was strange that a man would be walking around a public park in Dallas with a high-powered rifle like this, shooting leaves?

Mrs. De Mohrenschildt: I didn't know it was a high-powered rifle. I had no idea. I don't even know right now. (9H316)

The Commission did not see fit to include in the Report the fact that the extent of the De Mohrenschildts' knowledge of Oswald's "rifle practice" was that he fired at leaves while walking his baby daughter through public parks. Had this been included, no one could have believed the De Mohrenschildts.

7. Marina Oswald testified that in New Orleans in May of 1963, she observed Oswald sitting with the rifle on their screened porch at night, sighting with the telescopic lens and operating the bolt.

For this the Report cites Marina's testimony at 1H21-22, 53-54, and 65 and CE 1814, p. 736. However, CE 1814 has nothing to do with Marina Oswald, or rifle practice (23H471).

Marina's testimony about the bolt-working sessions
on the porch of the Oswald's New Orleans home was
another spectacle of blatant self-contradiction, again
none of which was reflected in the Report. In three
days, Marina give three opposing accounts represented
in the Report as consistent. On February 3, Marina
said:

> I know that we had a kind of a porch with a—a screened-
> in porch, and I know that sometimes evenings after dark
> he would sit there with his rifle. I don't know what he did
> with it. I came there only by chance once and saw him
> just sitting there with his rifle. I thought he is merely sit-
> ting there and resting. . .
> Mr. Rankin: From what you observed about his having
> the rifle on the back porch, in the dark, could you tell
> whether or not he was trying to practice with the tele-
> scopic lens?
> Mrs. Oswald: Yes. (1H21-22).

On February 4, Marina offered a version of the porch
practice different from that put forth in the Report:

> Mr. Rankin: Did you ever see him working the bolt, the
> action that opens the rifle, where you can put a shell in
> and push it back—during those times [on the porch]?
> Mrs. Oswald: I did not see it, because it was dark, and I
> would be in the room at that time. But I did hear the
> noise from time to time—not often. (1H54)

Finally, on February 5, Marina reached the height of
her confusion and merely retracted the statement attributed to her in the Report:

> Mr. Rankin: You have told us about his practicing with
> the rifle, the telescopic lens, on the back porch at New Or-
> leans, and also his using the bolt action that you heard
> from time to time. Will you describe that a little more
> fully to us, as best you remember?

Mrs. Oswald: I cannot describe that in greater detail. I can only say the Lee would sit there with the rifle and open and close the bolt and clean it. No, he didn't clean it at that time. Yes—twice he did clean it.

Mr. Rankin: And did he seem to be practicing with the telescopic lens, too, and sighting the gun on different objects?

Mrs. Oswald: I don't know. The rifle was always with this. I don't know exactly how he practiced, because I was in the house, I was busy. I just knew that he sits there with his rifle. I was not interested in it. (1H65)

It is important to note that Marina originally denied any such New Orleans porch practice to the FBI. An FBI report of an interview with Marina on December 16, 1963, states that "She never saw [Oswald] clean [the rifle] nor did he ever hold it in her presence [in New Orleans] as best as she can recall" (22H778).

If Marina's stories of porch practice are true (and here the reader may believe whichever version he likes), then Oswald practiced sighting with his rifle *in total darkness* on a screened porch. If this can be called "practice," it certainly cannot be applied to normal daylight firing.

The seven assertions as quoted above from the Report constitute the know extent of "Oswald's Rifle Practice." Only one had substantiation. The others are either misrepresentations of the evidence or are merely unsupported altogether. Oswald performed badly on the hunts in which he participated. He did not even use a rifle in Russia although, to the Commission, intent on associating Oswald with a rifle as frequently as possible, a shotgun was the same as a rifle. Marina's assertions that Oswald practiced with the Carcano are rendered invalid by her earlier statements that Oswald never practiced. Even if the one incident she finally conceded was true, Oswald would have had a total of

244   PRESUMED GUILTY

64 minutes to practice (26H61). The DeMohren-schildts' description of Oswald's target shooting at leaves in the park warrants no serious consideration. As Marina admitted to the Commission, she did not know what Oswald did with the rifle when he sat with it on the porch of their New Orleans home (if he ever did this at all, as Marina originally denied).

Taking the issue further than did the Commission, we can be reasonably certain that Oswald engaged in *no* rifle practice in New Orleans during the summer of 1963 or in Dallas up until the time of the assassination.

If Marina was consistent in any of her statements, it was her denial that Oswald practiced with the rifle in New Orleans. While she recalled no such incident, she felt that Oswald could not have practiced without telling her.

> because as a rule he stayed home when he was not working. When he did go out, she did not see him take the rifle. (22H778)

Marina told this to the FBI on December 16, 1963. She stuck to this story before the Commission, saying she knew "for sure" Oswald did not practice in New Orleans (1H21).

More reliable information relating to possible New Orleans practice comes from Adrian Alba, a New Orleans garage owner who spoke with Oswald about rifles during the summer of 1963. On November 25, 1963, Alba told the FBI that

> he knew of no rifle practice which OSWALD had engaged in while in New Orleans, adding that from his conversation with OSWALD he did not believe that OSWALD belonged to any of the local gun clubs. He added that it would have been almost impossible for OSWALD to prac-

tice with a rifle around New Orleans unless he belonged
to a gun club. (CD7:203)

Alba repeated this information in his deposition before
staff member Liebeler. He explained why Oswald could
not have practiced in New Orleans unless he belonged
to a gun club (which he did not). According to Alba, if
someone attempted to practice in the only possible reg-
ions other than the clubs, "they would either run you
off or arrest you for discharging firearms" (10H224).

There is no credible evidence in any form to indicate
that Oswald practiced with his rifle after moving back
to Dallas from New Orleans in October 1963. If the
rifle was stored in the Paine garage as the Commission
asserts (though proof of this is lacking), then the possibility that Oswald could have taken the rifle for practice is virtually nil. Likewise, Marina was emphatic
that Oswald never practiced during the time she lived
with the Paines. For what little reliance, if any, can be
put in her testimony, I quote her relevant words:

> he couldn't have practiced while we were at the Paine's,
> because Ruth was there. But whenever she was not at
> home, he tried to spend as much time as he could with
> me—he would watch television in the house. (1H53)

There is no evidence indicating that the rifle was in
Oswald's possession during this period. The woman
who cleaned his small room on North Beckley never
saw it there, although she did not go into the drawers
of the "little wooden commode or closet" in the room
(6H440-441). While several witnesses thought they had
seen Oswald practicing at a rifle range in Dallas
throughout September to November 1963, the evidence
strongly indicates that the man observed neither was
nor *could* have been Oswald, as the Report admits

(R318-30). Various FBI and Secret Service checks failed to turn up any evidence of rifle practice by Oswald in the Dallas area (see CEs 2694, 2908, 3049).

And this was Oswald the marksman—from the time he received his first weapons training in the Marines, where he went from a fairly good to a rather poor shot, to his few hunting trips with Robert Oswald, where he manifested his lack of skill with a rifle, to his presumed hunting in the Soviet Union with other than a rifle but the same absence of any proficiency, to the time of his assumed possession of the rifle, when no credible evidence indicated that he ever engaged in practice.

This obviously was not the caliber of shooter defined by expert Simmons as necessary to have pulled off the assassination alone. The presumed lone assassin, according to Simmons, had to have "considerable experience" in his background, especially "considerable experience with" the Carcano, and had to be "a proficient man with this weapon." Oswald was none of these. The only reliable evidence now known demonstrates that he was simply a poor shot who never did a thing to improve his capability.

As we have seen, the Commission consistently misrepresented the evidence relevant to Oswald's rifle capability. In its conclusion to this section of the Report, it retained its propensity for conjuring up what it wanted without regard to evidence. It concluded this:

> Oswald's Marine training in marksmanship, his other rifle experience and his established familiarity with this particular weapon show that he possessed ample capability to commit the assassination. (R195)

The Commission, in essence, told the public that "rather poor shot" Oswald did what shooters in the

NRA Master classification, the highest rating, could not do. It must have caused great concern among those who spend hours of concentrated practice each day trying to maintain proficiency with a rifle to learn that Oswald outdid the best and "established familiarity" with his rifle by *never* practicing, probably never even playing with his rifle!

Oswald did not have the capability to fire the assassination shots as the official theory proclaims. That he was a competent marksman is a pure myth created by the Commission in flagrant disregard of the evidence.

Conclusion

It is appropriate now to pull together the major points that have been raised throughout this discussion.

In Part I we saw that, from the time Oswald was in the hands of the authorities, he was presumed guilty. The Dallas Police wasted no time in announcing their verdict. Of course, it is preposterous to assume that even the most competent police force could have solved one of the century's most complex crimes overnight. Yet this was precisely the claim made by the Dallas police when, on the day after the assassination, they told the world that Oswald was beyond doubt the lone assassin.

Two weeks later the FBI claimed that it too had conclusively determined that Oswald was the lone assassin. This was indeed an unwarranted conclusion since, in its "solution" of the crime, the FBI failed to account for one of the President's wounds. The FBI seems never to have anticipated that concerned citizens would probe its thoroughly flawed report. It made sure that everyone knew the conclusion reached in the report by leaking to the press everything it wanted known. The report itself, however, the FBI decided to keep secret.

The Warren Commission claimed that it presumed neither Oswald's innocence nor his guilt, that it was merely searching for the facts and not building a prosecution case. The final Report and the once-secret working papers of the Commission disprove these claims. The Commission, from the very beginning of its investigation, planned its work under the presumption that Oswald was guilty, and the staff consciously endeavored to construct a prosecution case against Oswald. One Commission member actually complained to the staff that he wanted to see more arguments in support of the theory that Oswald was the assassin. There could have been no more candid an admission of how fraudulent the "investigation" was than when a staff lawyer secretly wrote, "Our intention is not to establish the point with complete accuracy, but merely to substantitate the hypothesis which underlies the conclusions that Oswald was the sole assassin." In its zeal to posthumously frame Oswald—and falsify history —the staff often considered ludicrous methods of avoiding the facts—as in the suggestion of one staff lawyer that "the best evidence that Oswald could fire as fast as he did and hit the target is the fact that he did so."

At the very least, the discussion of the medical evidence demonstrates that that evidence establishes *no* connection between Oswald and the crime. In reality, the medical evidence disassociates Oswald's rifle from the wounds suffered by President Kennedy and Governor Connally. The nature of the bullet fragmentation within the President's wounds rules out full-jacketed military bullets such as those allegedly fired by Oswald. Bullet 399, discovered at Parkland Hospital and traced to Oswald's rifle, could *not,* in any conceivable way, have produced any of the President's wounds. Likewise, 399 could not have produced the Governor's wounds without having suffered some form of multilation; bullets simply do not smash through two or three bones and emerge in the condition of 399, with no apparent distortions and no disruption of their microscopic markings.

The medical evidence leads one to believe that Oswald's rifle played no role in the shooting and that all of the evidence that seems to link Oswald to the shooting was in fact planted. The only evidence that could conclusively show whether bullet 399 and the two bullet fragments traced to Oswald's rifle were actually involved in the wounding of either victim is the spectrographic analyses, and they are withheld from the public. One need not be an expert analyst to deduce that the government would hardly suppress this evidence if it corroborated its account of the assassination. The only credible explanation for the suppression of the spectrographic analyses is that they must establish conclusively what the medical evidence establishes to but a reasonable degree—that Oswald's rifle played no role in the shooting.

The evidence of the rifle, the cartridge cases, and the bullets is significant because it creates the powerful assumption that Oswald was the assassin. The medical evidence, in disassociating Oswald's rifle from the crime, makes it apparent that unknown persons deliberately planted the recovered ballistics items with the intention of leaving evidence that would point to Oswald as the murderer. However, once it is established that Oswald's rifle was not involved in the shooting, there is not a shred of tangible or credible evidence to

indicate that Oswald was the assassin. The evidence
proves exactly the opposite.

In my examination of the circumstantial evidence relating to Oswald himself, the implications have crystal-
lized. It has been documented that, through its staff
and its Report, the Commission:

1. Drew undue suspicion to Oswald's return to Irving
on November 21, although the evidence indicated Oswald did not know the motorcade route and broke no
set pattern in making the return;

2. Ignored *all* evidence that could have provided an
innocent excuse for Oswald's visit;

3. Wrongly discredited the reliable and consistent
testimony of the only two witnesses who saw the package Oswald carried to work on the morning of the assassination; because their descriptions meant that the
package could *not* have contained the rifle, the Commission claimed to have made this rejection on the
basis of "scientific evidence," which did not exist;

4. Concluded that Oswald made a paper sack to conceal the rifle, citing no evidence in support of this notion and suppressing the information that disproved it;

5. Concluded that the sack was used to transport the
rifle, although its evidence proved that the sack never
contained the rifle;

6. Used the testimony of Charles Givens to place
Oswald at the alleged source of the shots *35 minutes
too early,* even though Givens described an event that
physically could not have taken place;

7. Claimed to know of no Depository employee who
saw Oswald between 11:35 and 12:30, basing its claim
on an inquiry in which it (through General Counsel
Rankin) had the FBI determine whether any employee had seen Oswald *only* at 12:30, completely sup-

pressing from the Report three distinct pieces of evidence indicating Oswald's presence on the first floor during the period in question.

8. Had no witness who could identify the sixth-floor gunman as Oswald; both rejected *and* accepted the identification of one man who admitted lying to the police, who constantly contradicted himself, and who described physically impossible events; and ignored evidence of clothing descriptions that might have indicated that Oswald was *not* the gunman;

9. Reconstructed the movements of Baker and Truly in such a way as to lengthen the time of their ascent to the second floor;

10. Reconstructed the movements of the "assassin" so as greatly to reduce the time of his presumed descent; a valid reconstruction would have proved that a sixth-floor gunman could *not* have reached the second-floor lunchroom before Baker and Truly;

11. Misrepresented Baker's position at the time he saw Oswald entering the lunchroom, making it seem possible that Oswald could have just descended from the third floor, although, in fact, the events described by Baker and Truly prove that Oswald must have been coming *up* from the *first* floor (as Oswald himself told the police he did);

12. Misrepresented the nature of the assassination shots by omitting from its evaluation, the time factor and other physical obstacles, thus making it seem that the shots were easy and that Oswald could have fired them;

13. Misrepresented the evidence relevant to Oswald's rifle capability and practice, creating the impression that he was a good shot with much practice, although the evidence indicated exactly the opposite.

The conclusion dictated by all this evidence en masse is inescapable and overwhelming: Lee Harvey Oswald never fired a shot at President Kennedy; he was not even at the Depository window during the assassination; and no one fired his rifle, the Mannlicher-Carcano, on that day. Beyond any doubt, he is innocent of the monstrous crime with which he was charged and of which he was presumed guilty. The official presumption of his guilt effectively cut off any quest for truth and led to the abandonment of the principles of law and honest investigation. At *all* costs, the government has denied (and, to judge from its record, will continue to deny) Oswald's innocence and perpetuated the myth of his lone guilt.

With this, a thousand other spiders emerge from the walls.

It can now be inferred that Oswald was framed; he was deliberately set up as the Kennedy assassin. His rifle was found in the Depository. We know that it had to have been put there; we also knew that it was not Oswald who put it there. *Someone else did.*

We know that a whole bullet traceable to Oswald's rifle turned up at Parkland Hospital; we also know that this bullet was never in the body of either victim. *Someone had to have planted it at the hospital.* The same applies to the two identifiable fragments found in the front seat of the President's limousine.

We know that someone shot and killed President Kennedy; we also know that Oswald did not do this. Thus the real presidential murderers have escaped punishment through our established judicial channels, their crime tacitly sanctioned by those who endeavored to prove Oswald guilty. The after-the-fact framing of Oswald by the federal authorities means, in effect, that the federal government has conspired to protect those who conspired to kill President Kennedy.

It is not my responsibility to explain why the Commission did what it did, and I would deceive the reader if I made the slightest pretense that it was within my capability to provide such an explanation. I have presented the facts; no explanation of motives, be they the highest and the purest or the lowest and the most corrupt, will alter those facts or undo what the Commission indisputably has done. If anyone has the responsibility for explaining why Oswald was presumed guilty and why presidential assassins were tacitly exculpated, it is the Commission members and the staff themselves.

Whatever new platitudes the accessories after the fact may concoct to portray themselves as honest and decent men, the implications of their actions remain. One implication is particularly obvious and threatening: the federal government has sacrificed its credibility. A government that lies without restraint about the death of its chief executive can not be believed on anything.

A government that exculpates presidential assassins and denies an accused man his every right can not be trusted to protect its presidents or the rights of its citizens. With democratic government, if the president and the rights of the people are not safe, then all of society is threatened. Government that denies its people the true story of their president's murder undercuts, if it does not prevent, the working of democracy.

Remedies are not clearly apparent or easily suggested. First and foremost, the people must recognize they have been lied to by their government and denied the truth about the murder of their former leader.

They must demand the truth, whatever the price, and insist that their government work honestly and properly.

Until then, the history of one of the world's most democratic nations must suffer the stigma of a frighteningly immoral and undemocratic act by its government.

Appendix A

Tentative Outline of the Work of the
President's Commission

Author's note: This "Tentative Outline" was attached to a "Progress Report" dated January 11, 1964, from Commission Chairman Earl Warren to the other Commission members, and reveals the extent to which the Commission's conclusions were formulated prior to its investigation.

I. *Assassination of President Kennedy on November 22, 1963 in Dallas*

    A. Trip to Texas—Prior to Assassination
        1. Initial plans for trip
            a. relevent dates
            b. itinerary
            c. companions
            d. motorcade to luncheon
            e. other
        2. Events of morning of November 22
            a. arrival at airport—time, etc.
            b. motorcade—crowds, time, etc.

B. Assassination (based on all available statements of witnesses, films, photographs, etc.)
  1. Shots
    a. number of shots fired
    b. time elapsed during shots
    c. direction of shots
    d. location of car at time
  2. Postures and apparent injuries to President Kennedy and Governor Connally
    a. President Kennedy
    b. Governor Connally

C. Events Immediately Following the Shooting
  1. Treatment at hospital
  2. Activities of Dallas law enforcement
  3. Return of entourage to Washington
    a. President Johnson's trip to airport
    b. trip of Mrs. Kennedy with body of late President to airport
    c. swearing-in
  4. Removal of President Kennedy's body to Bethesda Naval Hospital
  5. Removal of car to Washington—condition and repairs
D. Nature and Extent of Wounds Received by President Kennedy (based on examinations in Dallas and Bethesda)
  1. Number of individual wounds received by President Kennedy
  2. Cause of death
  3. Time of death
  4. Evaluation of medical treatment received in Dallas

II. *Lee Harvey Oswald as the Assassin of President Kennedy*
A. Brief Identification of Oswald (Dallas resident, employee of Texas School Book Depository, etc.)

B. Movements on November 22, 1963 Prior to Assassination
   1. Trip to work
      a. time
      b. package
      c. other significant facts, e.g. any conversations, etc.
   2. Entry into Depository
      a. time
      b. package
      c. other significant facts
   3. Activities during morning
      a. nature of his work
      b. location of his work
      c. other significant facts, e.g. any conversations, etc.
   4. Movements immediately prior to 12:29 P.M.

C. Movements after Assassination until Murder of Tippit
   1. Presence within building
      a. location
      b. time
      c. encounter with police
      d. other relevant facts
   2. Departure from building
      a. time
      b. direction of movement
      c. other relevant facts, e.g. crossing police line, etc.
   3. Boarding of bus
      a. time and place of boarding
      b. duration of ride
      c. other relevant facts, e.g. dress, appearance, conversations, etc.
   4. From bus to taxi
      a. time and place
      b. distance and route of cab

      c. time to destination

      d. other relevant facts obtained from cab driver or other witnesses or sources

  5. Arrival at rooming house

      a. time

      b. actions within rooming house

      c. departure and direction

  6. Route until encounter with Tippit

      a. time

      b. distance

D. Murder of Tippit

  1. Encounter of Oswald and Tippit

      a. time

      b. location

  2. Evidence demonstrating Oswald's guilt

      a. eyewitness reports

      b. murder weapon

      c. autopsy and ballistics reports

      d. paraffin tests

      e. other, e.g. statements (if any)

E. Flight and Apprehension in Texas Theater

  1. Movement until entry into theater

      a. time

      b. actions, e.g. reloading weapon

      c. other relevant facts, e.g. recovery of jacket

  2. Apprehension in theater

      a. movements of Oswald in theater

      b. notification and arrival of police

      c. arrest of Oswald

      d. removal to station

F. Oswald at Dallas Police Station

  1. Interrogation

      a. time, manner and number of interrogation
         sessions
      b. persons present
      c. persons responsible
      d. results
   2. Other investigation by Dallas police
      a. line-ups and eyewitness identification
      b. seizure of Oswald's papers
      c. other
   3. Denials and other statements by Oswald
   4. Removal to County Jail on November 24,
      1963
   5. Killing of Oswald by Ruby

G. Evidence Identifying Oswald as the Assassin of President
   Kennedy
   1. Room of Texas School Book Depository
      identified as source of shots
      a. eyewitness reports
      b. trajectory of shots
      c. evidence on scene after assassination
      d. other
   2. Oswald placed in Depository (and specific room?)
      a. eyewitness reports
      b. fingerprints on objects in room
      c. facts reviewed above
   3. Assassination weapon identified as Oswald's
      a. discovery of rifle and shells
      b. obtaining and possession of gun by Os-
         wald
      c. whereabouts of gun on November 21 and
         November 22
      d. prints on rifle
      e. photographs of Oswald and rifle
      f. General Walker ballistic report.

   4. Other physical evidence
      a. clothing tests
      b. paraffin tests
   5. Prior similar acts
      a. General Walker attack
      b. General Eisenhower threat
   6. Permissible inferences from Oswald's:
      a. flight from Depository
      b. statements on bus
      c. murder of Tippit

H. Evidence Implicating Others in Assassination or Suggesting Accomplices
   1. Evidence of shots other than from Depos-
      itory?
   2. Feasibility of shots within time span and
      with use of telescope
   3. Evidence re other persons involved in actual
      shooting from Depository
   4. Analysis of all movements of Oswald after
      assassination for attempt to meet associates
   5. Refutation of allegations

III. *Lee Harvey Oswald: Background and Possible Motive*
A. Birth and Pre-school Days
   1. Family structure (death of father; statements
      of persons who knew family; interviews of
      mother, brother, and members of family)
   2. Where family lived (statements as to child-
      hood character of Oswald from neighbors
      who recall family and child)
   3. Standard of living of family (document fac-
      tors which would have bearing upon develop-
      would have bearing upon development)

B. Education

1. Schools (reports from each school attended regarding demeanor, grades, development, attitude to fellow students, activities, problems, possible aptitude for languages, sex life, etc.)
2. Reports of fellow students, associates, friends, enemies at each school attended
3. Reports from various neighbors where Oswald lived while attending various schools
4. Special report from juvenile authorities in New York City concerning Oswald.

   a. report of case worker on Oswald and family

   b. psychiatrist who examined him, treatment and results, opinion as to future development

C. Military Service
   1. Facts regarding entry into service, assignments, stations, etc. until discharge
   2. Reports of personnel from each station regarding demeanor, character, competence, activities, sex life, financial status, attitude, etc.
   3. Report on all activities while in Japan
   4. Report and document study of Russian language
      a. where and when
      b. books used
      c. instruction or self-taught
      d. any indication of degree of accomplishment

Appendix B

Memorandum to J. Lee Rankin
from David W. Belin

Author's note: This memorandum by staff lawyer Belin speaks for itself. A month later, on February 25, 1964, Belin wrote in another memorandum, "At no time have we assumed that Lee Harvey Oswald was the assassin of President Kennedy." See chapter 2.

MEMORANDUM   January 30, 1964
TO: J. Lee Rankin
FROM: David W. Belin
SUBJECT: Oswald's knowledge that Connally would be in the Presidential car and his intended target.

According to the Secret Service Report, Document No. 3, page 11, the route of the motorcade was released on the evening of November 18 and appeared in Dallas newspapers on November 19 as shown in Exhibits 6D and 6E (Document No. 3 is the December 18 Secret Service Report).

In examining these exhibits, although the general route of the motorcade is shown, there is nothing that shows that Governor Connally would be riding in the Presidential car.

In determining the accuracy of Oswald, we have three major possibilities: Oswald was shooting at Connally and missed two of the three shots, the two misses striking Kennedy; Oswald was shooting at both Kennedy and Connally and all three shots struck their intended targets; Oswald was shooting only at Kennedy and the second bullet missed its intended target and hit Connally instead.

If there was no mass media coverage that Connally would be riding in the Presidential car, it would tend to confirm the third alternative that Kennedy was the only intended target. This in turn bears on the motive of the assassination and also on the degree of markmanship required, which in turn affects the determination that Oswald was the assassin and that it was not too difficult to hit the intended target two out of the three times in this particular situation.

In any event, I believe it would be most helpful to have the FBI investigate all newspaper, television and radio reports from November 18 to November 22 in Dallas to ascertain whether or not in any of these reports there was a public announcement that Connally would be riding in the Presidential car. If such public announcement was made, we should know specifically over what media and when.

Of course, there is another element of timing: If Connally's position in the motorcade was not released until the afternoon of November 21, then when Oswald went home to get the weapon, he would not have necessarily intended Connally as the target.

Finally, we would like to know whether or not there was any release to the public news media that Connally would ride in any car in the motorcade, regardless of whether or not it was the Presidential car.

Thank you.

Appendix C

Memorandum to J. Lee Rankin
from Norman Redlich

Author's note: This is one of many similar outlines of the Warren Report, drafted long before the Commission's "investigation" ended, and before virtually all of the relevant testimony was taken. It proves that the Commission worked to substantiate a preconceived conclusion naming Oswald as the sole assassin.

MEMORANDUM   March 26, 1964
TO: J. Lee Rankin
FROM: Norman Redlich
SUBJECT: Proposed Outline of Report

I attach a proposed outline of our final report. This plan envisages a main report and supplementary materials to be published as one volume. This will be followed by appendixes to be published when prepared. These appendixes will contain the supporting material for the report such as the transcript of testimony, important underlying investigatory material, and photos of important exhibits not published with the original report.

I have listed the staff members who I feel should have responsibility for the particular sections of the report. Although I have assigned small sections of the report to Mr. Williams, Mr. Eisenberg, and myself, the major responsibility lies with other members of the staff. I am assuming that Mr.

Williams as your Administrative Assistant, and I as your
Special Assistant, together with Mr. Eisenberg, will have
responsibility for review, editing, avoidance of duplication,
and other technical details of putting a report into publish-
able condition.

With your permission, I would like to distribute this
outline to the staff.

PROPOSED OUTLINE OF REPORT
(Submitted by Mr. Redlich)

I.   Statement of Objectives and Standards (Mr. Rankin)
     (The Report should start with a brief statement setting
     forth the Commission's view of its objectives and
     standards used to achieve them. It is important to clarify
     the Commission's position as a fact-finding body and to
     indicate wherein our findings differ from a judicial
     determination of criminal guilt.)

II. Brief Summary of Major Conclusions (Redlich and
     Willens)
     (The purpose of this section is to provide the reader with
     a short statement of our major conclusions without
     having to read through the entire document.)
     A. Basic Facts Concerning Assassination of President
         Kennedy and Shooting of Governor Connally
     B. Identity of the Assassin
     C. Conclusions Concerning Accomplices
     D. Conclusions Concerning Motive
     E. Ruby's Killing of Oswald and Conclusion as to
         Possible Link to Assassination
III. The Assassination — Basic Facts (Adams and Specter)
     A. Physical Setting
         1. Description of Motorcade
         2. Description of Area where Shooting Occurred

B. Shooting
   1. Number of Shots
   2. Medical Effect of Each Shot
   3. Point from which Shots Fired
   4. Statistical Data
      a. Elapsed time of shooting
      b. Distance travelled by Presidential car
      c. Speed of car
      d. Distance travelled by each bullet
   5. Events Immediately following Shooting
      a. Reaction of Secret Service
      b. Trip to Parkland
      c. Events in Parkland
      d. Trip to Love Field
      e. Return to Washington

IV. Lee H. Oswald as the Assassin (Ball and Belin)
(This section should state the facts which lead to the conclusion that Oswald pulled the trigger and should also indicate the elements in the case which have either not been proven or are based on doubtful testimony. Each of the factors listed below should be reviewed in that light.)
A. Identification of Rifle as Murder Weapon
B. Oswald's Ownership of Weapon
C. Evidence of Oswald Carrying Weapon to Building
   1. Fake Curtain Rod Stroy
   2. Buell Frazier's Story
   3. Possible Presence in Paine's Garage on Evening of November 21, 1963
D. Evidence of Oswald on Sixth Floor
   1. Palm Prints on Carton
   2. Paper Bag with Oswald Print
E. Eyewitness Testimony
F. Oswald After Assassination — Actions in Building
G. Oswald After Assassination — Actions up to Tippit Shooting

H. Shooting of Tippit and Arrest in Theatre
    1. Eyewitnesses
    2. Gun as Murder Weapon
    3. Oswald's Ownership of Gun
I. Statements After Arrest
J. Prior Actions
    1. Walker Shooting
    2. Possible Nixon Attempt
    3. Practice with Rifle
K. Evidence of any Accomplices in Assassination
L. Appraisal of Oswald's Actions on November 21 and 22 in Light of Assassination
    (This will be a difficult section, but I feel we must face up to the various paradoxical aspects of Oswald's behavior in light of his being the assassin. I suggest the following items for consideration.)
    1. Did He Have a Planned Escape?
    2. Why did he pass up the Opportunity to get money on November 21 when he returned to Irving?
    3. Discussion with Marina about getting apartment in Dallas
    4. Asking fellow employee, on morning of November 22, which way the President was coming.
V. Possible Motive (Jenner, Liebeler, Coleman, Slawson)
    A. Brief Biographical Sketch of Oswald (Fuller Biography in Supplement)
    B. Any Personal Animosity Toward Kennedy or Connally
    C. Do his Political Beliefs Furnish Motive
    D. Link to Domestic Left-Wing Groups
        1. Fair Play for Cuba
        2. Communist Party
        3. Conclusions to be Drawn from such Links
    E. Link to Right-Wing Groups
    F. Possible Agent of Foreign Power
    G. Possible Link to Underworld

VI. Killing of Oswald by Ruby (Hubert and Griffin)
   A. Facts of the Killing
      1. Actions of Ruby starting with November 22
      2. Description of Events on November 24
   B. Discussion of Possible Link with Assassination of President Kennedy
   C. Other Possible Motives
      1. Brief Biographical Sketch (Fuller Sketch in Supplement)
      2. Ruby as Self-styled Patriot, Hero, Important Man
      3. Possibility of Ruby being Mentally Ill

SUPPLEMENT TO BE PUBLISHED WITH REPORT
   A. Visual Aids To Help Explain Main Body of Report (All Staff Members Concerned)
   B. Organization and Methods of Commission (Willens)
   C. Security Precautions to Protect Life of President (Stern)
      1. What Was Done on This Trip
      2. Broader Recommendations in This Area
      (I recognize that this area has been the subject of extended discussion and it might be desirable to move this section to the main body of the Report)
   D. Detailed Facts About President's Trip up to Assassination (Adams, Specter, Stern)
   E. Biography of Oswald (Jenner, Liebeler, Coleman, Slawson)
   F. Biography of Ruby (Hubert and Griffin)
   G. Oswald Relationship with U.S. Government Agencies (Redlich, Stern, Coleman, Slawson)
   H. Discussion of Widely Circulated Theories (Redlich and Eisenberg)
   I. Other Important Documents We May Wish to Publish as Part of Supplement, I suggest the following:

1. Autopsy Reports
2. Summary of Testimony of Experts on Physical Evidence (Eisenberg)
3. Charts and Other Data Presented by Experts (Eisenberg)
4. Reports of Medical Examination on Governor Connally
5. Report of FBI and Secret Service on Location of President's car at Time of Shots (Redlich and Eisenberg)

Appendix D

A Later Memorandum to J. Lee Rankin
from Norman Redlich

Author's note: This memorandum by staff lawyer Redlich explicitly states that the object of the investigation was not to determine the truth as far as it could be known, but rather to substantiate a preconceived conclusion.

MEMORANDUM   April 27, 1964
TO: J. Lee Rankin
FROM: Norman Redlich

The purpose of this memorandum is to explain the reasons why certain members of the staff feel that it is important to take certain on-site photographs in connection with the location of the approximate points at which the three bullets struck the occupants of the Presidential limousine.

Our report presumably will state that the President was hit by the first bullet, Governor Connally by the second, and the President by the third and fatal bullet. The report will also conclude that the bullets were fired by one person located in the sixth floor southeast corner window of the TSBD building.

As our investigation now stands, however, we have not shown that these events could possibly have occurred in the manner suggested above. All we have is a reasonable hypothesis which appears to be supported by the medical testimony but which has not been checked out against the physical facts at the scene of the assassination.

271

Our examination of the Zapruder films shows that the fatal third shot struck the President at a point which we can locate with reasonable accuracy on the ground. We can do this because we know the exact frame (no. 313) in the film at which the third shot hit the President and we know the location of the photographer. By lining up fixed objects in the movie fram where this shot occurs we feel that we have determined the approximate location of this shot. This can be verified by a photo of the same spot from the point were Zapruder was standing.

We have the testimony of Governor and Mrs. Connally that the Governor was hit with the second bullet at a point which we probably cannot fix with precision. We feel we have established, however, with the help of medical testimony, that the shot which hit the Governor did not come *after* frame 240 on the Zapruder film. The Governor feels that it came around 230 which is certainly consistent with our observations of the film and with the doctor's testimony. Since the President was shot at frame 313, this would leave a time of at least 4 seconds between two shots, certainly ample for even an inexperienced marksman.

Prior to our last viewing of the films with Governor Connally we had assumed that the President was hit while he was concealed behind the sign which occurs between frames 215 to 225. We have expert testimony to the effect that a skilled marksman would require a minimum of time of 2¼ seconds between shots with this rifle. Since the camera operates at 18 1/3 frames per second, there would have to be a minimum of 40 frames between shots. It is apparent therefore, that if Governor Connally was hit even as late as frame 240, the President would have to have been hit no later than frame 190 and probably even earlier.

We have not yet examined the assassination scene to determine whether the assassin in fact could have shot the President prior to frame 190. We could locate the position on the ground which corresponds to this frame and it would then be our intent to establish by photography that the assassin could have fired the first shot at the President prior to this point. Our intention is not to establish the point with complete accuracy, but merely to substantiate the hypothesis which underlies the conclusions that Oswald was the sole assassin.

I had always assumed that our final report would be accompanied by a surveyor's diagram which would indicate the appropriate location of the three shots. We certainly cannot prepare such a diagram without establishing that we are describing an occurrence which is physically possible. Our failure to do this will, in my opinion, place this Report in jeopardy since it is a certainty that others will examine the Zapruder films and raise the same questions which have been raised by our examination of the films. If we do not attempt to answer these questions with observable facts, others may answer them with facts which challenge our most basic assumptions, or with fanciful theories based on our unwillingness to test our assumptions by the investigatory methods available to us.

I should add that the facts which we now have in our possession, submitted to us in separate reports from the FBI and Secret Service, are totally incorrect and, if left uncorrected, will present a completely misleading picture.

It may well be that this project should be undertaken by the FBI and Secret Service with our assistance instead of being done as a staff project. The important thing is that the project be undertaken expeditiously.

Appendix E

Report of the FBI's First
Interview with Charles Givens

Author's note: This is the actual report of the FBI's first interview with Charles Givens. Givens is reported as saying nothing about the alleged encounter with Oswald on the sixth floor that he was to describe to the Commission much later. Rather, he is reported to have told the FBI on the day of the assassination that he saw Oswald on the first floor at the same time he later told the Commission he saw Oswald on the sixth floor. This FBI report was not published by the Commission or mentioned in the Warren Report.

FEDERAL BUREAU OF INVESTIGATION

Date   11/23/63

CHARLES DOUGLAS GIVENS, 2511 Cochran Street, advised he was employed by the Texas School Book Depository, Houston and Elm Street, from October 1, 1963, to present time. GIVENS said he has worked at this same position as a wrapper on several occasions prior to this employment.

On November 22, 1963, GIVENS worked on the sixth floor of the building until about 11:30 A.M. when he used the elevator to travel to the first floor where he used the restroom at about 11:35 A.M. or 11:40 A.M. GIVENS then walked around on the first floor until 12 o'clock noon, at which time he walked onto the sidewalk and stood for several minutes, then walked to the Classified Parking Lot at Elm and Records Street. GIVENS then walked to Main Street to watch the parade and after the President and the group had passed, he walked back to the parking lot, at which time he heard several shots fired from the direction of the building at which he is employed. He attempted to return to work but was told that he had been released for the balance of the day.

GIVENS advised that a white male, known as LEE, was employed in the same building and worked as a wrapper or order filler. He said he saw this same person's picture on television on the afternoon of November 22, 1963, who was supposed to have been the person being investigated for the shooting of the President. LEE worked on all floors of the building, and on November 22, 1963, GIVENS recalls observing LEE working on the fifth floor during the morning filling orders. LEE was standing by the elevator in the building at 11:30 A.M. when GIVENS went to the first floor. When he started down in the elevator, LEE yelled at him to close the gates on the elevator so that he (LEE) could have the elevator returned to the sixth floor. GIVENS said that during the past few days LEE had commented that he rode to work with a boy named WESLEY.

GIVENS said all employees enter the back door of the building when JACK DOUGHERTY, the foreman opens the door at about 7 A.M. On the morning of November 22, 1963, GIVENS observed LEE reading a newspaper in the domino room where the employees eat lunch about 11:50 A.M.

_____

on ___11/22/63___ at ___Dallas, Texas___ File # __DL 89-43__

by Special Agent ___WILL HAYDEN GRIFFEN and___
___BARDWELL D. ODUM (HM)___

Date dictated   __11/23/63__

Appendix F

FBI Report on Mrs. R. E. Arnold

Author's note: The Warren Commission stated in its Report that it knew of no Book Depository employee who claimed to have seen Oswald between 11:55 and 12:30 on the day of the assassination. This was false, as this FBI report from the Commission's files reveals. The Warren Report never mentions Mrs. Arnold and this FBI document was omitted from the Commission's published evidence.

FEDERAL BUREAU OF INVESTIGATION

Date   11/26/63

Mrs. R. E. ARNOLD, Secretary, Texas School Book Depository, advised she was in her office on the second floor of the building on November 22, 1963, and left that office between 12:00 and 12:15 PM, to go downstairs and stand in front of the building to view the Presidential Motorcade. As she was standing in front of the building, she stated she thought she caught a fleeting glimpse of LEE HARVEY OSWALD standing in the hallway between the front door and the double doors leading to the warehouse, located on the first floor. She could not be sure that this was OSWALD, but said she felt it was and believed the time to be a few minutes before 12:15 PM.

She stated thereafter she viewed the Presidential Motorcade and heard the shots that were fired at the President; however, she could furnish no information of value as to the individual firing the shots or any other information concern-

276

ing OSWALD, whom she stated she did not know and had
merely seen him working in the building.

---

on __11/26/63__   at __Dallas, Texas__   File # __DL 89-43__

by Special Agent __RICHARD E. HARRISON /rmb__

Date dictated   __11/26/63__

Notes

Introduction

1. *E.g.,* see Rose De Wolf, "Four Children With Problem Parents," *Philadelphia Evening Bulletin,* May 19, 1972, p. 3; Boyce Rensberger, "Bremer's Way of Life Likened to Three Assassins," *New York Times,* May 21, 1972, p. 1; Harriet Van Horne, "Profile Shows Assassins Are Loners," *Philadelphia Inquirer,* June 4, 1972.

2. *New York Times,* March 19, 1967.

3. Harold Weisberg, *Frame-Up: The King/Ray Case* (New York: Outerbridge and Dienstfrey, 1971), chapt. 9.

4. See *e.g., New York Times,* March 11, 1969, p. 46.

5. The loose ends, contradictions, and indications of conspiracy in the Ray case were brought out by Harold Weisberg in *Frame-Up.*

6. Robert Blair Kaiser provides several grounds for challenging the official version of how Sirhan came to kill Robert Kennedy in *RFK Must Die* (New York: E. P. Dutton, 1970).

7. A Los Angeles County grand jury investigated the question of evidence tampering involving ballistics aspects of the case. The grand jury, which convened on August 16, 1971, "severely criticized the county clerk's office in its handling of evidence in the assassination of Sen. Robert F. Kennedy." (See *Los Angeles Times,* August 25, 1971, p. 1.) Two months later the Los Angeles county District Attorney said that an inquiry by his office had cleared a police criminologist of improperly handling evidence, but he agreed with the grand jury that the county clerk was guilty of "lax handling" of the evidence. (See *New York Times,* October 19, 1971.)

8. Broadcast by Group W commentator Rod MacLiesh, at approximately 6:33 P.M. on KYW News Radio, in Philadelphia.

9. *E.g.,* see Anthony Lewis's coverage of the Warren Report and editorial comment by James Reston, *New York Times,* September 28, 1964; *Washington Post* coverage of the same date, including praise by Robert Donovan, p. A14, Roscoe Drummond, p. A13, Marquis Childs, and an editorial saying the Report "deserves acceptance as the whole truth, and nothing but the truth"; a favorable editorial in the *Washington Evening Star,*

278

September 28, 1964, p. A-8; *Time* (October 2, 1964) and *Newsweek* (October 5, 1964) carried lenthy "news" features praising the Report.

10. Josiah Thompson, *Six Seconds in Dallas* (New York; Bernard Geis Associates, 1967), p. ix.

11. *E.g.*, see *Life*, November 25, 1966, pp. 38-48; *Ramparts*, October 1966, p. 3; *Saturday Evening Post*, January 14, 1967, and December 2, 1967, p. 88.

12. In May 1967 a Harris Survey revealed that 66 percent of the American public believed that the assassination was not the work of one man but was part of a broader plot.

13. *CBS News Inquiry: "The Warren Report"*, Parts I-IV, broadcast over CBS TV Network, June 25-28, 1967.

14. *Life*, November 25, 1966, p. 48.

15. *Philadelphia Inquirer*, November 25, 1966.

16. *Ibid.*, February 25, 1967.

17. *Washington Post*, February 23, 1967.

18. *Philadelphia Inquirer*, March 2, 1967.

19. *Ibid.*, March 2, 1969.

20. Harold Weisberg, *Whitewash: The Report on the Warren Report* (Hyattstown, Md.: Harold Weisberg, 1965), p. 189.

21. *Ibid.*

22. Sylvia Meagher, *Accessories After the Fact* (New York: The Bobbs-Merrill Co., Inc., 1967), p. xxiii.

23. *Ibid.*, p. 456.

24. The books by Weisberg are these: *Whitewash; Whitewash II: The FBI-Secret Service Coverup* (Hyattstown, Md.; Harold Weisberg, 1966); *Photographic Whitewash: Suppressed Kennedy Assassination Pictures* (Hyattstown, Md.: Harold Weisberg, 1967); *Oswald in New Orleans* (New York: Canyon Books, 1967); *Post Mortem I* and *Post Mortem III* (Frederick, Md.: Harold Weisberg, 1971). *Post Mortem* is a three-part copyrighted but unpublished study of the medical evidence.

25. Weisberg, *Whitewash*, p. ix.

26. *Ibid.*, p. 188.

27. Weisberg, *Whitewash II*, p. 7.

28. Weisberg, *Whitewash*, p. 189.

29. Weisberg, *Photographic Whitewash*, p. 137.

30. Mark Lane, *Rush to Judgement* (New York: Fawcett Publications, Inc., 1967), pp. 9-10.

31. *Ibid.*, p. 17.

32. *Ibid.*

33. *Ibid.*, p. 18.

34. *Ibid.*

35. Edward J. Epstein, *Inquest* (New York: Bantam Books, 1966), p. 1.

36. *Ibid.*, p. 2.

37. *Ibid.*, p. 125.

38. *Ibid.*

39. See Sylvia Meagher, p. xxxii; Josiah Thompson, p. viii.

40. Richard Popkin, *The Second Oswald* (New York: Avon Books, 1966), p. 12.

41. This quotation is from the blurb that appears on the back cover of Mr. Popkin's book.

42. Weisberg, *Whitewash*, pp. 137-54.

43. Popkin, p. 117.

44. *Philadelphia Inquirer,* May 29, 1972, p. 1.

1   Assassination: The Official Case

1. "Memorandum re Galley Proofs of Chapter IV of the Report," written on September 6, 1964, by Wesley J. Liebeler, p. 5. (Hereinafter referred to as Liebeler 9/6/64 Memorandum. This document is available from the National Archives.)

2. *Ibid.,* p. 7.

3. *Ibid.,* p. 20.

4. *Ibid.,* p. 21.

5. *Ibid.*

6. *Ibid.,* p. 22.

7. *Ibid.,* p. 21.

8. *Ibid.,* p. 23.

9. *Ibid.,* p. 25.

2   Presumed Guilty: The Official Disposition

1. *New York Times,* November 24, 1963, p. 1.

2. *Philadelphia Inquirer,* November 24, 1963.

3. *St. Louis Post-Dispatch,* November 24, 1963.

4. *New York Times,* November 25, 1963, p. 18.

5. *St. Louis Post-Dispatch,* November 24, 1963, p. 2.

6. Transcript of the December 5, 1963, Executive Session of the Warren Commission, pp. 10-11.

7. *Ibid.,* p. 8.

8. Letter from Nicholas Katzenbach to Chief Justice Warren, dated December 9, 1963. This letter is available from the National Archives.

9. *Washington Post,* December 1, 1963.

10. *Time,* December 13, 1963, p. 26.

11. *Newsweek,* December 16, 1963, p. 26.

12. *New York Times,* December 10, 1963, p. 1.

13. Transcript of the December 16, 1963, Executive Session of the Warren Commission, p. 11.

14. *Ibid.,* p. 12.

15. "Progress Report" by Chairman Warren, p. 4, attached to "Memorandum for Members of the Commission" from Mr. Rankin, dated January 11, 1964.

16. The "Tentative Outline of the Work of the President's Commission" was attached to the memorandum mentioned in note 15.

17. *Ibid.*

18. *Ibid.*

19. *Ibid.*

20. Transcript of the January 21, 1964, Executive Session of the Warren Commission, pp. 10-11.

21. Memorandum from W. David Slawson to Mr. Ball and Mr. Belin, dated January 27, 1964, "SUBJECT: Time of Rifle Shots," located in the "Slawson Chrono. File."

22. Memorandum from Arlen Specter to Mr. Rankin, dated January 30, 1964, concerning the questioning of Marina Oswald, p. 3.

23. "Memorandum to the Staff," from Mr. Rankin, dated January 13, 1964, p. 3.

24. "Memorandum" from David W. Belin to J. Lee Rankin, dated January 30, 1964. This document was discovered in the National Archives by Harold Weisberg and was first presented in *Post Mortem I,* pp. 61-62.

25. *Ibid.*

26. "Ball-Belin Report #1," dated February 25, 1964, p. 233.

27. *Ibid.,* pp. 1-2.

28. See   "Truth Was My Only Goal," by David Belin in *The Texas Observer,* August 13, 1971, p. 14.

29. "Memorandum" from Alfred Goldberg to J. Lee Rankin, dated "approx 3/14," 1964.

30. "Proposed Outline of Report," attached to the memorandum referred to in note 29. This outline was discovered in the National Archives by Harold Weisberg and is presented in *Post Mortem I,* p. 123.

31. "Proposed Outline of Report (Submitted by Mr. Redlich)," attached to "Memorandum" from Norman Redlich to J. Lee Rankin, dated March 26, 1964. This document was discovered in the National Archives by Harold Weisberg and is presented in *Post Mortem I,* p. 132.

32. "Memorandum" from Norman Redlich to J. Lee Rankin, dated April 27, 1964. This document was discovered in the National Archives by Harold Weisberg and is presented in *Post Mortem I,* pp. 132-34.

33. *Ibid.*

34. Transcript of the April 30, 1964, Executive Session of the Warren Commission, p. 5891.

35. Memorandum from Mr. Belin to Mr. Rankin, dated May 15, 1964, p. 5.

36. Liebeler 9/6/64 Memorandum, p. 25.

3   Suppressed Spectrography

1. See "Spectrography" in *Encyclopaedia Britannica* (Chicago: William Benton Publishers, 1963), vol. 21, and "Photography" in vol. 17; Herbert Dingle, *Practical Applications of Spectrum Analysis* (London: Chapman and Hall, Ltd., 1950), pp. 1-3, 74-75, 122-24.

2. A. Lucas, *Forensic Chemistry and Scientific Criminal Investigation* (New York: Longmans, Green and Co., 1935), pp. 265-66.

3. Author's interview with Dr. John Nichols on April 16, 1970. See also Nichols's statement in the *Dallas Morning News,* June 19, 1970.

4. *The Winchester-Western Ammunition Handbook* (New York: Pocket Books, Inc., 1964), p. 120. (Hereinafter referred to as "Winchester Handbook.")

5. First public attention drawn to the spectrographic analyses and their omission from the Commission's record was by Harold Weisberg in *Whitewash,* p. 164. Sylvia Meagher later discussed this topic in her book, pp. 170-72.

6. Transcript of court proceedings of February 21, 1969, in *State of Louisiana* v. *Clay L. Shaw,* p. 40. (Hereinafter referred to as "Frazier 2/21/69 testimony.")

7. *Ibid.,* p. 41.

8. Weisberg, *Oswald in New Orleans,* pp. 148-49.

9. Weisberg's attorney in this case, Bernard Fensterwald, requested that his client be furnished with the spectrographic analyses in a letter to Justice Department lawyer Joseph Cella, dated October 9, 1969. Then Deputy Attorney General Richard Kleindienst responded to this request in a letter dated November 13, 1969; he refused to disclose the document, (These letters are a part of the public record. They are part of the set of exhibits appended to the "COMPLAINT'" dated March 11, 1970, filed in U.S. District Court for the District of Columbia in the case of *Harold Weisberg* v. *U.S. Department of Justice and U.S. Department of State,* Civil Action No. 718-70.)

Weisberg has attempted to obtain the report of the spectrographer through a series of written requests dated May 23, 1966, March 12, 1967, January 1, 1969, June 2, 1969, April 6, 1970, May 15, 1970, and an official request form submitted on May 10, 1970. In a letter dated June 4, 1970, then Attorney General John Mitchell personally denied Weisberg's request for access. Richard Kleindienst, in a letter dated June 12, 1970, also denied Weisberg's request. (These letters are also a part of the public record. They are contained in the appendix to Appeal No. 71-1026, *Weisberg* v. *U.S. Department of Justice,* filed by attorney for plaintiff-appellant in the U.S. Court of Appeals for the District of Columbia Circuit.)

4   *The President's Wounds*

1. The best published discussions of the limitations of the medical evidence may be found in the following sources: Weisberg, *Whitewash,* chap. 13; Meagher, chap. 5; Cyril Wecht, "A Critique of President Kennedy's Autopsy," in Thompson, pp. 278-84.

The most definitive exposé of the medical evidence is contained in a three-part book by Weisberg called *Post Mortem.* This is a copyrighted study based on Weisberg's exhaustive research over a period of about eight years; however, it is not commercially published.

2. *Winchester Handbook,* p. 121, and A. Lucas, pp. 241-42.

3. Rowland H. Long, *The Physician and the Law* (New York, 1968), p. 239.

4. Author's interview with Dr. John Nichols on April 16, 1970.

5. Author's taped interview with Dr. Halpert Fillinger on January 14,

1970. (Hereinafter referred to as "Fillinger Interview.") See also Long, p. 239.

6. Report of the Ramsey Clark panel, p. 11.

7. R. Long, p. 231. This phenomenon is also described and illustrated in Thomas Gonzales, Milton Helpern, Morgan Vance, and Charles Umberger, *Legal Medicine, Pathology and Toxicology* (New York: Appleton-Century-Crofts, Inc., 1954), pp. 396 and 423.

8. LeMoyne Snyder, *Homicide Investigation* (Springfield, Mass., 1953), p. 132.

9. Fillinger Interview.

10. Clark Panel Report, pp. 10-11.

11. The lead used in most military projecticles is an alloy of antimony with small quantities of arsenic and bismuth added for hardening to resist expansion. See Lucas, pp. 241-42.

12. Fillinger Interview.

13. Clark Panel Report, p. 7.

14. *Ibid.*, p. 10.

15. Thompson, p. 110.

16. Fillinger Interview.

17. *Ibid.*

18. *Ibid.*

19. *Ibid.*

20. *Winchester Handbook,* p. 123; C. E. Hagie, *The American Rifle for Hunting and Target Shooting* (New York: The Macmillan Co., 1946), pp. 69, 73, 83.

The possibility that a frangible bullet produced the massive head wound was first suggested by Vincent Salandria in an article that appeared in *Liberation* magazine, March 1965, p. 32. The specification of a varminting bullet was first introduced to me by Dick Bernabei, who has done much admirable and worthwhile work on the medical/ballistics aspects of the case.

21. See Weisberg, *Whitewash,* pp. 178-86; Meagher, pp. 139-59; David Welsh and David Lifton, "A Counter-Theory: The Case For Three Assassins," *Ramparts,* January 1967, section II: "The Bullet in the Back." Much of the original research can be found in Vincent Salandria, "The Warren Report," *Liberation,* March 1965, pp. 14-22, Part I: A Philadelphia Lawyer Analyzes the President's Back and Neck Wounds.

22. Fillinger Interview, and Thompson, p. 50.

23. Transcript of court proceedings of February 24, 1969, in *State of Louisiana* v. *Clay L. Shaw,* p. 115. (Hereinafter referred to as "Finck 2/24/69 testimony.")

24. Fillinger Interview.

25. Clark Panel Report, p. 13.

26. Letter to the author from Dr. Russell Morgan, dated November 12, 1969.

27. Fillinger Interview.

28. This case and the accompanying illustrations can be found in

LeMoyne Snyder, pp. 135-39.

29. Frazier 2/21/69 testimony, pp. 159-60.

30. See CD 7, p. 284; 2H93; Thompson, p. 167.

31. See CD 7, p. 284; 2H367.

32. See the first FBI report on the assassination, CD 1, and the Supplemental Report, dated January 13, 1964; Thompson, pp. 165-70.

33. Sir Sydney Smith and Frederick Fiddes, *Forensic Medicine* (London: J. and A. Churchill, Ltd., 1955), p. 174.

34. Major Sir Gerald Burrard, *The Identification of Firearms and Forensic Ballistics* (London: Herbert Jenkins, 1951), p. 51. The scheme I use in the text is adapted from this book, p. 52.

35. Author's taped interview with Charles Dickey at Frankford Arsenal. July 16, 1968. (Hereinafter referred to as "Dickey Interview.")

36. Thompson, pp. 167-68.

37. Dickey Interview.

38. *E.G.,* see R193 and *International Surgery* 50, no. 6 (December 1968): p. 529.

5   The Governor's Wounds and the Validity of the Essential Conclusions

1. "Memorandum for the Record," dated April 22, 1964, written by Melvin Eisenberg about a conference held on April 14, 1964.

2. "Memorandum for the Record," dated April 22, 1964, written by Melvin Eisenberg about a conference held on April 21, 1964.

3. Dickey Interview.

4. *CBS News Inquiry: "The Warren Report"*, Part II, broadcast over the CBS Television Network on June 26, 1967, p. 18 of the transcript prepared by CBS News.

5. Fillinger Interview.

6. Marshall Houts, *Where Death Delights* (New York: Coward-McCann, 1967), pp. 62-63.

7. Nichols Interview and letter to author from Dr. John Nichols, dated September 5, 1969.

8. Thompson, p. 153.

9. Fillinger Interview; Weisberg, *Post Mortem I,* p. 25.

10. *Ibid.*

11. Weisberg, *Oswald in New Orleans,* pp. 292-93.

12. *E.g.,* see Jesse Curry, *Personal JFK Assassination File* (Dallas: American Poster and Printing Co., Inc., 1969), pp. 34-37. The *Dallas Morning News* of November 23, 1963, estimated that a crowd of 200 had gathered outside the hospital (p. 9).

13. See Weisberg, *Whitewash II,* p. 35.

6   The Rifle in the Building

1. Weisberg, *Whitewash,* p. 23.

2. *Ibid.,* pp. 13-14.

3. Meagher, pp. 37-38.

4. Liebeler 9/6/64 Memorandum, p. 4.

5. Meagher, p. 37.

6. Letter from J. Lee Rankin to J. Edgar Hoover, dated August 31, 1964, found in the Truly "K.P." (Key Persons) file.

7. Letter to the author from Gene Daniels, received March 19, 1970. Quoted by permission.

8. Leo Sauvage, *The Oswald Affair* (Cleveland: The World Publishing Co., 1965), pp. 363-67.

9. Meagher, p. 38.

10. The first critical analysis of the questioning of witnesses Frazier and Randle appeared in Weisberg's *Whitewash,* pp. 17-19.

11. West's testimony was first noted by Harold Weisberg and published in *Whitewash,* p. 21.

12. According to Marina, Oswald overslept on the morning of the assassination and did not get up until 7:10, at which time he dressed and left (18H638-39). Oswald arrived at Frazier's home at 7:20 that morning (24H408). Thus, he had only ten minutes to get ready for work and walk to Frazier's, which would not have allowed him time to disassemble the rifle, place it in the sack, and replace the blanket.

7 Oswald at Window?

1. It was Sylvia Meagher who brought the shortcomings of Givens's story to light in her book, pp. 64-69.

Since her initial disclosure in 1967, Mrs. Meagher has discovered several unpublished documents in the National Archives that leave little doubt that Givens's story of seeing Oswald on the sixth floor *was* fabricated and that staff lawyer David Belin knew this when he took Givens's testimony. The documents tell a shocking story, which Mrs. Meagher incorporated in an impressive article published in the *Texas Observer,* August 13, 1971.

When Givens was interviewed by the FBI on the day of the assassination, he not only failed to mention having seen Oswald on the sixth floor, but he actually said he saw Oswald on the *first* floor at 11:50, reading a newspaper in the domino room (CD 5, p. 329). On February 13, 1964, Police Lt. Jack Revill told the FBI "he believes that Givens would change his story for money" (CD 735, p. 296). A lengthy memorandum by Joseph Ball and David Belin dated February 25, 1964, acknowledges that Givens originally reported seeing Oswald on the first floor reading a paper at 11:50 on the morning of November 22 (p. 105). On April 8, 1964, Givens testified for Belin in Dallas and said for the first time that he saw Oswald on the sixth floor at 11:55 when he returned for his cigarettes (Givens had never before said that he returned to the sixth floor) (See 6H345-56). Belin twice asked Givens if he ever told anyone that he "saw Lee Oswald reading a newspaper in the domino room around 11:50...that morning?" On both occasions, Givens denied ever making such a statement (6H352, 354). Finally, on June 3, 1964, when the FBI reinterviewed him, Givens "said he *now* recalls he returned to the sixth floor at about 11:45 A.M. to get his cigarettes. . .[and] it was at this time he saw Lee Harvey Oswald" (CD 1245, p. 182; emphasis added).

Belin apparently found nothing unusual in Givens's failure to mention the sixth-floor encounter until he testified in April 1964, contradicting a previous statement that he denied making. Givens's denial does not prove he actually never made his early statement, although for Belin the pro forma denial was sufficient, despite the caution of Lt. Revill that Givens would change his story for money. The Report (R143) mentions only the later Givens story and says nothing of the original version. This is consistent with the constant suppression of evidence exculpatory of Oswald.

2. Letter from J. Lee Rankin to J. Edgar Hoover, dated March 16, 1964, in the "Reading File of Outgoing Letters and Internal Memoranda."

This letter was based on a request for additional investigation by staff lawyers Ball and Belin. In their lengthy "Report #1," dated February 25, 1964, they suggested that "everyone who had a reason to be in" the Depository on November 22, 1963, be interviewed. "Each of these persons should be asked: 1) to account for his whereabouts at the time the President was shot. . . . 3) if he saw Lee Oswald at that time" (p. 125).

3. The episode with Jarman and Norman was first brought to light by Harold Weisberg in *Whitewash,* p. 73. Sylvia Meagher later discussed the issue in more detail in her book, p. 225.

4. The Report mentions this incident in a context other than one of Oswald's defense. It assures that Jarman neither saw nor ate with Oswald at the times involved (R182). This in no way disproves the validity of Oswald's claim that he saw Jarman, for it would not have been unusual for Jarman or any other employee not to have noticed Oswald.

5. Harold Wesiberg, *Photographic Whitewash,* pp. 74-75, 210-11.

6. *Ibid.,* p. 74.

7. Mark Lane, chap. 6.

8. The possibility that the sixth-floor gunman was a decoy was first suggested by Sylvia Meagher in her book, p. 9.

9. E.G., see Weisberg, *Whitewash,* pp. 39-42, and Lane, chap. 5.

10. *CBS News Extra: "November 22 and the Warren Report",* broadcast over the CBS Television Network, September 27, 1964, p. 20 of the transcript prepared by CBS News.

11. *Ibid.* At page two of the transcript, Walter Cronkite specifies that CBS interviewed various witnesses a month before the release of the Report.

12. *Life,* October 2, 1964, pp. 42, 47.

13. E.G., see CEs 1769, 1797, 2964, 2965; CD 1405 (reproduced in *Photographic Whitewash,* p. 209); Curry, pp. 72, 73, 77; *Life,* October 2, 1964, p. 48.

14. Baker testified to this at 3H257. In December 1963, Truly, who also saw Oswald within 90 seconds after the shots, said that Oswald had been wearing "light" clothing *and* a T-shirt (CD 87, Secret Service Control No. 491).

8   The Alibi: Oswald's Actions after the Shots

1. The first critical analysis of these reconstructions appeared in *Whitewash*, pp. 36-38.

2. *CBS News Extra: "November 22 and the Warren Report"*, p. 28.

3. To my knowledge, the Couch film is not commercially available. I was fortunately able to obtain numerous stills made from individual frames of a copy of the Couch film, which was originally obtained from the Dallas television station for which Couch worked. Due to the legalities involved, these pictures can not be reproduced here.

4. I obtained numerous frames from the Weigman film in the same manner as described above. These can not be reproduced either.

5. Weisberg, *Whitewash*, p. 37.

6. *CBS News Inquiry: "The Warren Report"*, Part I, p. 9.

9   Oswald's Rifle Capability

1. Analyses of the nature of the shots and related topics have appeared in *Whitewash*, chap. 4; Lane, chap. 9; Epstein, chap. 9; Meagher, chap. 4.

2. Frazier 2/21/69 testimony, p. 67.

3. *Ibid.*, p. 148.

4. See also the excerpts from the Liebeler 9/6/64 Memorandum as discussed in chap. 1.

5. U.S. Department of Commerce, Weather Bureau, *Local Climatological Data*, for San Diego, California, May 1959, and Los Angeles, California, May 1959.

6. I have seen this rifle at the National Archives and it does appear rather dilapidated. Fingerprint expert Latona called it "a cheap old weapon" (4H29). Ballistics expert Robert Frazier went into more detail on the condition of the rifle:

Mr. Eisenberg. . . .How much use does this weapon show?

Mr. Frazier. The stock is worn, scratched. The bolt is relatively smooth, as if it had been operated several times. I cannot actually say how much use the weapon has had. The barrel is—was not, when we first got it, in excellent condition. It was, I would say in fair condition. In other words, it showed the effects of wear and corrosion. (3H394)

7. Liebeler 9/6/64 Memorandum.

8. CD 344 was discovered in the National Archives by Harold Weisberg and is discussed in *Whitewash II*, pp. 15-19.

9. This memorandum was shown to Epstein by Liebeler. References to it may be found in *Inquest*, p. 146, and the *Saturday Evening Post*, April 6, 1968, p. 72.

Bibliography

Books

Belin, David. *November 22, 1963: You Are the Jury.* New York: Quadrangle Books, 1973.

Bishop, Jim. *The Day Kennedy Was Shot.* New York: Funk and Wagnall, 1968.

Bonner, Judy. *Investigation of a Homicide.* Anderson, S.C.: Drake House, 1969.

Buchanan, Thomas. *Who Killed Kennedy?* New York: Putnam's Sons, 1964.

Burrard, Major Sir Gerald. *The Identification of Firearms and Forensic Ballistics.* London: Herbert Jenkins, 1951.

Central Broadcasting System. *CBS News Inquiry: "The Warren Report."* Parts I-IV, broadcast over CBS Television Network June 25-28, 1967.

———. *CBS News Extra: "November 22 and the Warren Report,"* broadcast over CBS Television Network September 27, 1964.

Chapman, Gil and Ann. *Was Oswald Alone?* San Diego: Publisher's Export Co., 1967.

Curry, Jesse, *Personal JFK Assassination File.* Dallas: American Poster and Printing Co., Inc., 1969.

Cutler, R.B. *The Flight of CE 399: Evidence of Conspiracy.* Manchester, Mass.: R. B. Cutler, 1969.

Dingle, Herbert. *Practical Applications of Spectrum Analysis.* London: Chapman and Hall, Ltd., 1950.

Epstein, Edward J. *Inquest.* New York: Viking Press, 1966.

———. *Counterplot.* New York: Viking Press, 1969.

Fiddes, Frederick and Smith, Sydney. *Forensic Medicine.* London: J. and A. Churchill, Ltd., 1955.

Flammonde, Paris. *The Kennedy Conspiracy.* New York: Meredith Press, 1969.

Ford, Gerald and Stiles, John. *Portrait of an Assassin.* New York: Simon and Schuster, 1965.

Fox, Sylvan. *The Unanswered Questions About President Kennedy's Assassination.* New York: Award Books, 1965.

Garrison, Jim. *A Heritage of Stone.* New York: Putnam, 1970.

Gonzales, Thomas, Helpern, Milton, Vance, Morgan, and Umberger, Charles. *Legal Medicine, Pathology and Toxicology.* New York: Appleton-Century-Crofts, Inc., 1954.

Hagie, C. E. *The American Rifle for Hunting and Target Shooting.* New York: The Macmillan Co., 1946.

Houts, Marshall. *Where Death Delights.* New York: Coward-McCann, 1967.

Jay, David, ed. *The Weight of the Evidence: The Warren Report and Its Critics.* New York: Meredith Press, 1968.

Joesten, Joachim. *Oswald: Assassin or Fall Guy?.* New York: Marzani and Numsell Publishers, 1964.

Jones, Penn Jr. *Forgive My Grief I.* Midlothian, Tex.: Midlothian Mirror, Inc., 1966.

———. *Forgive My Grief II.* Midlothian, Tex.: Midlothian Mirror, Inc., 1967.

———. *Forgive My Grief III.* Midlothian, Tex.: Midlothian Mirror, Inc., 1969.

Kaiser, Robert Blair. *"RFK Must Die".* New York: E. P. Dutton, 1970.

Kirkwood, James. *An American Grotesque.* New York: Simon and Schuster, 1970.

Lane, Mark. *Rush To Judgement.* New York: Holt, Rinehart and Winston, 1966.

———. *A Citizen's Dissent.* New York: Holt, Rinehart and Winston, 1968.

Lewis, Richard and Schiller, Lawrence. *The Scavengers and Critics of the Warren Report.* New York: Dell Books, 1967.

Lifton, David. *Document Addendum to the Warren Report.* El Segundo, Calif.: 1968.

Long, Rowland H. *The Physician and the Law.* New York:

1968.

Lucas, A. *Forensic Chemistry and Scientific Criminal Investigation.* New York: Longmans, Green and Co., 1935.

Manchester, William. *The Death of a President.* New York: Harper and Row, 1967.

Marcus, Raymond. *The Bastard Bullet.* Los Angeles, Calif.: Rendell Publications, 1966.

Meagher, Sylvia. *Accessories After the Fact.* New York: The Bobbs-Merrill Co., Inc., 1967.

————. *Subject Index to the Warren Report and Hearings and Exhibits.* New York: Scarecrow Press, 1966.

Morin, Relman. *Assassination: The Death of President John F. Kennedy.* New York: Signet Books, 1968.

Nash, George and Patricia. *Critical Reactions to the Warren Report.* New York: Marzani and Munsell, 1964.

National Broadcasting Company. *There Was a President.* New York: Random House, 1966.

Newman, Albert. *The Assassination of John F. Kennedy: The Reasons Why.* New York: Clarkson N. Potter, Inc., 1970.

Popkin, Richard. *The Second Oswald.* New York: Avon Books, 1966.

Roberts, Charles. *The Truth About the Assassination.* New York: Grosset and Dunlap, 1967.

Sauvage, Leo. *The Oswald Affair.* Cleveland: The World Publishing Co., 1965.

Smith, Merriman, et al. *Four Days.* New York: United Press International and American Heritage, 1964.

Snyder, Le Moyne. *Homicide Investigation.* Springfield, Mass.: 1953.

Sparrow, John. *After the Assassination: A Positive Appraisal of the Warren Report.* New York: Chilmark Press, 1967.

Thompson, Josiah. *Six Seconds in Dallas.* New York: Bernard Geis Associates, 1967.

Warren, Earl, et al. *Report of the President's Commission on the Assassination of President Kennedy.* Washington, D.C.: Government Printing Office, 1964.

————. *Hearings Before the President's Commission on the Assassination of President Kennedy.* Washington, D.C.: Government Printing Office, 1964.

Weisberg, Harold. *Whitewash: The Report on the Warren Report. Hyattstown, Md.: Harold Wesiberg, 1965.

———. *Whitewash II: The FBI-Secret Service Cover-Up.* Hyattstown, Md.: Harold Weisberg, 1966.

———. *Photographic Whitewash: Suppressed Kennedy Assassination Pictures.* Hyattstown, Md.: Harold Weisberg, 1967.

———. *Oswald in New Orleans.* New York: Canyon Books, 1967.

———. *Post Mortem.* Frederick, Md.: Harold Weisberg, 1971.

———. *Frame-Up: The King/Ray Case.* New York: Outerbridge and Dienstfrey, 1971.

Winchester-Western Ammunition Handbook. New York: Pocket Books, Inc., 1964.

Articles

Bickel, Alexander. "The Failure of the Warren Report." *Commentary* (October 1966).

Epstein, Edward J. "The Final Chapter in the Assassination Controversy." *New York Times Magazine* (May 20, 1969).

Fonzi, Gaeton. "The Warren Commission, the Truth, and Arlen Specter." *Philadelphia Magazine* (August 1966).

Ford, Gerald. "Piecing Together the Evidence." *Life* (October 2, 1964).

Garrison, Jim. "Playboy Interview: Jim Garrison." *Playboy* (October 1967).

Jackson, Donald. "The Evolution of an Assassin." *Life* (February 21, 1964).

Kempton, Murray. "Warren Report: Case for the Prosecution." *The New Republic* (October 10, 1964).

Knebel, Fletcher. "A New Wave of Doubt." *Look* (July 12, 1966).

Lane, Mark. "Playboy Interview: Mark Lane." *Playboy* (February 1967).

Lattimer, John K. and Jon. "The Kennedy-Connally Single Bullet Theory: A Feasibility Study." *International Surgery* (December 1968).

Lifton, David and Welsh, Robert. "A Counter-Theory: The Case For Three Assassins." *Ramparts* (January 1967).

Lynd, Staughton and Minnis, Jack. "Seeds of Doubt: Some

Questions About the Assassination." *The New Republic* (December 21, 1963).

MacDonald, Dwight. "A Critique of the Warren Report." *Esquire* (March 1965).

"A Matter of Reasonable Doubt." *Life* (November 25, 1966).

Meagher, Sylvia. "The Curious Testimony of Mr. Givens." *The Texas Observer* (August 12, 1971).

"November 22, 1963, Dallas: Photos by Nine Bystanders." *Life* (November 24, 1967).

———. "The Warren Commission's Private Life." *The Texas Observer* (April 3, 1970).

Olson, Don and Turner, Ralph. "Photographic Evidence and the Assassination of President John F. Kennedy." *Journal of Forensic Sciences* (October 1971).

Oswald, Robert L. "Oswald: He was my Brother." *Look* (October 17, 1967).

Salandria, Vincent. "The Warren Report." *Liberation* (March 1965).

———. "The Impossible Tasks of One Assassination Bullet." *The Minority of One* (March 1966).

"Truth About Kennedy Assassination: Questions Raised and Answered." *U.S. News and World Report* (October 10, 1966).

Turner, William. "The Inquest." *Ramparts* (June 1967).

———. "The Garrison Commission on the Assassination of President Kennedy." *Ramparts* (January 1968).

Welsh, David. "In the Shadow of Dallas." *Ramparts* (November 1966).

Wise, David. "Secret Evidence on the Kennedy Assassination." *Saturday Evening Post* (April 16, 1968)

Index

Accessories after the fact in assassination, 30

Accomplices in assassination, 81-82

Alba, Adrian, 244-5

Alibi for Oswald, 221, 225

Ammunition. *See* Military ammunition; Sporting ammunition

Anderson, Eugene, 231

Arce, Danny, 183

Archives. *See* National Archives

Arnold, Mrs. Carolyn, 184-87, 276-77

Assassination of President Kennedy as political crime, 26-27

Assassin's rifle. *See* Rifle

Autopsy on President Kennedy, 121

Bag. *See* Paper bag

Baker, Mrs. Donald, 186

Baker, M. L., 63, 199, 201-9, 213, 218-21, 252

Ball, Joseph, 33, 84-86, 163, 181, 205

Ballistics evidence, 48

Ballistics tests, 50; simulating head wounds, 111-14

Belin, David, 33, 84-86, 90, 169, 196, 197-98, 222, 288-89

Bernabei, Richard, 126, 129, 283

Blanket, 170-71

Boggs, Hale, 20, 80, 222

Bolt practice by Oswald, 242-43

Bookhout, James, 182

Boone, Eugene, 212, 213

Boswell, Dr. J. Thornton, 118-19

Bremer, Arthur, 17

Brennan, Howard, 61-62, 188, 190-98, 199

Buchanan, Thomas, 22

Bullet fragments: in car, 98, 107, 114, 146; from Governor Connally, 99-100, 103, 131, 132; in President Kennedy's head, 117; in President Kennedy's neck, 121-25, 145

Bullet 399, 95-96, 99-101, 103, 121, 124, 128, 129, 131, 133, 134, 136-45, 250; planted, 253

Bullet wounds, 50; of Governor Connally, 131-45; of President Kennedy's anterior neck, 79, 123, 125, 145; of President Kennedy's back, 126, 145; of President Kennedy's head, 108-20; of President Kennedy's neck, 120-29

Bullets. *See also* Military ammunition; Sporting ammunition

Bullets and fragments, 48

Bullets, high-velocity, 119

Cabell, Mrs. Earle, 188

Cadigan, James, 171-72

Calvery, Gloria, 204-5

Cartridge cases, 49, 69, 107, 127-28, 129, 147

CBS News, 24, 193, 197, 205, 213

Central Broadcasting System. *See* CBS News

Central Intelligence Agency. *See* CIA

CIA, 28

Clark, Ramsey, 105, 114-15; panel assembled by, 115, 117, 118, 121

Clothing: description, 286; worn by gunman, 198-99; worn by President Kennedy, 99, 103; worn by Oswald, 198-99

Congress, 9, 11

Connally, John, 19, 84; views on Warren Report, 24

Cooper, Sen. John Sherman, 80, 134-35, 222, 238

293